International Dispute Resolution and the Public Policy Exception

Despite the unprecedented growth of arbitration and other means of ADR in treaties and transnational contracts in recent years, there remains no clearly defined mechanism for control of the system. One of the oldest yet largely marginalized concepts in law is the public policy exception. This doctrine grants discretion to courts to set aside private legal arrangements, including arbitration, which might be considered harmful to the "public." The exceptional and vague nature of the doctrine, along with the strong push of actors in dispute resolution, has transformed it, in certain jurisdictions, into a toothless doctrine. At the international level, the notion of transnational public policy has been devised in order to capture norms that are "truly" transnational and amenable for application in cross-border litigations. Yet, despite the importance of this discussion—a safety valve and a control mechanism for today's international and domestic international dispute resolution—no major study has ventured to review and analyze it.

This book provides a historical, theoretical, and practical background on public policy in dispute resolution with a focus on cross-border and transnational disputes. Farshad Ghodoosi argues that courts should adopt a more systemic approach to public policy while rejecting notions such as transnational public policy which limit the application of those norms with mandatory nature. Contrary to the current trend, the book invites the reader to re-conceptualize the role of public policy in transnational dispute resolution, in order to have more sustainable, fair, and efficient mechanisms for resolving disputes outside of national courts.

The book sheds light on one of the most important yet often-neglected control mechanisms of today's international dispute resolution and will be of particular interest to students and academics in the fields of International Investment Law, International Trade Law, Business, and Economics.

Farshad Ghodoosi holds J.S.D (Doctor of the Science of Law) from Yale Law School where he was a Howard M. Holtzmann Fellow in international dispute resolution. He also served as a Weinstein fellow in alternative dispute resolution, as co-president of the Yale Society of International Law and as a senior editor of the *Yale Journal of International Law*.

Routledge Research in International Commercial Law

Available titles in this series include:

International Commercial and Marine Arbitration
Georgios I. Zekos

International Commercial Arbitration and the Arbitrator's Contract
Emilia Onyema

Jurisdiction and Arbitration Agreements in International Commercial Law
Zheng Sophia Tang

Forthcoming:

Progressive Commercialization of Airline Governance Culture
Jan Walulik

International Dispute Resolution and the Public Policy Exception

Farshad Ghodoosi

LONDON AND NEW YORK

First published 2017 by Routledge

2 Park Square, Milton Park, Abingdon, Oxfordshire OX14 4RN
711 Third Avenue, New York, NY 10017

Routledge is an imprint of the Taylor & Francis Group, an informa business

First issued in paperback 2018

Copyright © 2017 Farshad Ghodoosi

The right of Farshad Ghodoosi to be identified as author of this work has been asserted by him in accordance with sections 77 and 78 of the Copyright, Designs and Patents Act 1988.

All rights reserved. No part of this book may be reprinted or reproduced or utilised in any form or by any electronic, mechanical, or other means, now known or hereafter invented, including photocopying and recording, or in any information storage or retrieval system, without permission in writing from the publishers.

Notice:
Product or corporate names may be trademarks or registered trademarks, and are used only for identification and explanation without intent to infringe.

British Library Cataloguing in Publication Data
A catalogue record for this book is available from the British Library

Library of Congress Cataloging-in-Publication Data
Names: Ghodoosi, Farshad, author.
Title: International dispute resolution and the public policy exception/
  Farshad Ghodoosi.
Description: Abingdon, Oxon ; New York, NY : Routledge, 2016. | Series:
  Routledge research in international commercial law | Based on author's
  thesis (J.S.D. - Yale Law School, 2015).
Identifiers: LCCN 2016001405 | ISBN 9781138183612 (hbk)
Subjects: LCSH: International commercial arbitration. | Public policy (Law)
Classification: LCC K2400.G54 2016 | DDC 347/.09—dc23
LC record available at http://lccn.loc.gov/2016001405

ISBN: 978-1-138-18361-2 (hbk)
ISBN: 978-1-138-61419-2 (pbk)

Typeset in Baskerville
by Swales & Willis Ltd, Exeter, Devon, UK

Dedication

I am dedicating this Book to my wife, Monica Sharif, Ph.D., whose support and patience has made this possible. She stood by me without hesitation when I went through doubts, stress, and intellectual struggles. It was with her kindness as well as intellectual support that I could successfully finish my doctoral academic journey.

I also would like to dedicate this Dissertation to my parents, Mr. Mahmoud Ghoddosi and Mrs. Fatemeh Mahmoudiyeh. They taught me the critical values necessary for my life and always encouraged me to think progressively and freely. I left my home to pursue knowledge and education. Nevertheless, they unconditionally and consistently supported me in this decision and throughout my life.

Contents

Foreword   x
Acknowledgements   xii

Introduction   1

1   A brief history of the notion of public policy in English common law   5

     A. *Paradigm shift*   5
     B. *Unruliness of public policy*   8
     C. *Definition*   11
     D. *Taxonomy*   14

2   A brief history of public policy as regulatory planning in the United States   21

     A. *The classical approach*   22
        1. Formalism   22
        2. Rationalism   25
     B. *Age of statutes*   27
        1. Emergence of a welfare state   27
        2. American legal realism   29
     C. *A need for a new approach*   31
        1. The age of multiculturalism   31
        2. The revisionist approach   32
        3. Beyond revisionism   32

3   Economics of the public policy doctrine   34

     A. *The law and economics approach in law*   34
     B. *The law and economics of public policy*   37
        1. Protecting parties   37
        2. Protecting third parties   39
        3. Protecting redistributive justice   41

C. *The leading role of public policy*   43
  1. Incompleteness of the law and economics approach   43
  2. Policy arguments in courts   45

4   Public policy in arbitration   49

A. *Why people arbitrate: three paradigms*   49
  1. Structural tension   50
  2. Consent-based   52
  3. Interest-based   55
  4. Resistance-based   59
B. *The doctrine of public policy in arbitration*   62
  1. Role of the public policy exception   62
  2. Courts' approach to public policy exceptions   63
  3. Concluding remarks   73
C. *The United States Supreme Court*   73

5   The trajectory of international dispute resolution   78

A. *Pre-modern developments*   78
B. *Developments in the early modern era*   80
C. *Emergence of the notion of public policy*   85

6   Theorizing international arbitration   91

A. *Judicialization and state power*   91
B. *Two schools of international arbitration*   93
  1. The transnationalist approach   94
  2. The statist approach   99
  3. Practical significance   104

7   Transnational public policy in contemporary international commercial arbitration   108

A. *Public policy in international commercial arbitration*   110
  1. The complicated picture of choice of law   110
  2. Empirical data on the success rate   113
B. *Three approaches to transnational public policy*   117
  1. Common values among nations   119
  2. National courts' international public policy   121
  3. *Lex mercatoria*   123
C. *Transnational public policy in enforcement*   128

8 The development of transnational public policy in international law **131**

  A. Established norms 131
      1. *Jus cogens* 131
      2. Human rights 133
      3. Corruption and fraudulent conduct 136
  B. Transnational public policy in the twenty-first century 140
      1. Economic sanctions 140
      2. Sovereign debt 142

Conclusion 145

Index 147

Foreword

The New York Convention on the Recognition and Enforcement of Foreign Arbitral Awards establishes the legal infrastructure for international commercial arbitration. Its centerpiece is Article V which confirms the recruitment of national courts for the enforcement of awards. After that provision carefully spells out the few grounds on which a national court may refuse enforcement, it ends rather surprisingly by stating that recognition or enforcement may be refused if "the award would be contrary to the public policy of that country." Public policy is not defined in the Convention; its content is apparently left to the determination of each state-party's national courts, where it is also not *lex scripta*.

For an international effort designed to mobilize national courts as the ultimate enforcers of awards, the public policy exception may have been a concession necessary to secure the consent of states (now more than 150) to a treaty regime which compels them to use state power to enforce private – and foreign – awards.

Considering that all law is policy, the public policy exception may have been a big concession. For a long time, however, it was a relatively minor feature, infrequently used. Of late, however, it is not. In addition to the diversity among "national" public policies, a number of national courts have also developed a notion of transnational public policy. In contrast to the use of national public policy to justify non-enforcement of awards that fall under the purview of the Convention, "transnational public policy" (which is also undefined) has sometimes been used to support national enforcement of international awards that might otherwise have been unenforceable under relevant national law, sometimes for what would have been core national values! Now even that has come under stress, as some national courts have demanded that transnational public policy, as they define it, may also be used to justify non-enforcement of valid awards.

With remarkable prescience, Burroughs J., almost 200 years ago, cautioned about the judicial use of public policy: "It is an unruly horse," he said, "and when once you get astride it, you never know where it will carry you." International commercial arbitration seems to be unsteadily astride that horse and we are uncertain as to where it is carrying us.

With this thoughtful book, Dr. Ghodoosi brings the international community a long way toward taming that unruly horse. Unlike much of the literature in the field, his is not an uncritical paean to international commercial arbitration with public policy a danger to it. Rather he presents a probing and original examination of the origins of public policy doctrines in relation to private dispute resolution and their implications for social order, viewed through the prisms of political philosophy and history, doctrinal writings in the United States and abroad and detailed reviews of case law. He concludes that there are systemic benefits as well as deficits to the public policy exception.

This book is rich in innovative insights and is an important contribution to both international legal scholarship and policy clarification.

W. Michael Reisman
Yale Law School
New Haven, Connecticut.

Acknowledgements

I am extremely grateful for the help and support of my advisor Professor Michael Reisman. Not only did he supervise my dissertation but also, and more importantly, he taught me how to think critically. Our many sessions and intellectual exchanges has left a lasting mark on my intellectual view towards international law and more importantly changed me as a person.

I am also greatly appreciative of the endless support of Professor Susan Rose-Ackerman. Her office was always open for me to bounce around ideas, receive feedback on my work, and re-energize myself to go through the process of researching and writing.

Also, I would like to extend my gratitude to Professor David Grewal for his support and help throughout my doctoral program.

I also want to thank the Graduate Program at Yale Law School, the administrative staff and in particular Cina Santos for her continuous help.

Introduction

On a daily basis—and even for mundane purchases—people often waive an important right: the right to go to courts. From plan contracts with AT&T[1] to sophisticated international economic relations[2] to major international conflicts,[3] one can trace the alternative dispute resolution (ADR) system and most importantly arbitration. In short, by signing arbitration clauses, contracting parties promise to pursue their future disputes not at the courts but before a private single arbitrator or arbitral tribunal. Despite its importance, this area of law, as well as its relation with public law and policy, has remained understudied, particularly from a theoretical perspective.

An unresolved tension lies at the heart of private conflict resolution mechanisms and public law and policy. This tension is detectable in three phases of arbitration (and other forms of ADR): pre-referral, proceeding, and post-decision. The pre-referral phase determines the disputes that qualify to be referred to arbitration, pursuant to public policy (so-called arbitrability).[4] The proceeding phase deal with challenges stemming from a wide range of issues mainly from a constitutional perspective (e.g., due process).[5] Lastly, in the post-decision phase, the enforceability of decisions might be in contention with the public policy of states. My research focuses on the enforcement stage, with important consequences for the first two phases.

---

1 *See, e.g.*, AT&T Mobility v. Concepcion, 131 S. Ct. 1740 (2011).
2 A good example would be the series of cases brought against Argentina following its economic crisis in 1998–2002. *See, e.g.*, CMS Gas Transmission Company v. The Republic of Argentina, ICSID Case No. ARB/01/8, Award (12 May, 2005), Impregilo S.p.A v. Argentine Republic, ICSID Case No. ARB/07/17, Award (June 21, 2011), Sempra Energy International v. Argentina Republic, ICSID Case No. ARB/02/16., Award (June 29, 2010).
3 The Alabama Arbitration between the United States and Great Britain over disputes that arose out of the US Civil War is a good example. *See e.g.*, ADRIAN COOK, THE ALABAMA CLAIMS: AMERICAN POLITICS AND ANGLO-AMERICAN RELATIONS (1975).
4 *See, e.g.*, Jeffery W. Stempel, *Pitfalls of Public Policy: The Case of Arbitration Agreements*, 22 ST. MARY'S L.J. 259 (1992). *See also* George A. Bermann, *The "Gateway" Problem in International Commercial Arbitration*, YALE J. INT'L L. 1 (2012).
5 *See, e.g.*, Edward Brunet, *Arbitration and Constitutional Rights*, 71 N.C. L. REV. (1992).

Investigating the tension between ADR mechanisms and public law and policy is intertwined with other crucial discussions. First and foremost, the notion of "public" in the discussion should be delineated. This book revisits the concept of public policy, as it is pertinent to the discussion of enforcement of contractual terms, arbitral awards and foreign judgments. The other side of the equation is the notion of alternative dispute resolution and arbitration. I lay out three approaches to the ADR system as a whole as well as a theory of public policy in arbitration. Lastly, I explore the extra-territoriality of public policy as it applies to international litigation and arbitration.

Private arbitral bodies are now adjudicating critical disputes, including those involving areas that traditionally fell exclusively within the absolute discretion of national sovereignty, e.g., national regulations on monetary matters.[6] Yet, challenges posed by the arbitration and its benefits remain to be explored. The most important challenge is the inherent tension between the private nature of arbitration and the important public matters it resolves.[7]

The doctrine of public policy is a channel through which public law enters private law and bars it from actualizing its normal legal consequences. Although public policy is an old doctrine in common law and other legal systems, it is not clear which aspects of public law could enter the arena of contract (private) law and make it unenforceable. The phrase public policy is used and pled in various national and international tribunals on a daily basis. Despite its importance, the literature surrounding the doctrine of public policy is extremely limited. This book first briefly traces the genealogy and paradigm shifts of the doctrine of public policy in the history of common law. Subsequently, it scrutinizes the ramifications emanating from developments of legal theory as well as the emergence of the welfare state in transformation of the notion of public policy. It then explains the doctrine of public policy from the law and economics

---

[6] For instance, in the context of investor arbitration, in a recent study Gus Van Harten states that in 162 international investment cases coded, arbitrators reviewed executive measures in all of them and 37% and 44% of cases respectively involved a domestic legislative or judicial decision. Gus Van Harte, *Beware of the Discretionary Choices of Arbitrators*, VALE COLUMBIA CENTER ON SUSTAINABLE INTERNATIONAL INVESTMENT, http://academiccommons.columbia.edu/catalog/ac:168302 (last visited, Dec. 24, 2013)

[7] Imagine the following case: Australia decides to impose a stricter regulation on cigarette packaging based on multiple studies showing that buyers are less likely to purchase cigarettes if packaging is bland. A major cigarette manufacturer who has invested in Australia is clearly unhappy about the recent regulation because it has to change its packaging and, after all, it is entitled to the trademark of its products. The investor brings a case against Australia for violating an investment treaty. The arbitral panel is now faced with assessing a national regulation, a matter that historically was exclusively within the authority of states. In other words, the tribunal is evaluating a regulation directly related to public health in Australia. *See* Philip Morris Asia Limited v. The Commonwealth of Australia, PCA Case no. 2012-12, Notice of Arbitration (2011).

perspective and shows its shortcomings. The concept of public policy is a not a single concept but consists of three distinct strands—public interest, public morality, and public security—each with a separate pedigree and logic requiring a separate method for its analysis. The public interest category refers to instances where the public policy exception can be determined by employing cost–benefit analysis, weighing the interests of private parties against societal interest. The second strand, public morality, attempts to safeguard the communal values by allowing the judiciary not to lend its enforcement apparatus to private legal arrangements that are injurious to common morality. Lastly, public security is structured around the exceptionalist logic of modern statehood, which aims to protect states' survival interest. In instances where public morality and public security are severely at stake, private law is subsumed by the mandate of public policy. However, in the majority of cases, which fall under the category of public interest, courts should follow the balancing approach with the single test of avoiding negative externalities.

Alternative dispute resolution is a mechanism by which states outsource their distribution of justice function. A brief look at recent American political tradition shows how alternative dispute resolution gained momentum at the time the political paradigm shifted towards "making the government smaller." Yet, national courts still have the final say in regard to enforcement of arbitral awards, mainly through the doctrine of public policy. Furthermore, arbitral bodies are overly cautious not to step on aspects of a case with strong public law implications. Chapter 4 starts off by investigating the underpinning political philosophy of arbitration. It argues, firstly, that it is a form of political philosophy despite current narration which observes it as a simple alternative technique to courts' procedures. Second, it suggests that the idea of arbitration challenges the prevailing paradigm of modern statehood, a contention which places it in a structural tension with not only the judicial system but the very notion of modern statehood. Subsequently, by looking at various jurisdictions, it analyzes and categorizes the various instances in which arbitral awards are set aside due to violation of public policy under four paradigms. It posits that the holistic approach of courts to public policy produces inefficient and contradictory results. It concludes that arbitral bodies should begin to assess public policy (at least in its public interest sense) through balancing. Following the US Supreme Court case *Mitsubishi v. Soler*, it is sufficient for an arbitral body to pay due consideration to public policy matters without any need for courts to re-consider the case on merits at the enforcement stage.

The legal scene is changing both domestically and internationally. This is largely due to unprecedented growth in alternative dispute resolution, a mechanism that aims to resolve disputes outside courts and through private legal institutions and arrangements. With the staggering increase in treaties and transnational contracts referring to arbitration and other methods of alternative dispute resolution, the distinction between national and international is murkier than ever. The fast paced expansion of dispute resolution utilization outside of courts coupled with the lethargic response of courts renders the issue of mechanisms for control of such a system as timely as ever. One of the old yet largely marginalized concepts in law is the public policy exception. This doctrine grants discretion to courts to set aside private legal arrangements, including arbitration agreements and awards, which harm the "public." The ad hoc and vague nature of the doctrine, along with the strong push by actors in dispute resolution, has transformed it, in certain jurisdictions, into a toothless doctrine. At the international level also, some tribunals and scholars have devised the notion of transnational public policy in order to capture norms that are "truly" transnational and amenable for application in cross-border litigations. Yet, despite the importance of this discussion—a safety valve and a control mechanism for today's international and domestic dispute resolution—no major study has ventured to review and analyze it. Despite the exuberance about the emergence of transnationalism in international dispute resolution, the increasing application of the transnational public policy notion does in fact limit the application of mandatory laws emanating from national and international law. Moreover, this trend might lead to a worrisome practice in which public policy concerns remain under-litigated and under-analyzed. By drawing from empirical data and doctrinal analysis, the book invites scholars and practitioners to revisit the role of the public policy exception in transnational litigation as one of the very few available internal control mechanisms.

1 A brief history of the notion of public policy in English common law*

A. Paradigm shift

The word public policy did not appear until the eighteenth century in common law. Prior to that, there were general references to "*encounter commone ley*," which meant prejudicial to the community or against the benefits of the commonwealth. Knight, a legal historian, considers *John Dyer's case* (1413)[1] as one of the oldest cases referring to "*encounter commone ley*."[2] This case reflects what I call the traditional approach to public policy: a notion designed to guard against violations of communal values and mores.[3]

One of the first instances in which courts employed the term "public policy" was in the case of *Mitchel v. Reynolds*.[4] In that case Lord Macclesfield invalidated a contract that would result in restraint of trade: " . . . to obtain the sole exercise of any known trade throughout England, is a complete monopoly, and against the policy of law."[5] The doctrine of public policy first appeared explicitly here in a case involving the restraint of trade.[6] Later, it extended to other areas such as the rule against perpetuities, sales of offices, marriage contracts, and wagers.

In 1750 Lord Hardwicke offered one of the first definitions of public policy that was illuminating: contracts against public policy are of no effect,

---

* The content of the following chapter has appeared previously in Farshad Ghodoosi, *The Concept of Public Policy in Law: Revisiting the Role of the Public Policy Doctrine in the Enforcement of Private Legal Arrangements*, 94 Neb. L. Rev. 685 (2016).
1 *Yearbook*, 2 Hen. V, fol. 5, pl 26. This case was about a non-compete clause in which John Dyer promised not to use his art for half a year or else the other party could forfeit Dryer's deposit bond. The court rejected this arrangement, Keith N. Hylton, Antitrust Law: Economic Theory and Common Law Evolution 33 (2003).
2 W.S.W.Knight, Public Policy in English Law, 38 L.Q.R. 207 (1922). Robert F. Brachtenbach, *Public Policy in Judicial Decisions*, 21 Gonz. L. Rev. 1, 4 (1985–1986).
3 Winfield believes that the history of the doctrine of public policy predates even the equity system. Long before that, in considering new writs judges would consider the benefit of the public. Percy H. Winfield, *Public Policy in the English Common Law*, 42 Harv. L. Rev. 76, 77–79 (1928); Knight, *supra* note 27 at 209–10; Kent Murphy, *Traditional View of Public Policy and Ordre Public in Private International Law*, 11 Ga. J. Int'l & Comp. L. 591 (1981).
4 Brachtenbach, *supra* note 2 at 5.
5 Mitchel v. Reynolds, 1 P. WMS. 187, 24 Eng. Rep. 349 (1711).
6 Amasa M. Eaton, *Contracts in Restraint of Trade*, 4 Harv. L. Rev. 128, 129–130 (1890).

6 *Brief history of the notion of public policy*

not because either of the parties has been deceived but because they are a "general mischief" to the public."[7] More importantly, Lord Hardwicke transformed the concept from being simply against the community to being against *res publica*, i.e., public affairs. In other words, he politicized the concept of public policy in such a way that sovereign considerations would receive significant weight in the courts:

> political arguments in the fullest sense of the word, as they concern the government of a nation, must, and have always been, of great weight in the consideration of this court, and though there may be no *dolus malus*, in contracts as to other persons, yet if the rest of mankind are concerned as well as the parties, it may properly be said, that it regards the public utility.[8]

This could be marked as the start of the modern approach to the doctrine of public policy.[9] Lord Mansfield's interpretation of the doctrine of "*ex dolo malo non oritur actio*" laid another important foundation for the modern doctrine of public policy: Courts should not lend their resources to aid a man whose cause of action is based on illegal or immoral ground.[10] As Knight noted, the eighteenth century reshaped the doctrine of public policy as something distinct from bare immorality or illegality.[11] The modern approach to public policy entailed political considerations, not merely shared communal values, for its justification and its substance.

The politicization of the doctrine of public policy provoked the resistance and hesitation of nineteenth century common law. The paradigm shift from "*encounter commone ley*" to counter *res publica* incited two main reactions. One group was dismissive of the notion and believed it should lie within the authority of the legislative body to decide the policies related to the public. For instance, in *Richardson v. Mellish*, Justice Burrough famously called public policy "a very unruly horse" as "when you get astride of it, you never know where it will carry you."[12] This has become the most-often-quoted sentence on the doctrine of public policy.[13]

---

7 Knight, *supra* note 2 at 209.
8 *Id.*
9 The shift seems to be in line with the emergence of modern contract law, according to some legal historians. Contract law underwent two major paradigms: up to the late eighteenth century contract law was centered on the fairness of the bargain. Afterwards the focus shifted to the will theory of contract law and less so on the very fairness of the bargain, Morton J. Hortwitz, *The Historical Foundation of Modern Contract Law*, Harv. L. Rev. 917, 917–19 (1974).
10 *Id.*, *see also* The Bishop of London v. Fytche Cunn. 52 (1783), Fletcher v. Sondes, 3 Bing. 590 (1826), Rex v. Waddington, 1 East 143 (1800).
11 "The departure lies in the confusion of the principle of public policy with bare immorality and illegality . . . ", Knight, *supra* note 2 at 210.
12 Richardson v. Mellish, 130 Eng. Rep. 294, 303; 2 Bing. 229, 251–52 (1824) (Burrough J.).
13 This case has been cited in various contexts; in the area of law and economics *see, e.g.*, Richard A. Epstein, *Unconscionability: A Critical Reappraisal*, 18 J. Law and Econ. 293, 293

There were similar doubts in the famous case of *Egerton v. Brownlow.* Lord Alderson found it to be "inexpedient" in the opinion of sensible man.[14] Lord Parke opined that it should be the legislator, not the parties and the courts, which determine public good and public policy. *Egerton* is an important case because for the first time the conflicting views of judges on public policy were shaped and articulated clearly. One view conceptualized public policy as only a guide for ascertaining the object and purpose of statutes whereas the opposite view saw it as an abstract legal standard independent of time and circumstances.[15] The thrust of the dissenting argument revolved around the same concerns as voiced earlier by Justice Burrough: public policy lies in the discretion of legislature, not the judicature. In short, with a multitude of statutes, there was no need for judicially crafted public policy.[16]

The second group suggested that the courts concentrate on the state's interests in cases involving a public policy exception. For instance, in the old case *Cooke v. Turner*, in deciding the enforceability of a will the Judge declared that a condition could be void on the ground of public policy, if it restrained a party "from doing some act which it is supposed the State has or may have an interest to be done," as, for instance, to conduct trades or to marry.[17] However, if "the State has no interest whatsoever apart from the interest of the parties themselves"[18] the court's involvement would not be necessary, particularly under the rubric of public policy.

Lord Watson's opinion in *Nordenfeldt v. Maxim* serves as another example for the second group approach:

(1975). In the area of criminal law and contract law *see, e.g.,* John Shand, *Unblinkering the Unruly Horse: Public Policy in the Law of Contract,* 30 CAMBRIDGE L.J. 144 (1972). In the field of conflict of laws *see, e.g.,* Nicholas deBelleville Katzenbach, *Conflicts on an Unruly Horse: Reciprocal Claims and Tolerances in Interstate and International Law,* 65 YALE L.J. 1087 (1956). In the area of alternative dispute resolution *see, e.g.,* Jeffrey W. Stempel, *Pitfalls of Public Policy: The Case of Arbitration Agreements,* 22 MARY'S L.J. 259, 259 (1990). In the area of family law *see, e.g.,* Harry G. Prince, *Public Policy Limitations on Cohabitation Agreements: Unruly Horse or Circus Pony?* 70 MINN. L. REV. 163 (1985). In the area of tax law *see, e.g.,* Cathryn V. Deal, *Reining in the Unruly Horse: The Public Policy Test for Disallowing Tax Deductions,* 9 VT. L. REV. 11, 11 (1984). In the area of international arbitration *see, e.g.,* W. Michael Reisman, *Law, International Public Policy (So-called) and Arbitral Choice in International Commercial Arbitration* in INTERNATIONAL ARBITRATION 2006: BACK TO BASIC? 849, 854–55 (Albert Jan van den Berg ed., 2008); Loukas Mistelis, *Keeping the Unruly Horse in Control or Public Policy as a Bar to Enforcement of (Foreign) Arbitral Awards,* 2 INT'L L. FORUM DU DROIT INT'L 248 (2000).

14   Egerton v. Brownlow, 4 H. L. Cas. U, 196, 10 Eng. Rep. 359, 437 (1853). The case involved a contingent interest in an estate in the form of condition subsequent. The House of Lords found the arrangement void. RULING CASES 118 (Vol. 24, Irving Browne et al. eds., 1901).

15   Winfield, *supra* note 3 at 88.

16   *Id.* at 88–89.

17   Cooke v. Turner, 60 E. R. 449, 502 (1845).

18   *Id.*

A series of decisions based upon grounds of public policy, however eminent the judges by whom they were delivered, cannot possess the same binding authority as decisions which deal with and formulate principles which are purely legal. The course of policy pursued by any country in relation to, and for promoting the interests of, its commerce must, as time advances and as its commerce thrives, undergo change and development from various causes *which are altogether independent of the action of its courts*. [Emphasis added][19]

A distinction between these two approaches—most notably—lies in the fact that the former endorses a more passive role in the assessment of the public policy exception whereas the later encourages courts to actively assess and enforce the state's interests in this context. Still, today similar approaches are traceable in court's position towards this topic.

B. Unruliness of public policy

As discussed in the previous section, some judges started to cast doubt on the applicability of the doctrine of public policy. Most notably Justice Burrough called it a "very unruly horse." Yet, despite the multitude of references to the unruliness of public policy,[20] it is not clear why the resistance towards the notion of public policy emerged. In other words, this section investigates the unruly characteristic of the doctrine of public policy as it has subsisted until today in our legal culture.

The unruliness of public policy relates to its exogenous nature vis-à-vis the logic of legal reasoning. Simply put, the constitutive narrative of public policy departs from the structure of legal reasoning. Historically, the discussion of public policy has been enmeshed with contract law.[21] The law of contracts is the bedrock on which many legal systems have developed throughout history. Simply put, contract is a result of correspondence between an offer and an acceptance.[22] There are formation defects preventing the agreement from coming into existence, commonly as a result of lack or defect in consent. For example, there will be no contract if

---

19 Nordenfeldt Guns & Ammunition Co. L.R. [1894] App. Cas. 535, 553.
20 *See supra* note 13.
21 Brachtenbach, *supra* note 2 at 5; Arthur Nussbaum, *Public Policy and the Political Crisis in the Conflict of Laws*, 49 Yale L.J. 1027, 1029 (1940) ("the contracts use of the public policy concept can be traced back to the fifteenth century and its conflict use to the eighteenth century.")
22 Historically and in English common law, the modern conception of the contract came as result of recognition of the notion of assumpit. In short, assumpit, which emerged in the sixteenth century, allowed for the non-breaching party in an agreement to claim damages from the breaching party in the event of mere non-performance. Before, the non-breaching party would be liable only if (s)he was at fault, Grant Gilmore, The Ages of American law 40–43 (2d ed. 2014).

acceptance does not unconditionally match the essential terms of an offer,[23] or, if acceptance is expressed while the person is intoxicated to an extreme level.[24] In these instances, no contract or agreement is ever formed between the parties.

On the other hand, there are instances where a contract, after being fully formed by the parties, does not yield its usual consequences. Illegality of a contract is one of the prime instances in which the contract is devoid of legal impact. Usury is a good example in the history of contract law. Following Christianity[25] and Greek economic theory, receiving extra payment for the use of a loan was prohibited. As a result, contracts that led to usury were found to be unlawful and, thus, void.[26]

The public policy exception belongs to the second category. It does not bear on the formation of contracts but on their effects. Historically, for Medieval lawyers the contract was either illegal or not. No other categories, such as public policy, existed.[27] Similarly, during the sixteenth and early seventeenth centuries in common law, illegality was a general category encompassing contracts rendered void by statute, contracts contrary to public policy, contracts to commit crimes, and other categories.[28] It was later in history that public policy became an independent category from illegality. Parties could not evade public policy by entering into private contracts. In other words, private contracts were not to be avenues to circumvent the public policy of states. As a result, private legal arrangements became systemically subject to public affairs thanks to the doctrine of public policy. At the time, three types of contracts were deemed to be against public policy: 1) contracts to oust the jurisdiction of the court; 2) contracts that tend to prejudice the status of marriage; and 3) contracts in restraint of trade.[29]

---

23 *See, e.g.*, Iselin v. United States, 46 S. Ct. 458, 459 (1926) ("A proposal to accept, or an acceptance of, an offer, on terms varying from those offered, is a rejection of the offer, and ends the negotiation unless one making the original offer renews it or assents to the suggested modification."

24 *See, e.g.*, Seminara v. Grisman, 137 N.J. Eq. 307, 312–13 (1945) ("A contract should not be enforced where the mind of the party was so disqualified by excessive and complete intoxication that he was at the time mentally incapable of understanding the subject of the agreement, its nature, and probable consequences").

25 St Thomas Aquinas famously argues that usury is double payment because the person who loans receives extra payment for something that does not have an independent existence, *see* ALFRED WILLIAM BRIAN SIMPSON, A HISTORY OF THE COMMON LAW OF CONTRACT: THE RISE OF ACTION OF ASSUMPSIT 510 (vol. 1, 1987).

26 *See, e.g.*, Sanderson v. Warner, Palmer 291, 2 Rolle Rep. 239 (1622); *cited in* ALFRED WILLIAM BRIAN SIMPSON, A HISTORY OF THE COMMON LAW OF CONTRACT: THE RISE OF THE ACTION OF ASSUMPSIT 514 (1975); *see generally* MARK ORD, AN ESSAY ON THE LAW OF USURY (1809).

27 ALFRED WILLIAM BRIAN SIMPSON, LEGAL THEORY AND LEGAL HISTORY: ESSAYS ON THE COMMON LAW 129 (1987).

28 *Id.* at 508.

29 M.P. FURMSTON, CHESHIRE FIFOOT & FURMSTON'S LAW OF CONTRACT 470 (2007).

Courts gradually employed the category of public policy as separate from illegality in contract law,, holding that if a contract is against public policy, it is not void, yet it is unenforceable. It is best described in the words of Denning LJ in the *Bennett v. Bennett* case:

> They are not "illegal", in the sense that a contact to do a prohibited or immoral act is illegal. They are not "unenforceable", in the sense that a contract within the Statute of Frauds is unenforceable for want of writing. These covenants lie somewhere in between. They are invalid and unenforceable.[30]

This excerpt attests to the exceptional nature of public policy in contract law. Also, and more importantly, it is exogenous: it is imposed by an external necessity or force and has not been duly integrated into the fabric of contract law jurisprudence. It is "somewhere in between", as Denning opines, because it does not entirely fit within contract law's traditional *illegality* doctrine.

Contract law is primarily a matter of private law, in which the parties are deemed to be of equal footing. Neither party has privilege because of social or political status. Yet, the modern doctrine of public policy rests on the idea that enforcing a contract is a matter of public law. Delivering justice is a public affair and is done at public expense and, therefore, should be monitored. Public resources should not be employed for the execution of an agreement which is injurious to public morality or interest.[31] The words of Wilmot C. demonstrate this approach:

> It is the duty of all courts of justice to keep their eye steadily upon the interests of the public, even in the administration of commutative justice; and when they find an action is founded upon a claim injurious to public . . .[32]

Henceforth, contract law had to confront an entity which was beyond the logic resulting from the offer–acceptance paradigm. Even if all four corners of the documents complied with provisions of jurisprudence of contract law, an external moral or legislative concern could render it unenforceable. The very exogenous feature of the public policy doctrine has differentiated it from other similar doctrines such as the unconscionability doctrine. An unconscionable term goes to the heart of consideration in a bargain; public

---

30 [1952] 1 KB 249, 260, [1952] 1 All ER 413, 421, *reprinted in* Michael Furmston, Cheshire, Fifoot and Furmston's Law of Contract 460 (2012).

31 "The strength of every contract lies in the power of the promise to appeal to the courts to appeal to the courts of public justice for redress for its violation. The administration of justice is maintained at the public expense: the courts will never, therefore, recognize any transaction which, in its object, operation, or tendency, is calculated to be prejudicial to the public welfare." Elisha Greenhood, The Doctrine of Public Policy in the Law of Contracts: Reduced to Rules 2 (1886).

32 Wilmot's opinion, 377, *quoted in* Crawford & Murray v. Wick, 18 Ohio St. 190, 204 (1868); Gleason v. Chicago, 43 N.W. 517, 518 (1889).

policy doctrine does not concern itself with the logics of contract law, such as consideration. This is what's unruly about public policy. It has a logic of its own separate from the internal logic of private legal acts of citizens.[33] More importantly, it could prevent a lawful act from yielding results. Public policy is also distinct from illegality. It is external, exceptional, and rather haphazard. Scholars find it almost impossible to pin down an overarching theory regarding this doctrine. All these factors demonstrate the general tendency to contain the public policy doctrine. In addition, in a globalized world in need for predictability, the public policy doctrine has remained the most unpredictable aspect of global judicialization.

C. Definition

We hear the phrase public policy on a daily basis from media outlets to scholarly debates in law and other fields. Yet, the doctrine of public policy in law has a distinct and nuanced framework that needs to be delineated before we embark on analyzing it. This section provides an overview of various applications and definitions of the phrase 'public policy'.

The phrase is discussed in four contexts: 1) public policy in a modern sense, i.e., policies pursued and enacted by governments, and mainly referring to the administrative aspects of governments;[34][35] 2) public policy as a mandatory rule which trumps the parties' contractual agreement; 3) public policy as it appears in conflict of laws limiting the application of foreign rules;[36]

---

33 "To base a decision on the ground of public policy, however, introduces into the judicial process an element with different characteristics than the other grounds. It brings into the case an element extrinsic from the conduct of the parties—the exercise of community control quite apart from statute, judicial precedent or doctrine." James D. Hopkins, *Public Policy and the Formation of a Rule of Law*, 37 BROOK. L. REV. 323, 323 (1970).

34 Here are some leading definitions in this category: "The term public policy always refers to the actions of government and the intentions that determine those actions," CLARKE E. COCHRAN ET AL., AMERICAN PUBLIC POLICY: AN INTRODUCTION (1999); "Whatever governments choose to do or not to do," THOMAS R DYE, UNDERSTANDING PUBLIC POLICY (1992); "Stated most simply, public policy is the sum of government activities, whether acting directly or through agents, as it has an influence on the life of citizens," B. GUY PETERS, AMERICAN PUBLIC POLICY: PROMISE AND PERFORMANCE (1999).

35 *See, e.g.*, Richard H.W. Maloy, *Public Policy: Who Should Make It in America's Oligarchy?* 1998 DET. C. L. REV. 1147, 1147 (1998). Often, the term public policy does not refer to specific laws and regulations but a practice by the government that has not been incorporated into law, P.C.A. Snyman, *Public Policy in Anglo-American Law*, 19 COMP. & INT. L. J. OF S. AFR. 220, 221 (1986) (citing Nashville C & St L v. Browning 310 U.S 362 (1940); Nussbaum, *supra* note 21 at 1027 ("public policy is relied upon in order to solve doubts as to the interpretation of legal rules").

36 *See, e.g.*, Herbert F. Goodrich, *Public Policy in the Conflict of Laws*, 36 W. VA. L. Q. 156 (1930); Ernest G. Lorenzen, *Territoriality, Public Policy and the Conflict of Laws*, 33 YALE L. J. 736 (1924); Arthur Nussbaum, *supra* note 21; Charles B. Nutting, *Suggested Limitations of the Public Policy Doctrine*, 19 MINN. L. REV. 196 (1935); John Corr, *Modern Choice of Law and Public Policy: The Emperor Has the Same Old Clothes*, 39 U. MIAMI L. REV. 647 (1985); Conrad G. Paulsen & Michael I. Sovren, *"Public Policy" in Conflict of Laws*, 56 COLUM. L. REV. 969 (1956); Herbert

and 4) public policy which bars the enforcement of foreign judgments or arbitral awards.

Public policy, in its first sense, encompasses general '*public*' policies pursued by the government. Governments try to achieve certain '*public*' goals, such as promotion of education, prohibition of drug usage, increasing the efficiencies of their economies, and protection of basic rights, among many other policies. What public policies best suit each government is a science and a field of study. Almost all well-reputed universities offer a degree or a non-degree program in public policy.

Courts often utilize the aforementioned meaning of public policy. For example, a quick survey of US Supreme Court decisions demonstrates that this usage of the phrase has been quite common. For example, in the classic *Marbury v. Madison* case the Supreme Court found public policy provided an underlying ground for the writ of mandamus.[37] In *U. S. v. Procter & Gamble Co* the Court confirmed "the strong public policy of preserving the secrecy of grand jury proceedings."[38] In *Owen v. City of Independence* and *Malley v. Briggs*, the Supreme Court favored qualified immunity because of, *inter alia*, considerations of public policy.[39] Another example is the *Mitsubishi* case in

---

W. Greenber, *Extrastate Enforcement of Tax Claims and Administrative Tax Determinations under the Full Faith and Credit Clause*, 43 BROOK L. REV. 630 (1977); Robert A. Leflar, *Extrastate Enforcement of Penal and Government Claims*, 46 HARV. L. REV. 193 (1932); Willis L.M. Reese, *Full Faith and Credit to Statutes: The Defense of Public Policy*, 19 U. CHI, L. REV. 339 (1952); for more recent discussions, *see e.g.*, Thomas G. Guedj, *The theory of the Lois de Police: A Functional Trend in Continental Private International Law—A Comparative Analysis with Modern American Theories*, 39 AM. J. COMP. L. 661 (1991); Barbara Cox, *Same-Sex Marriage and the Public Policy Exception in Choice of Law: Does It Really Exist?* 16 QUINNIPIAC L. REV. 61 (1996); Todd C. Hilbig, Will New York Recognize Same-Sex Marriage?: An Analysis of the Conflict-of-Laws' Public Policy Exception, 12 U. J. Pub. L. 333 (1998); Lynn L. Hogue, *State Common-Law Choice of Law Doctrine in Same Sex Marriage: How Will States Enforce the Public Policy Exception?* 32 CREIGHTON L. REV. 29 (1998); Kent Murphy, *Traditional View of Public Policy and Ordre Public in Private International Law*, 11 GA. J. INT'L & COMP. L. 591 (1981).

37 Marbury v. Madison, 5 U.S. 137,169–70 (1803) ("Lord Mansfield, in 3d Burrow's 1266, in the case of *The King v. Baker, et al.* states with much precision and explicitness the cases in which this writ may be used. 'Whenever,' says that very able judge, 'there is a right to execute an office, perform a service, or exercise a franchise (more especially if it be in a matter of public concern, or attended with profit) and a person is kept out of possession, or dispossessed of such right, and has no other specific legal remedy, this court ought to assist by mandamus, upon reasons of justice, as the writ expresses, and upon reasons of public policy, to preserve peace, order and good government.' In the same case he says, 'this writ ought to be used upon all occasions where the law has established no specific remedy, and where in justice and good government there ought to be one.'")
38 U. S. v. Procter & Gamble Co., 78 S. Ct. 983, 989 (1958). ("I fully subscribe to the view that the strong public policy of preserving the secrecy of grand jury proceedings should prevent the general disclosure of a grand jury transcript except in the rarest cases.")
39 Owen v. City of Independence, 445 U.S. 622, 667 (1980): "Important public policies support the extension of qualified immunity to local governments." Malley v. Briggs, 475 U.S. 335, 335 (1986) ("Neither the common law nor public policy affords any support for absolute immunity. Such immunity cannot be permitted on the basis that petitioner's function

which the Supreme Court declared that the law endorsed the public policy in favor of competition.[40]

Public policy, as used in other contexts, refers to an aspect of '*public*' life, emanating from various sources including public policy in the above-mentioned sense, that holds a trump card against contracts, judgments, and foreign rules. While its multi-dimensional character makes it very difficult to define public policy, Lord Truro put forward a much reiterated definition in 1853, when he said in the landmark case of *Egerton v. Brownlow* that it is

> that principle of law which holds that no subject can lawfully do that which has a tendency to be injurious to the public, or against the public good, which may be termed ... the policy of law or public policy in relation to the administration of the law.[41] [42]

In the literature, Winfield has provided a basic definition for the concept of public policy: "a principle of judicial legislation or interpretation founded on the current needs of the community."[43]

Yet, only certain types of public policies—in the first sense—could exert an impact on the enforceability and legality of private contracts as well as foreign judgments and awards. The vexing question is how to draw the line between the two and how to frame the public policy exception both descriptively and normatively. Descriptively, it has become almost impossible to find a pattern which the courts have followed when finding contracts against public policy. From the normative standpoint, it remains a challenging task to find an all-encompassing theory that they should follow in cases involving the public policy defense.

In this chapter, public policy refers to situations where private legal acts such as contracts become unenforceable due to their conflict with a '*public*' policy deduced from legislation or judge-made rules. Rationales put forward for the functionality of this theory are manifold. In the area of

---

in seeking the arrest warrants was similar to that of a complaining witness, since complaining witnesses were not absolutely immune at common law. As a matter of public policy, qualified immunity provides ample protection to all but the plainly incompetent or those who knowingly violate the law"); Imbler v. Pachtman, 424 U.S. 409, 409 (1976) ("The same considerations of public policy that underlie the common-law rule of absolute immunity of a prosecutor from a suit for malicious prosecution likewise dictate absolute immunity under § 1983.")

40 Mitsubishi Motors Corp. v. Soler Chrysler-Plymouth, Inc., 105 S. Ct. 3346, 3367 n.21 (1985) ("The plaintiff who reaps the reward of treble damages may be no less morally reprehensible than the defendant, but the law encourages his suit to further the overriding public policy in favor of competition.")
41 Egerton v. Brownlow, *supra* note 14.
42 Earlier, Tindal C.J. provided a similar definition: "Whatever is injurious to the interests of the public is void, on the grounds of public policy." Hornor v. Graves, 131 Eng. Rep. 284, 287 (1831).
43 Winfield, *supra* note 3 at 92.

contract law, historically, courts have leaned towards three main justifications. First, the justification has been that public policy punishes wrongful behavior by refusing to enforce the agreement.[44] Second, it proscribes lending help to those who have violated an important public interest.[45] Third, and primarily relevant to legal acts that are contrary to criminal law, is the deterrent effect of the doctrine of public policy.[46] [47]

One final note is necessary regarding the contours of the public policy doctrine as it appears in this chapter. This piece does not address the situations in which the law explicitly declares the contrary agreements to be unenforceable, i.e., in which a statute declares unequivocally that contrary agreements are void and unenforceable.[48] These are easy cases, requiring no significant discussion and analysis. In fact, these cases do not even belong in the discussion of public policy and invoking the doctrine in these instances seems to be an erroneous practice.

D. Taxonomy

In this section we look at the taxonomy and classifications suggested in the literature for the public policy exception. Despite its importance, the existing literature has not addressed the matter thoroughly, and except for a few notable recent pieces the majority of the scholarship predates the 1950s. In 1935, Walter Gellhorn wrote a classic piece, published in the *Columbia Law Review*, in which he favored what could be called the legislation-based doctrine of public policy.[49] Criticizing the judicial-based approach to public policy, he argues that the role of courts is to discover public policies underlying statutes

---

44 Shand, *supra* note 13 at 148.
45 *Id.* at 151.
46 *Id.* at 154. The Supreme Court of the United States in the case *McMullen v. Hoffman* refers to it as a rationale underlying doctrine of public policy: "to refuse to grant either party to an illegal contract judicial aid for the enforcement of his alleged rights under it tends strongly towards reducing the number of such transactions to minimum. The more plainly parties understand that when they enter into contracts of this nature they place themselves outside the protection of the law . . . " McMullen v. Hoffman, 174 U.S. 639, 669–70 (1899).
47 In situations where contracts impose costs on third parties, legislatures and courts face a dilemma: whether they should hold them subject to criminal or civil liability while leaving the contract intact or declare the contract unenforceable. For example in *Mincks Agri Center, Inc., v. Bell Farms, Inc.*, the court had to decide whether imposing criminal penalties for lack of license would be sufficient deterrence. The court decided that the contract concluded during the time the plaintiff did not have a property license was unenforceable, Mincks Agri Center, Inc., v. Bell Farms, Inc, 611 N.W. 2d 270, 270 (Iowa Super. Ct. 2000). In contrast, in the case *Hirman Ricker & Sons v. Students International Mediation Society* the court did not declare the contract unenforceable, even though the plaintiff did not have a sanitation license; the court found the additional penalty of non-enforceability as harsh and unsound in that case, Hirman Ricker & Sons v. Students International Mediation Society, 342 A. 2d 262, 267 (Me. Super. Ct. 1975).
48 *See infra* note 71.
49 Walter Gellhorn, *Contracts and Public Policy*, 35 COLUM. L. REV. 679, 679–80 (1935).

rather than foisting new policies. What falls under public policy "is for the legislature to determine," according to Gellhorn, whereas the judiciary is limited to investigating the content of public policy.[50]

He also found penal code provisions to be one effective way of ascertaining legal acts that are detrimental to public interest. Even absent clear-cut legislative intent, contracts assisting or resulting in certain prohibited criminal acts should be declared unenforceable as contrary to public policy.[51] This argument was a response to those who viewed unenforceability of contracts as an additional sanction to a prohibited act, not stipulated by the legislature.[52]

Gellhorn's piece marks the start of the American approach to the doctrine of public policy. It essentially seeded skepticism towards the judicially-based public policy doctrine. Paradoxically, in a common law system encouraging judicial review, the determination of public policy was viewed primarily as a task of statutory interpretation. The judge's task was reduced to eliciting non-legal policy deductions from essentially non-legal materials.[53] This approach probably was the reason behind the general popularity of the case *Richardson v. Mellish* among courts, and its often-quoted description of public policy as an "unruly horse."[54] [55] This view yields to a transcendental view of public policy, a hidden wisdom that judges should extract from legislation.[56] In sharp contrast, in the same period, Justice Oliver Wendell Holmes was

---

50 *Id.* at 685.
51 *Id.* at 683–84.
52 *Id.* at 683.
53 MORRIS R. COHEN & FELIX S. COHEN, READINGS IN JURISPRUDENCE AND LEGAL PHILOSOPHY VOLUME I 187 (1951).
54 *See supra* note 13.
55 Justice Burrough differed from Chief Justice Abbott, who had taken an opposite view in an earlier case, *Card v. Hope*, on the issue of public policy. Winfield, *supra* note 3, at 87; Richardson v. Mellish, *supra* note 12 at 251. Interestingly enough, his views have been rarely invoked in the discourse on public policy doctrine. Winfield, *supra* note 3 at 87.
56 The suggested passive role of judges regarding public policy has a notable consequence for alternative dispute resolution. For the purpose of this section, Gellhorn's theory attracted a group of scholars and practitioners in international arbitration. With the reduced role for judges in this area, it remains less of a challenge to prove that arbitrators not only have the authority to adjudicate public policy related matters, but courts would have limited judicial review discretion, JAN PAULSSON, THE IDEA OF ARBITRATION 134–35 (2013). Arbitrators are as competent as judges to discover the intent of the legislative body as to the underlying public policy of a certain act or regulation. We will discuss the merits of this argument in a separate chapter. Yet, one point is worth considering: this approach seems to dodge the very vexing question of discovering the nature of "*public*" in public policy. The role of arbitrators is inextricably linked to the conceptualization of public policy. The public nature of these policies needs to be dissected and investigated. The exiting literature on alternative dispute resolution shuns away from probing into the hard task of the nature of "*public*." As I lay out in this chapter, public policy is not simply a constructed policy behind legislation but consist of at least three distinct notions.

laying the foundation of American jurisprudence by relying heavily on the role of judges in policy-making.[57] This has remained an important component of American jurisprudence ever since. For instance McDougal and Lasswell find it inevitable—and even desirable—that lawyers engage in shaping policies.[58] In spite of this theoretic and practical turn, the public policy doctrine remained an outlier in the discourse of American legal realism. The skeptic view of the unruliness of public policy, whether articulated by the legislature or the courts, has become the prevailing narrative.

Not all scholars, however, share this view. While Gellhorn's theory summed up—and by one account initiated—a long-lasting tradition vis-à-vis public policy, opposing theories challenged his reductionist view. Roscoe Pound probably furnished the most important counter-argument to Gellhorn's approach. Pound's theory rests on the social implications of law and not on any abstract notions, meaning natural rights or positivism. His general theoretical interest lies in the ways through which law controls the social sphere. In his seminal piece in the *Harvard Law Review*, *A Survey of Social Interests*, he grapples with the doctrine of public policy in common law, pointing out that from the seventeenth to the end of the nineteenth century public policy focused on the individual's natural rights. Social interests, according to Pound, were marginalized due to the prevailing public policy approach or were construed in the shadow of the abstract individual right paradigm.[59] Consequently, the notion of public policy routinely conjured up the image of an "unruly horse"—"you never know where it will carry you."[60] Courts became too apprehensive to apply, or too hostile to seriously engage, the notion of public policy. They only paid lip service to it, as Pound mentions:

> In truth, the nineteenth-century attitude toward public policy was itself only the expression of a public policy. It resulted from a weighing of the social interest in the general security against other social interests which men had sought to secure through an overwide magisterial discretion in the stage of equity and natural law.

---

57 "I recognize without hesitation that judges do and must legislate but they can do so only interstitially; they are confined from molar to molecular motions. A common-law judge could not say I think the doctrine of consideration a bit of historical nonsense and shall not enforce it in any court." Southern Pacific Co. v. Jensen, 244 U.S. 205, 231 (1917) (dissenting opinion).
58 Justin Zaremby, Legal Realism and American Law 99 (2014).
59 Roscoe Pound, *A Survey of Social Interest*, 57 Harv. L. Rev. 1, 5 (1943).
60 Richardson v. Mellish, *supra* note 12.

As a result, the courts forged a few judicial public policies[61] in light of the enlightenment teachings,[62] and the rest of what constitutes public policy was left with the legislature to decide. According to Pound, the courts retained their status as a guardian of "general security exclusively in terms of individual rights" and did not find it cumbersome to weigh "social interest in terms of the general security" in the sense described. Yet, they voiced their skepticism about the courts' role in the advancement of other social interests, finding those interests to be too vague and ill-defined.[63] Furthermore, the courts noted that they were restricted to adjudicating the merits of the cases before them, which limited their ability to further or establish public policies.

Pound's piece shed light on the shortcomings of the doctrine of public policy in common law and specifically in American jurisprudence. Juxtaposing it with Gellhorn's theory, one can understand the conceptual framework underlying the treatment of public policy in American jurisprudence. In this framework courts are tasked with protecting mainly individual rights under the doctrine of public policy whereas for other public interests the legislature sets the policies and the court's task is to investigate them. Pound's piece aims to demonstrate that the reductionist view undermines other forms of social interests which, for him, are manifold. First, general security, which consists of general safety and general health as well as the security of transactions, is of paramount importance.[64] The security of social institutions such as marriage and religious institutions are the second important social interest.[65] Third is the social interest

---

61 Pound enumerates the most prominent judicial public policies created by the courts over the nineteenth century: "First and most numerous are policies with reference to the security of social institutions. As to political institutions, there is a recognized policy against acts promotive of crime or violation of law—in other words, a policy of upholding legal institution—and a policy against acts prejudicially affecting the public service performed by public officers. As to domestic institutions, there is the well-known policy against acts affecting the security of the domestic relations, or in restraint of marriage. As to economic institutions, there is the policy against acts destructive of competition, the policy against acts affecting commercial freedom, and the policy against permanent or general restrictions on the free use and transfer of property. Secondly, there are policies with reference to maintaining the general morals. Thus there is a recognized policy against acts promotive of dishonesty. Also there is a recognized policy against acts offending the general morals. Thirdly, there are policies with reference to the individual social life: a policy against things tending to oppression, and a policy against general or extensive restrictions upon individual freedom of action" [footnotes omitted]. *Id.* at 8.
62 Hegel's idea of liberty influenced nineteenth century jurisprudence and as a result the notion of public policy. *Id.* at 5.
63 *Id.* at 12.
64 *Id.* at 17–20.
65 *Id.* at 20–23.

in the general morals; the so called *boni mores* of Roman law.[66] Fourth, he identifies the conservation of social resources as a public interest which should be preserved against individual desires.[67] Public interest in general progress is the fifth social interest.[68] Last, and most important for Pound, is the very value of individual life, such that every human should be able to enjoy rights such as individual self-assertion, individual opportunity, and individual conditions of life.[69]

Pound was the first scholar to provide a taxonomy of public policy under the rubric of social interests. He aimed to broaden the perspective of what constituted public interests and change the discourse on legal order "as one of adjusting the exercise of free wills to one of satisfying wants, of which free exercise of will is but one."[70] He was probably the first who viewed public policies as graded and not as a monolithic or an untouchable notion.

There have also been several attempts to formulate public policy by its sources. This classification is premised on the clarity of legislative intent. The first category belongs to public policies declared explicitly by the legislature. Often statutes proclaim unequivocally their objectives in the preamble of the document or in the text.[71] For instance, the Public Housing Law of New York State devotes a section to describing in detail the policy and purpose of the law.[72] The task of judges in these instances is minimal since the public purpose of the statute has been declared by the legislature. In most cases, judges have to extrapolate the intent of the legislature re. the prevailing policy underlying the statute. Judges investigate the legislative history and the context in which the legislation was passed to identify the policy behind it.[73] Lastly, in the absence of a legislative or constitutional declaration or a reasonable inference thereupon, courts are permitted to venture into the area of declaring public policy.[74] Antitrust law is a good example: due to the vagueness of the Sherman Act, judges gradually crafted a body of public policies to protect society from unfair competition.[75]

A taxonomy based on the sources of public policy as described above oversimplifies the complicated problem of public policy. Not only does it

---

66 *Id.* at 25. He opines that in cases involving moral issues "we much reach a balance between social interest in the general morals, and the social interest in general progress, taking form in a policy of free discussion."
67 *Id.* at 26.
68 *Id.* at 30.
69 *Id.* at 33.
70 *Id.* at 1.
71 Hopkins, *supra* note 33 at 325–26.
72 McKinney's Public Housing Law § 2, NY PUB HOUS § 2 (Policy of State and purpose of chapter.)
73 Hopkins, *supra* note 33 at 326. Brachtenbach, *supra* note 2, at 18.
74 Hopkins, *supra* note 33 at 330.
75 *See generally* KEITH N. HYLTON, ANTITRUST LAW: ECONOMIC THEORY AND COMMON LAW EVOLUTION (2003).

not provide any substantive guide as to the nature of public policy, but its classification might also be easily deconstructed. For instance, the preamble to the Patriot Act clearly lays out the purpose of the statute: "to deter and punish terrorist acts in the United States and around the world." Even if, according to the taxonomy above, the policy here is clearly declared, that does not render any help to judges. The judges confront a multitude of statutes with conflicting public policies, making it almost impossible to use a statute's declared policy as a guideline. In the example above, the Patriot Act's public policy turned out to be in conflict with other documents including the Constitution.[76] The conflicting policies as well as the vague language of statutes leaves almost all categories open to a judicially-based public policy. In addition, statutory interpretations by various courts would routinely result in conflicting outcomes. Therefore, we can hardly accept that public policy is a matter exclusively for the legislature to decide. Judicial public policy and legislative policies serve inherently distinct functions: the former resolves disputes at micro level whereas the latter aims to set broader policies.[77]

A few scholars have proposed several substantive classifications of public policy, mainly in the field of contract law. Furmston divides the doctrine of public policy into five categories. First, he pays attention to instances where contracts are not illegal but only unenforceable due to public policy concerns. The example he provides is the case *Beresford v. Royal Insurance Company Limited*,[78] in which the House of Lords held that an insurance company did not need to pay out on a life insurance contract because the beneficiary had committed suicide, which was illegal. The decision was based on public policy in that the contract on its face supported the view of the beneficiary's family.[79]

The second category pertains to instances where contracts lead to prohibited acts, notably crimes. These are easy cases where, for instance, contracts prescribe committing a crime.[80] The third category is the opposite of the second one. In instances where the policy of law is to promote a particular act, no legal acts including contracts can restrain or prohibit it. The paramount examples are contracts in restraint of marriage or in restraint of trade.[81] The next category belongs to situations where a contract does not

---

76 *See, e.g.*, John W. Whitehead & Steven H. Aden, *Forfeiting "Enduring Freedom" for Homeland Security": A Constitutional Analysis of the USA Patriot Act and the Justice Department's Anti-Terrorism Initiatives*, 51 Am. U. L. Rev. 1081 (2001).
77 Daniel A. Farber & Philip P. Frickey, *In the Shadow of the Legislature: The Common Law in the Age of the New Public Law*, 89 Mich. L. Rev. 875, 889.
78 [1938] A.C. 586; affirming [1937] 2 K.B. 197.
79 M.P. Furmston, *The Analysis of Illegal Contract*, 16 U. Toronto L.J., 267, 268 (1965).
80 *Id.* at 280. For instance, in *Evert v. Williams* an individual sued for a financial dispute arising out of a partnership formed to commit a robbery, 9 L.Q.R. 197 (1893).
81 *Id.* at 292.

lead to an illegal act but rather promotes a tendency that is contrary to the policy of the law. An example is where a couple signs a separation agreement for their potential future divorce. This very contract might induce divorce, a matter that is contrary to the marriage law policy.[82]

Lastly, a contract might violate public policy if the intention of one party or both is to use it as a preparation for an unlawful act. For instance, if a person rents a place with the intention to use it for prostitution, the lease is lawful yet the intention makes the contract contrary to public policy.[83]

Furmston's study is illuminating as to the various ways that public policy could affect legal acts. Yet, it is a descriptive study and does not provide a theoretical ground on which a general public policy could be premised.

In another recent case, Friedman endeavors to bring order to complicated public policy matters by analyzing data collected from court decisions. He finds that, in practice, public policy defenses rooted in a statute or regulation had a 59% success rate whereas general appeals to public policy resulted in only a 31% success rate.[84] Among the first category, those cases involving an agreement in direct contravention of licensure or a code had the higher success rate (75%). The rest belongs to criminal agreements (57%), agreements that limit or shift liability (58%), and others (50%).[85] This study confirms the special status of the legislative branch in setting public policy and the heavy weight courts place on such declared policy. In spite of illuminating empirical data, this piece leaves pressing questions about the nature of public policy unanswered.

As noted, the current literature does not engage itself with rigorous and substantive analysis of the doctrine of public policy. It is still the case that most of the important works on this issue predate 1950, and go as far back as opinions in eighteenth and nineteenth century England. New changes in conflict of laws, contract law, and, more importantly, alternative dispute resolution necessitate serious scholarship on this front. Integration of the world economy, globalization, and increasing cross-border disputes are among the many factors that render public policy a pivotal doctrine and a pressing issue. It could serve as a guardian for national values and also as a deterrent for cross-border trade, if used disproportionately.

---

82 *Id.* at 297–98.
83 *Id.* at 306.
84 David Adam Friedman, *Bringing Order to Contracts against Public Policy*, 39 Fla. St. U. L.R. 563, 581 (2011).
85 *Id.* at 583.

2 A brief history of public policy as regulatory planning in the United States

This section aims to show the ebb and flow of the notion of public policy in twentieth-century legal thought. It also endeavors to demonstrate that one's approach to the public policy doctrine is inextricably linked to one's chosen legal theory. Many legal theories do not explicitly address the effects of their approach on the public policy doctrine. This section aims to redress that.

The American legal system in the twentieth century had to confront a complicated challenge. While the courts lagged behind in expanding the common law in proportion to the needs of the growing society and economy, Congress introduced an ever-increasing number statutes to the legal system. This coincided with the interference of various other crucial factors including the emergence of the concept of a welfare state with its accompanying massive regulation as well as a new policy-based school of legal thought commonly referred to as American Realism.

Three phases are identifiable in twentieth century American legal history. In the first period, dating back to pre-World War II, courts showed a reluctance to analyze statutes from a policy-based approach. As will be explained in the first section, the courts remained formalistic in their approach to common law versus statutes. However, this classical approach, in practice, allowed more discretion for courts to determine public policy as applied to private agreements and foreign judgments.

In the second phase, following World War II, the prevailing approach of courts was to interpret statutes in line with the expressed or implied (public) policies. More recently, in the third phase, the idea that statutes set rather immutable public policies became the interpretive standard. This approach came under criticism as it limits the maneuvering of courts in cases and it would change the nature of common law. The last section will address the most recent scholarly reactions to this problem.

A. The classical approach

1. Formalism

One's view of the role of public policy in law is tied to the role of the state vis-à-vis its citizens. Classical liberalism, which existed at the early stages of modern statehood, held that there should be a minimal role for states. In a nutshell, classical liberalism does not go further than assigning to states the task of protecting citizens and their civil rights. Early philosophers such as Thomas Hobbes[1] and John Locke[2] laid the foundational theories for modern statehood, framing the function of states quite narrowly. This view can be summed up, using Robert Nozick's language, as advocating a "night-watchman" state.[3]

For classical liberalists, states cannot have much say in determining public policy especially in issues other than security and protection of civil liberties.[4] This view allows for broader court discretion to set certain public policies through the *stare decisis* mechanism. Unlike the policies declared by the legislator, the courts' policies are bottom-up, deriving from disputes between parties. These policies emerge as a result of parties' arguments and remain fact-specific and fact-sensitive. This is in sharp contrast with legislator-set policies contained in statutes; these are top-down and not necessarily related to any particular sets of facts.

We should note that determining public policy is an interpretive task—particularly when private agreements can be compromised due to conflict with public policy. In cases where the language of a statute conveys a clear meaning as to the invalidity of contrary private agreements, arbitral awards, and foreign judgments, judges do not need to resort to the doctrine of public policy. The notion of public policy as understood in the legislative phase remains broader than public policy as applied in the adjudicative phase. Government representatives tend to call the outcome of the legislative process public policy while the courts, with some differences, take a much narrower approach.

---

1 *See* CARL SCHMITT, THE LEVIATHAN IN THE STATE THEORY OF THOMAS HOBBES 31 (George Schwab & Erna Hilfstein trans., Greenwood Press 1996) (1938): "The starting point of Hobbes' construction of the state is fear of the state of nature, the goal and terminus is security of the civil, the stately (*staatlichen*) condition." THOMAS HOBBS, LEVIATHAN: OR, THE MATTER, FORME, & POWER OF A COMMON WEALTH ECCLESIASTICAL AND CIVIL (1904).
2 JOHN LOCKE, TWO TREATISES OF GOVERNMENT § 131 (1821). "But though men when they enter into society give up the equality, liberty, and executive power they had in the state of Nature into the hands of society . . . yet it being only with an intention in every one the better to preserve himself his Liberty, Property . . . "
3 ROBERT NOZICK, ANARCHY, STATE, AND UTOPIA 25 (1974).
4 Consent plays a critical role in liberalist ideas. Government cannot enter into regulating people's lives without prior consent from them. In the United States context, "we the people" consented to be bound by Congress' statutes as stipulated in the Constitution, WILLIAM N. ESKRIDGE, DYNAMIC STATUTORY INTERPRETATION 111–12 (1994).

The formal supremacy of statutes over judicial decisions has remained a cornerstone of the traditional American "legisprudence."[5][6] This is more or less similar to other major legal systems in the world. Pursuant to the Constitution of the United States, legislative power rests at the discretion of Congress. Article II declares that the President and the executive branch ensure that the laws are "faithfully executed." On the other hand, the judicial branch has been tasked with adjudicating cases and controversies. Although no explicit language in the Constitution lays out the supremacy of the statutes over judicial decisions, this principle is inferred from the separation of power doctrine and the nature of the judicial task.

However, as several authors have pointed out, the supremacy of statutes over judicial decisions did not carry much weight in the classical approach.[7][8] Courts would still limit the scope of statutes by resorting to the Constitution (specifically, Ex Post Facto,[9] Bill of Attainder,[10] and Contract Clauses[11]).[12] More importantly the courts in the classical era would not

---

5 This term refers to the study of law-making by legislators using legal theory and philosophy, Julius Cohen, *Legisprudence: Problems and Agenda*, 11 HOFSTRA L. REV. 1163 (1983); Julius Cohen, *Towards Realism in Legisprudence*, 59 YALE L. J. 886 (1950); *see also* William N. Eskridge, Jr. & Philip P. Frickey, *Legislation Scholarship and Pedagogy in the Post-Legal Process Era*, 48 U. PITT. L. REV. 691, 693 (1987); LUC J. WINTGENS ET AL., LEGISPRUDENCE: A NEW THEORETICAL APPROACH TO LEGISLATION (Luc J. Wintgens ed., 2002); *see also* GRANT GILMORE, THE AGES OF AMERICAN LAW 62 (2d ed. 2014). ("The post-Civil War judicial product seems to start from the assumption that the law is a closed, logical system. Judges do not make law: they merely declare the law which, in some Platonic sense, already exists.")

6 Some authors believe that the American legal system had three periods: from 1800 until the Civil War, Civil War until World War I and from World War I until the present time. The pre-Civil War is considered to be the Golden age of the American legal system because of its non-formalistic approach to law, KARL LLEWELLYN, THE COMMON LAW TRADITION: DECIDING APPEALS, 35–39 (1960).

7 For instance, Guido Calabresi states, "in the nineteenth century the United States is said to have developed a unique solution to meeting the two requirements. The principal instruments of this system were the common law courts, for most law was court-made. Legislatures did, of course, possess the ultimate authority, subject to constitutional requirements, to make law; however, that authority was exercised sparingly, by modern standards, and in largely revisionary capacity. In such a world, the law could normally be updated without dramatic breaks through common law adjudication and revision of precedents," GUIDO CALABRESI, A COMMON LAW FOR THE AGE OF STATUTES 3–4 (1999) (footnotes omitted).

8 The early Anglophobia of the American society also caused a revolt against the Blackstone hard-and-fast rule of adherence to precedents. Instead American courts embraced the idea of Mansfield on judicial law-making: "In this country, however, a pure Mansfieldianism flourished: not only were his cases regularly cited but his lightheaded disregard for precedent, his joyous acceptance of the idea that judges are supposed to make law—the more the better—became a notable feature of our early jurisprudence," GILMORE, *supra* note 5 at 24.

9 US CONST. art.1, § 9, cl. 3.
10 US CONST. art.1, § 9, cl. 3.
11 US CONST. art.1, § 10, cl.1.
12 *Id.* at 587–88.

envisage an underlying public policy in statutes. The statutes were considered to be alien creatures imposed on judicial decisions. Henceforth, this alien should be confined as much as possible, so as to minimize interference with reasoned judicial decisions. As mentioned in the literature, in the classical era the idea was that:

> Judges apply statutes, not because they reflect principle of natural order, but because they are dictates of sovereign will; as opposed to "reasoned" judicial decisions, statutes are intrusions into the organize law. They are political not principled.[13]

As discussed, courts would not consider the public policy embedded in statutes. In other words, statutes would not necessarily be interpreted according to their underlying public policy. As a consequence, the preferred method of interpretation was textual, i.e., interpretation based on the plain and clear meaning of the statutes. The formalistic approach in the US, and common law in general, was different from its counterpart in civil law systems. In common law, judges were not merely limited to infer the law and legislative intent from the plethora of statutes. Judges had a well-settled and ingrained principle of resorting to precedents. Therefore, the mechanical approach of formalism in common law would not necessarily lead to a rigid interpretative method in civil law.

A brief survey of decisions rendered in the early half of the twentieth century reveals the classical approach to the notion of public policy in US courts.[14] In *Marcus Brown Holding Co. v. Feldman*, the Southern District Court of New York rejected the argument in briefs that "statutes are justified because consonant with the state's public policy."[15] In contrast, the court declares, "no state can have a public policy except what is to be found in its Constitution and its laws constitutionally enacted."[16] This decision followed the majority opinion in *People v. Hawkins*. In that case the question was whether prisoner-made goods could be sold in light of a statute that considered the act a misdemeanor and a then-new amendment to the state's constitution. The minority argued, *inter alia*, that states establish a public policy, under the police power of the state, and the legislation

---

13 *Id.* at 589.
14 In the nineteenth century, in the landmark case, *Swift v. Tyson*, the US Supreme Court established the authority of federal courts to create a common law through precedents. Pursuant to the Court's opinion the federal courts could venture into law-making, absent conflict with statutes, even if no legislation warrants it. GILMORE, *supra* note 5 at 60–61.
15 Marcus Brown Holding Co. v. Feldman, 269 F. 306, 317 (1920).
16 *Id.* The court continues to elaborate its position by delineating its liberal view of statehood: "Applied to a state, this means its reserved sovereignty, inherent and incapable of being bartered away, because necessary for the state's existence, and lessened only by what the people of the state joined with all the other people of the other states in conveying to and consolidating in the United States," *Id.*

should be interpreted in light of that.[17] The majority, however, viewed the statute and the constitution as carrying no public policy in this regard.[18] This limited view conforms to the prevailing classical approach at the time that viewed statutes and public policy as an intrusion into the common law system. Other courts have also invoked the notion of public policy in a limited fashion.

In brief, in the classical period much of the discussion and usage of the phrase public policy relates to the first meaning of the term, i.e., the policies that the government pursues through the process of legislation. This is an *ex ante* approach to the notion of public policy. The *ex post* phase or the second meaning of public policy relates to its effects on the legal system, judicial decisions, and private agreements. In the *ex post* phase, the classical approach remained formalistic and rigid about the effects of public policy. As discussed, the statutes should be construed narrowly and in a textualistic fashion. Statutes and, consequently, their underlying public policy are not sources of legal reasoning. Even further, the classical approach does not believe in viewing law as a body of policies. As we will see in the next section, this approach came under attack from American Realism as well as the necessity of establishing a welfare state.

2. Rationalism

Rationalism refers to a group of scholars who have joined the anti-formalism movement. Yet, instead of emphasizing the notion of policy like legal realists, they focused on the role of principles in the law. Unlike Holmes and other realists, rationalists do not believe in the separation of morality and law. In fact, moral reality lies at the heart of their viewpoint on law and statutory interpretation. For them, judges should not deviate from certain moral principles in deciding their cases. Hence, the notion of public policy in law, which can trump private agreements, derives from these moral realities.

This school of thought traces back to the ideas of Benjamin Cardozo and, later, Lon Fuller. Cardozo believed that judges should, first and foremost, rule based on shared values and common morality:

> His duty is to declare the law in accordance with reason and justice is seen to be a phase of his duty to declare it in accordance with custom. It is the customary morality of right-minded men and women which he is to enforce by his decree.[19]

---

17 People v. Hawkins, 157 N.Y. 1, 30 (1898).
18 *Id.* at 13 ("the term public policy is frequently used in a very vague, loose, or inaccurate sense. The courts have often found it necessary to define its juridical meaning, and have held that a state can have no public policy except what is to be found in its constitution and laws.")
19 Benjamin N. Cardozo, The Nature of the Judicial Process 106 (1922).

In a lecture series at Northwestern University Law School, Lon Fuller elaborated on rationalism, primarily relying on the normative approach to law. According to him, the descriptive ("is") aspect of law is intertwined with the normative ("ought") aspect of it. Any interpretive task inevitably links to the underlying normative stance of the interpreter.[20] Fuller's theory embraces the possibility of divergent views on the normative interpretation of statutes.[21] He does not offer a substantive moral view that could serve as a guideline for statute interpretation. Fuller, however, emphasizes "procedural natural law." By this term, Fuller endeavors to achieve a process-based ethical guideline without which no law and legal system exist.

Other scholars have followed this school of thought, including Heidi Hurd[22] and Michael Moore.[23] Ronald Dworkin has latterly taken up the challenge of trying to formulate a legal theory contrary to positivism with an emphasis on principles and normativity. For Dworkin, as with others in this school of thought, law and morality are inseparable, in that morality occupies an independent domain which should be respected and followed by law.[24] Rejecting legislative intent as political, Dworkin proposes an interpretive school based on the "law as integrity" method; he views law as composed of rules as well as principles and policies.[25] For Dworkin, law, through his imaginative "Hercules" judge, ultimately has one right answer to legal questions under ideal circumstances.[26] [27]

---

20 For instance, the dispute between Georgetown University, as a Roman Catholic university, and the Gay Rights Coalition of Georgetown University Law Center in Gay Rights Coalition of Georgetown University Law Center v. Georgetown University, 536 A.2d 1 (D.C. 1987) can be illuminating. Georgetown University denied the application of the Gay Rights Coalition to serve as student body and center at the University. Scholars show that the normative stance of judges in the ensued case at the District's Court of Appeals shaped their reasoning. In other words, this case is a good example of the interconnectedness of normative and descriptive aspect in law, William N. Eskridge & Gary Peller, *The New Public Law Movement: Moderation as a Postmodern Cultural Form*, 89 MICH. L. REV. 750–52 (1990).
21 WILLIAM N. ESKRIDGE, DYNAMIC STATUTORY INTERPRETATION 178–79 (1994).
22 Heidi Hurd holds a more radical yet inspiring view on the relationship between law and morality. For her, statutes that are not comprised of any moral reality should not be treated as authoritative. In fact, statutes are mere advices and reflective of a moral reality. Statutes do not hold an independent normative force just because they are coming from a higher authority, ESKRIDGE, *Id.* at 179–180.
23 Michael Moore takes the Fuller view to the next level. For Moore, one moral reality exists, even though we might not be able to access it. Through time, we know more about the moral reality. Judges should not remain in the past and should embrace the possibility of normative interpretation of statutes. Moore emphasizes that the normative stance should not be the conventional values but what he calls "real" values, ESKRIDGE *Id.* at 178–79.
24 RONALD DWORKIN, JUSTICE FOR HEDGEHOGS 99–102 (2011).
25 RONALD DWORKIN, LAW'S EMPIRE 313–316 (1986).
26 RONALD DOWRKIN, TAKING RIGHTS SERIOUSLY 335–37 (1997).
27 Ronald Dworkin's theory is indebted to the new language theories by scholars such as Hilary Putnam and Saul Kripke. For an analysis of the effect of linguistic theories on legal theories in the twentieth century, *see* Farshad Ghodoosi, *Objectivity in Law* (Feb. 2, 2008) (unpublished master's thesis, University of Tehran).

Rationalists follow a teleological approach to law, i.e., law has an end goal. For instance, for Cardozo the final cause of law is the "welfare of society."[28] Or, for Heidi Hurd, the goal of statutes should be to advance moral reality. The teleological approach to law has a critical implication for our discussion on public policy.

Public policy under rationalism is not and should not be limited to the policies promulgated by parliament through statutes. Judges are not bound by the intent of the legislator in order to discover and apply public policy. The notion of public policy under rationalism carries a moral, rather than regulatory, weight. Thus, in cases where the doctrine of public policy is allegedly at conflict with contracts or arbitral awards, it is the courts which should determine a public policy based on moral grounds.

B. Age of statutes

1. Emergence of a welfare state

The world has changed tremendously since World War II. Two destructive wars and the Great Depression of the 1920s, along with the rise of the United States as a superpower, brought about many unprecedented changes. The Great Depression paved the way for the idea of social regulation through legislation.[29] The influence of economists such as Keynes convinced the rule makers that a laissez-faire economic approach would result in catastrophic

---

28 *Id*, at 66.
29 The idea of social regulation first entered into the American Legal system in labor laws and regulations. Towards the end of the nineteenth century some states embarked on regulating the working condition including the laws on wages, hours, and compensation for workplace injury. The courts reacted rather erratically to these laws. For instance in *Holden v. Hardy*, 169 U.S. 366, 18 S.Ct 383, 42 L.Ed. 780 (1896), the Supreme Court upheld a law in Utah that limited work hours in mines, invoking by way of justification the policing power of states. On the other hand, a few years later, the Supreme Court, in *Lochner v. New York*, 198 U.S. 45, 25 S.Ct. 539, 49 L.Ed. 937 (1905), found a New York law setting maximum working hours to be unconstitutional, declaring that the law violated the Fourteenth Amendment as a guarantee for personal liberty and the right to contract. Holmes issued a dissenting opinion in the latter case, suggesting that the state law should be upheld because the Constitution does not support a particular economic theory, STEPHEN B. PRESSER & JAMIL S. ZAINALDIN, LAW AND JURISPRUDENCE IN AMERICAN HISTORY: CASES AND MATERIALS 734–735 (1989). The economic prosperity of the early years of the twentieth century assured the public and courts that no socioeconomic engineering was needed. The Great Depression of the 1920s shocked American society, resulting in ideas of social and economic regulation; these eventually took the form of the New Deal during the Franklin D. Roosevelt administration. The Agricultural Adjustment Administration (AAA) and the National Industrial Recovery Act (NIRA) served as the two most important New Deal measures, the former aimed at regulating the agricultural sector and the latter addressing fair competition as well as wage and working conditions regulations *Id*. at 735–37.

consequences. All these factors contributed to the emergence of a welfare state that required massive regulation on many aspects of society.

The headlong rush to the regulatory government transformed the classical dynamic between judicial decisions and statutes.[30] Guido Calabresi calls this process the "statutorification" of American law.[31] Due to the intricacy of matters involved, the style of writing statutes has undergone a dramatic change as well. Instead of the rather general language of statutes of the classical period, the drafters of statutes from the New Deal onwards tend to use more detailed and specific language. As Grant Gilmore observes, with the New Deal, "a style of drafting which aimed at unearthly and superhuman precision came into vogue, on the state as well as the federal level."[32]

The inundating flow of detailed laws and regulation necessitated a new approach to legisprudence by the courts. Statutes were narrowing the maneuvering capability of courts in individual cases. More importantly, and related to our discussion, the government eventually nailed its colors to the mast of public policy. Through introducing sophisticated and technical statutes, the government conveyed the message that "the purpose of all branches of government is to cooperate in the creation of *dynamic* and *rational* public policy."[33]

Several legal scholars laid the ground for developing the notion of the regulatory state. The forefathers of this viewpoint were Louis Brandeis and Felix Frankfurter.[34] These two figures had an immense impact both on the executive and the judicial system. The leading idea behind the regulatory state was that the law should create institutions necessary to implement policies needed by society. Due to the complexities of the society we live in, the legislature and judiciary are both technically incapable and too sluggish to

---

30 "The New Deal represents a significant watershed in American legal and constitutional history. Not only did it elevate the federal government to a position of dominance over the states, but it also subordinated judicial precedents in economic matters to the public policies enunciated by the executive and legislative branch of the federal government," HERBERT A. JOHNSON, AMERICAN LEGAL AND CONSTITUTIONAL HISTORY: CASES AND MATERIALS 615–16 (2001).
31 Calabresi, *supra* note 7 at 1; LINDA D. JELLUM & DAVID CHARLES HRICIK, MODERN STATUTORY INTERPRETATION: PROBLEMS, THEORIES, AND LAWYERING STRATEGIES 3–5 (2006). But cf. Duncan Kenney, *The Stakes of Law, or Hale and Foucault!*, 15 LEGAL STUD. F. 327, 334: "It is a long-running cliché that statutes have 'proliferated' and that we face a legislation 'explosion.' In the realist sense, these developments do not increase the distributive importance of law, but only bring to visibility what was there all along.")
32 GILMORE, *supra* note 5; Grant Gilmore, *The Age of Anxiety* 84 YALE L. J. 1022 (1975); *See also* James D. Miller, *Holmes, Pierce, and Legal Pragmatism* 84 YALE L. J. 1123 (1975).
33 ESKRIDGE, *supra* note 4 at 588.
34 For an overview of the scholarship and contribution of these two authors, *see* NELSON L. DAWSON, LOUIS D. BRANDIS, FELIX FRANKFURTER, AND THE NEW DEAL (1980). Another prominent scholar who contributed to the emergence of legal culture of regulatory state was James Landis, *see* JUSTIN O'BRIEN, THE TRIUMPH, TRAGEDY AND LOST LEGACY OF JAMES M. LANDIS: A LIFE ON FIRE (2014).

put into effect the required policies. Brandeis's dissent in *International News Service v. Associated Press*[35] best encapsulates the skepticism of the theoreticians of the regulatory state towards the judiciary:

> But with the increasing complexity of society, the public interest tends to become omnipresent; and the problems presented by new demands for justice cease to be simple. Then the creation or recognition by courts of a new private right may work serious injury to the general public, unless the boundaries of the right are definitely established and wisely guarded. In order to reconcile the new private right with the public interest, it may be necessary to prescribe limitations and rules for its enjoyment; and also to provide administrative machinery for enforcing the rules. It is largely for this reason that, in the effort to meet the many new demands for justice incident to a rapidly changing civilization, resort to legislation has latterly been had with increasing frequency . . . [36]
>
> Courts would be powerless to prescribe the detailed regulations essential to full enjoyment of the rights conferred or to introduce the machinery required for enforcement of such regulations. Considerations such as these should lead us to decline to establish a new rule of law in the effort to redress a newly disclosed wrong, although the propriety of some remedy appears to be clear.[37]

In a nutshell, the idea of a welfare state had a pivotal impact on the notion of public policy in the American legal system. In the *ex ante* phase (enactment), the framers of the idea mistrusted the ability of the legislature to pass suitable and well-crafted statutes that reflected the best public policy needed for society. In the *ex post* phase (enforcement), they also could not remain sure that the judiciary would enforce the public policies appropriately.

2. American legal realism

In Legal Realism, a movement that started in the first half of the twentieth century, America experienced a new approach to law and jurisprudence, one which has left its mark on the American legal system ever since.[38] Whether the movement was primarily inspired by the American Pragmatism

---

35 248 U.S. 215 (1918).
36 *Id.* at 262–63.
37 *Id.* at 267.
38 "After World War I the formalistic approach which had been dominant in American legal thought for fifty years went into a protracted period of break-down and dissolution. There appears to be a general agreement that a principal feature of the new approach, which became manifest during the 1920s, was a root-and-branch rejection of the formalism or (in a term which came to have wide vogue) the conceptualism of the preceding period," GILMORE, *supra* note 5 at 12.

school of thought or emerged as a revolt against the rigidity of the formalism of the time, American Realism was an unprecedented movement. Other legal systems with a relatively similar legal and political environment did not undergo such a transformation in legal approach.

American Legal Realism had a lasting impact on the idea of public policy. It is premised on the view that law is policy. Law does not offer a rigid closed system that judges should follow blindly. Conversely, law pursues certain policies that define the scope and the correct interpretation of law in each case. Law is a living entity that owes its life to the policies that shape it, not to its language and text. As a corollary of this view, the public policies underlying statutes become guidelines for courts.

Justice Oliver Wendell Holmes, the United State Supreme Court judge, served as the first and most important critic of the formalism of the time.[39] He paved the way for other legal scholars—such as Roscoe Pound, Wesley Hohfeld, Felix Cohen, Jerome Frank, Robert Hale, and Karl Llewellyn—to develop his ideas and edify a new jurisprudence. Each legal realist scholar crafted a different approach to law. Some emphasized the ultimate indeterminacy of law and the influence of other factors, mainly politics, on the outcome of judicial decisions.[40] Others endeavored to explore factors deriving from sociological or psychological phenomena that determine the outcome of judicial proceedings.[41] Putting the vagaries and intricacies of these theories aside, one important point is clear: law was largely viewed as an instrument to develop social policy. As some have put it: "many of the

---

[39] Holmes had an undeniable impact on the development of the American jurisprudence. He put forward a new look and methodology for studying the law. The object of study for legal scholars should be "the prediction of the incidence of the public force through the instrumentality of the courts," Oliver Wendell Holmes, *The Path of the Law* in COLLECTED LEGAL PAPERS 167, 167 (1942). On the one hand, Holmes distinguishes between law and morality. Morality theories are simply "putting the cart before the horse" while in practice it is the prediction of consequences related to breach of law that determines the legal duties and rights, *Id.* at 168–69. In short, moral theories do not get us far in understanding and analyzing law according to Holmes. On the other hand, Holmes shows that analysis of law is different from analysis of its logic. He opines radically, "you can give any conclusion a logical form," *Id.* at 181. Thus, studying the logics employed in legal reasoning does yield little fruit for understanding law. It is not the logical development that determines the content and growth of law; neither is it the moral development. Instead, Holmes emphasizes the "social end" of each law and the underlying policy that should determine the development of rule of law, *Id.* at 187. The best analysis of law comes from "weighing considerations of social advantage which judges and courts have been neglecting by focusing on moral and logical aspects of their decisions," *Id.* at 184. Holmes thus called for a fresh look on the legal system by putting the emphasis on the social end and the underlying policy of laws.

[40] Wesley Newcomb Hohfeld, *Some Fundamental Legal Conceptions as Applied in Judicial Reasoning*, 23 YALE L. J. 16 (1913); Felix Cohen, *Transcendental Nonsense and the Functional Approach*, 35 COLUM. L. REV. 809 (1935); JEROME FRANK, COURTS ON TRIAL: MYTHS AND REALITY IN AMERICAN JUSTICE (1949).

[41] Karl Llewellyn, *A Realistic Jurisprudence—the Next Step*, 30 COLUM. L. REV. 431 (1930); Roscoe Pound, *A Survey of Social Interest*, 57 HARV. L. REV. 1, 5 (1943).

realists, especially those who served in the New Deal, believed that law's legitimacy rested upon its instrumental value, its ability to deliver good policy."[42] As a result of this movement, the idea of policy has turned into the focal point of American legal thought.

Although Legal Realism has helped the legal system break free from the inflexibility of formalism, it has subjugated it to the abstract notion of policy. In Holmesian scholarship, judges would infer and form the policy behind laws and would employ them to give spirit to the law. Through time, however, with the emergence of the welfare state and its accompanying regulatory state scholarship, judges' room to maneuver has become limited.

C. A need for a new approach

1. The age of multiculturalism

The world has changed tremendously since the era in which the idea of the welfare state was introduced. The end of the Cold War and the emergence of the US as the sole superpower transformed the dynamics of international relations. At the domestic level, the civil rights movement and the upsurge in immigration, along with the unprecedented boost in the economy, have changed American society.

These changes, domestically and internationally, have necessitated a fresh look at law and the issue of public policy. The socio-economic dynamics of post-Cold War American society differ significantly from the post-WWII period in which a regulatory state was found to be the solution to avoiding another depression and war. Diversity in American life, along with the achievements of the civil rights movement, meant that marginal groups had more scope to voice their opinions. Furthermore, with the surge in immigration to the US, American society became more diverse, resulting in fresh and new opinions and voices. The improvement in the economic well-being of society also paved the way for new demands to arise.

Consequently, in the area of public policy, there was felt to be a need for new theories that could correspond with the dynamics of this new society. Two approaches could be identified. The first group believed in the law-is-policy view, yet with revisions stemming mainly from the principle-based natural law theories. The second group was not satisfied with mere revision; they desired a new legal system in which diverse groups could partake. In the following two sections I will discuss these two approaches.

Despite the recent intellectual efforts by the new generation of legal scholars, the legacy of the regulatory state era still remains the prevailing approach. In numerous examples, including the famous *Chevron* case,[43] the

---
42 ESKRIDGE, *supra* note 4 at 593.
43 Chevron USA, Inc. v. Natural Resources Defense Council, Inc., 467 U.S. 837 (1984) (establishing a strong deference for administrative matters to agencies and limiting the scope of judicial review on this front).

judiciary has shown that courts should give deference to the public policies pursued by the government. This approach still leaves public policy as an exogenous entity imposed on the judiciary while leaving little discretion to the courts to challenge and set new public policies.

2. The revisionist approach

Recent scholarship has undermined the centrality of public policy in determining the outcome of cases. The move towards the importance of principles and fair process in law has opened the door for more discretion for courts in issues related to public policy. The intellectual endeavors of scholars such as Ronald Dworkin,[44] Bruce Ackerman,[45] Robert Cover,[46] Owen Fiss,[47] Cass Sunstein[48] and Lawrence Tribe[49] aimed to revise the law-as-policy approach of American Legal Realism. The purpose of the law is not only limited to the will of the sovereign, as reflected in governmental public policies. A legal system should protect certain principles that come before public policies.

Defining the principles that law should pursue has proven to be an extremely difficult task. From the ancient natural law approach to the new rationalist approach of scholars such as Ronald Dworkin, efforts to define the boundaries of these principles have continued. However—and relevant to our discussion—following this approach, the notion of (*ex post*) public policy is defined according to these principles and not the will of the sovereign. The legal system and the judiciary should not become the mouthpiece of the policies of the government. No matter how sophisticated the policies are, the judiciary should be able to test them against a set of basic principles. This view could be aptly categorized as a revisionist approach, aiming to restrict American Realism to the contours of a few basic principles.

3. Beyond revisionism

On the other side of the spectrum, a new movement started in the 1950s that questioned the legitimacy of the entire legal system. Critical Legal scholars challenged the objectivity of the law-making process as well as the judiciary decision-making. They developed an anti-legal process view

---

44 RONALD DWORKIN, LAW'S EMPIRE (1986).
45 *See, e.g.*, Bruce Ackerman, *The Storrs Lectures: Discovering the Constitution* 93 YALE L. J. 1013 (1984); Robert Cover, *The Supreme Court, 1982 Term, Foreword: Nomos and Narrative*, 97 HARV. L. REV. 4 (1983).
46 Robert Cover, *The Supreme Court, 1982 Term, Foreword: Nomos and Narrative*, 97 HARV. L. REV. 4 (1983).
47 Owen Fiss, *The Supreme Court, 1978 Term, Foreword: The Forms of Justice*, 93 HARV. L. REV. (1978).
48 Cass Sunstein, *Interest Groups in American Public Law*, 38 STAND. L. REV. 29 (1985).
49 Lawrence Tribe, *Constitutional Calculus; Equal Justice or Economic Efficiency?* 98 HARV. L. REV. 592, 617 (1985).

on the public law.[50] According to Critical Legal scholarship, politics lie at the center of the legal system and all laws are subjective and intermediate. Furthermore, they questioned the soundness of the law-making process in which many marginal groups have no or limited participation. Groups such as women, people of color, immigrants, gay men and lesbians, and other marginal groups do not partake in the process of law-making and policy-making of the government. Critical Legal scholarship holds a strong skepticism towards the notion of public policy. Policies that are pursued by the government and are passed by the legislation in forms of laws do not reflect the demands and aspirations of the body politic. One of the major arguments of the pro-policy group rests on the fact that policies are a result of a democratic process in which various interest groups voice their opinion. Critical Legal scholars attack this very argument by showing that this democratic process is biased and political. Henceforth, public policies cannot be impartial and should not be blindly followed by courts.[51]

Postmodern thinkers challenge the underlying assumptions of various legal schools of thoughts. They attack the notion of consent in a liberalist paradigm, procedure in legal process theories, and morality underlying classical theories of law.[52] Unlike Critical Legal scholars, the postmodernists do not put forward any solution. Their aim is to foster vigilance on the inherent intermediacy of policy and law-making.[53]

This section aimed to show different approaches to the public policy doctrine in the twentieth century. As explained, legal philosophy plays an indispensable role in delineating the boundaries of the doctrine of public policy. Contrary to the prevailing conception, the doctrine is nuanced and requires an in-depth discussion of the philosophy of law, a matter that is missing in both scholarship and court practice.

An important paradigm that defines public policy in today's legal system is the "law and economics" approach. It endeavors to provide a value-free and objective justification for the notion of public policy. Due to its importance and impact on the literature, we will analyze this approach to public policy in the next section.

---

50 *See, e.g.,* CATHERINE A. MACKINNON, FEMINISM UNMODIFIED: DISCOURSES ON LIFE AND LAW (1986); ROBERTO M. UNGER, KNOWLEDGE AND POLITICS (1975); Paul Brest, *Interpretation and Interest*, 34 STAN. L. REV. 765 (1982); Duncan Kennedy, *Form and Substance in Private Law Adjudication*, 89 HARV. L. REV. 1685 (1976); Richard Parker, *The Past of Constitutional Theory—and Its Future*, 42 OHIO ST. L. J. 223, 239–456 (1981); Gary Peller, *The Metaphysics of American Law*, 73 CALIF. L. REV. 1152 (1985); Joseph Singer, *The Player and the Cards: Nihilism and Legal Theory*, 94 YALE L. J. 1 (1984); Mark Tushnet, *Darkness on the Edge of the Town: The Contribution of John Hart Ely to Constitutional Theory*, 89 YALE L. J. 1037 (1980).
51 John S. Dryzek, *Policy Analysis as Critique* in THE OXFORD HANDBOOK OF PUBLIC POLICY 190, 191–92 (Michael Moran ed., 2008). MARK KELMAN, A GUIDE TO CRITICAL LEGAL STUDIES 64–66 (1987); ANDREW ALTMAN, CRITICAL LEGAL STUDIES: A LIBERAL CRITIQUE 49 (1990).
52 ESKRIDGE, *supra* note 4 at 175.
53 *Id.*; JOSEPH A. SCHUMPETER, CAPITALISM, SOCIALISM, AND DEMOCRACY 242 (1961).

3 Economics of the public policy doctrine*

A. The law and economics approach in law

If philosophy in the twentieth century is marked by its linguistic turn, law has experienced an economic turn. This came about as a result of the intellectual contribution of Holmes and other scholars who desired to impose general standards for legal problems in lieu of moral blameworthiness.[1] In short, the endeavor of law and economics intellectuals is to institute an economic method for the analysis of legal problems.[2] The ultimate goal is economic efficiency.

The practice of contracting between parties is highly cherished because, by properly allocating resources, the total wealth of a society can be increased. Prices are most efficiently determined through a free market, which allows for freedom of contract among various players in the market. However—unlike some judicial opinions including the US Supreme Court in *Baltimore & Ohio Southwestern v. Voight*—contracts are not sacred from the law and economics perspective. They are the means to an ultimate goal, which is efficiency and increase of wealth.[3]

Scholars in this field, however, have rarely engaged the doctrine of public policy directly although their entire field of research is directed toward promoting the particular public policy of efficiency.[4] Yet, one relevant problem has

---

* The content of the following chapter has appeared previously in Farshad Ghodoosi, *The Concept of Public Policy in Law: Revisiting the Role of the Public Policy Doctrine in the Enforcement of Private Legal Arrangements*, 94 NEB. L. REV. 685 (2016).
1 "The general principle of our law is that loss from accident must lie where it falls, and this principle is not affected by the fact that a human being is the instrument of misfortune," HOLMES, THE COMMON LAW 77 (1963); GRANT GILMORE, THE AGES OF AMERICAN LAW 54 (2d ed. 2014).
2 *See generally* Susan Rose-Ackerman, *Economics, Public Policy and Law*, 26 VICTORIA UNIV. WELLINGTON L. REV. 1 (1996).
3 Baltimore & Ohio Southwestern Ry. v. Voight, 176 U.S. 498, 505 (1899). "If there is one thing which more than another public policy requires it is that men of full age and competent understanding shall have the utmost liberty of contracting and their contracts, when entered into freely and voluntarily, shall be held sacred and shall be enforced by court of justice." Quoting Printing & Co. v. Sampson, 19 LR. Eq. 462, 465 (1975). This is a moralistic approach to contract law according to some authors, Harry G. Prince, *Public Policy Limitations on Cohabitation Agreements: Unruly Horse or Circus Pony?* 70 MINN. L. REV. 163, 164 (fn. 4) (1985).
4 The notable exception is a note at Harvard Law Review: Note, *A Law and Economics Look at Contracts against Public Policy*, 119 HARV. L. REV. 1145–1466 (2006).

turned out to be a vexing issue for them: providing justifications for bans on certain types of contracts and transactions. In other words, why should certain external prohibitions bar contracts from yielding their normal legal consequences? Borrowing from this scholarship, I will show that there are three strands of public policy conceivable under the law and economics approach:

1   public policy as a protection for parties in the contract (paternalism);
2   public policy as a protection for third parties outside the contract (negative externalities); and
3   public policy as a means for redistributive justice.

Synchronically, policy considerations are imposed on contract law in two stages: 1) *ex ante*: when parties are contracting; and 2) *ex post*: when there is a dispute about the contract. At the *ex ante* stage, contract law divides rules into two categories: default rules and mandatory rules. What differentiates the two types of rules is the parties' ability to contract around them. Parties can contract around default rules, while mandatory rules are not contractible. Mandatory rules refer to rules derived from public policy; parties cannot deviate from these rules by entering into a private contract.[5] Policy considerations prevent these rules from being the subject of a contract.

There is controversy over whether mandatory rules produce economic efficiency.[6] In the case of market failures, for instance where there is asymmetry of information, mandatory rules may foster efficiency as well as distributive goals.[7] Willy Rice, after analyzing state Supreme Court decisions on insurance contracts—specifically implied covenant of good faith clauses—from 1900 to 1991, concluded that the courts unwittingly discriminate against the litigants. One of the study's aims is to show that mandatory rules such as the covenant of good faith do not necessarily lead to efficiency or distributional goals, especially because of "disparate-impact discrimination."[8] Similarly, the skepticism towards mandatory rules

---

5   Alan Schwartz & Robert E. Scott, *Contract Theory and the Limits of Contract Law*, YALE L.J. 541, 609–610 (2003).
6   *Id.*
7   Daniel P. Kessler & Daniel L. Rubinfeld, *Empirical Study of the Civil Justice System in* HANDBOOK OF LAW AND ECONOMICS: VOLUME 1 343, 350 (A. Mitchell Polinsky & Steven Shavell eds., 2007).
8   This is a term coined by the United States Supreme Court in the context of employment discrimination. *See, e.g.*, International Bhd. of Teamsters v. United States, 431 U.S. 324 (1977); Albermarle Paper Co. v. Moody, 422 U.S. 405 (1975); Griggs v. Duke Power Co., 401 U.S. 424 (1971). Under the court's "disparate impact" analysis, a Title VII plaintiff may state a *prima facie* employment discrimination claim by making a statistical showing that the neutral scheme caused the hiring disparity, *see* Lee M. Modjeska, EMPLOYMENT DISCRIMINATION LAW 30, § 1.8 (2d ed. 1988). But in the context of the present discussion, a "disparate impact" analysis permits a presumption, based on a statistical showing, that a state supreme court's neutral rule, practice, or policy harms members of a certain group, such as female policy-holders, automobile insurers, life insurance insurers, or excess liability insurers.

exists among those scholars who view the firm as a contract or a "nexus of contracts."[9] These scholars believe that mandatory rules are only justified to prevent adverse effects on third parties. Contracts that result in pollution and contracts negatively affecting competition are among these contracts, which should not be enforceable.[10] Yet, contracts related to business and/or governance do not involve substantial effects for third parties and, therefore, should not be limited. Justification for state intervention is not applicable to intra-corporate affairs.[11] [12]

In contrast, Ayres aims to show that mandatory provisions lead to efficiency. He analyzes mandatory disclosure by sending 203 testers to negotiate for the purchase of a new car. He finds out that mandatory disclosure leads to economic efficiency and reduced price discrimination.[13] However, the latter study goes to the heart of the asymmetry of information problem rather than the first study, which deals with a traditional covenant of good faith in contracts. In other words, it does not refute the presumption that some mandatory rules do not necessarily increase economic efficiency.

In the enforcement stage, considerations related to public affairs are part of the doctrine of public policy. As discussed, public policy concerns the enforcement of contracts. There are significant overlaps between mandatory rules and the doctrine of public policy. However, they are distinct from each other. An example will clarify this distinction: even if the legislature did not criminalize prostitution, a contract for prostitution would remain unenforceable.[14] In other words, the illegality of prostitution is recognized only if judicial resources are used for enforcement. Mandatory rules are designed to shape parties' behavior while contracting, and public policy is a bar to enforcing their contractual terms where the overall objective or outcome of the contract is against public policy.

So far we have realized that three possible explanations or scenarios can be found in the law and economics approach regarding the issue of the public policy exception: 1) protecting parties in the contract; 2) protecting third parties; or 3) advancing redistributive goals. In the following section I will analyze each explanation in depth and at the end try to show why, in my

---

9 Harold Demsetz, *The Theory of the Firm Revisited* in THE NATURE OF THE FIRM: ORIGINS, EVOLUTION, AND DEVELOPMENT 159,169–171 (Oliver E. Williamson & Sidney G. Winter eds., 1993); MICHAEL JENSEN & WILLIAM MECKLING, THEORY OF THE FIRM, MANAGERIAL BEHAVIOR, AGENCY COSTS AND OWNERSHIP STRUCTURE 8–10 (1976); For the limits of contract theory of firm, *see* Ian Ayres, *Making a Difference: The Contractual Contribution of Easterbrook and Fischel*, 59 U. CHI. L. REV. 1391, 1395–97 (1992).
10 FRANK H. EASTERBROOK AND DANIEL R. FISCHEL, THE ECONOMIC STRUCTURE OF CORPORATE LAW 23 (1996).
11 *Id.*
12 For the opposite view *see* Ian Ayres, *Making a Difference: The Contractual Contributions of Easterbook and Fischel*, 59 U. CHIC. L. REV. 1391 (1992).
13 Ian Ayres, *Fair Driving, Gender and Race Discrimination in Retail Car Negotiations*, 104 HARV. L. REV. 817, 817–22 (1991).
14 R. A. BUCKLEY, ILLEGALITY AND PUBLIC POLICY 90 (2d ed., 2009).

opinion, public policy in the enforcement state (the *ex post* phase) should be mainly applied in cases involving protection of third parties.

B. The law and economics of public policy

1. Protecting parties

In the real world, parties almost never enjoy an equal footing at the time of contracting. People around the world hold diverse social, political, as well as cultural status. For example, the dealer of a famous Japanese car brand has relative economic leverage over his buyers and could more or less incorporate his preferences in the sales contracts. It is similarly true of a cable service provider which does not face formidable competitors in a certain area. However, these differences and leverages do not render the contract unenforceable. The law protects the weaker party—in the language of law and economics—only in cases where there is serious asymmetry of information between the parties. One assumption of law and economics is that contracts maximize welfare if made with perfect information about parties' payoffs. Protection against formation defects—such as the infancy of a party, fraud, and, to a great extent, unconscionable contractual terms—occur because one party is gravely under-informed compared to the other party. In other words, asymmetry of information exists when one party has informational privilege over the other side. This informational advantage might lead to market failure. In a seminal article, economist George Akerlof explains how asymmetry of information leads to market failure.[15]

The question is whether the doctrine of public policy should concern itself with asymmetry of information between parties in contracts or agreements. The controversy over unconscionability terms helps us to frame the issue more accurately. Pursuant to the unconscionability doctrine, courts should invalidate contracts with egregious and unjust terms for a contracting party.[16] One instance of unconscionable contracts is where one party is economically and socially feeble to the point that that the other party could easily exert influence on him/her. A contract for the sale of an umbrella on a rainy day for $200 instead of a normal $10 is an example of unconscionability.[17] Law and economics scholars have grappled with this doctrine because they believe courts impose their views on the rights and duties of parties by invoking this doctrine.[18] Alan Schwartz endeavored to limit its scope while remaining silent about situations where unconscionability results from a

---

15 George A. Akerlof, *The Market for "Lemons": Quality Uncertainty and the Market Mechanism*, 84 Q. J. ECON. 488, 488–89 (1970).
16 Guido Pincione, *Welfare, Autonomy, and Contractual Freedom* in THEORETICAL FOUNDATIONS OF LAW AND ECONOMICS 219, 224 (Mark D. White ed., 2009).
17 Some frame it as economic duress. The discussion on this matter is beyond the scope of this book.
18 Richard A. Epstein, *Unconscionability: A Critical Reappraisal*, 18 J. LAW AND ECON. 293 (1975).

lack of information.[19] Richard Epstein voices a stronger objection to this doctrine, arguing that it does not serve any function beyond prohibition against fraud, duress, and incompetence. The only difference is that the bar for the standard of proof is set lower in the doctrine of unconscionability. This will reduce the total error in enforcement of unjust contracts.[20] Epstein's approach is dismissive of substantive unconscionability (i.e. invalidation on grounds of unjust terms; for instance, unfair prices).[21] In short, for Epstein the doctrine of unconscionability is acceptable only in circumstances where there is some incapacity of a contracting party that results in that party's informational deficiency. His theory allows the courts to police the incompetency of parties, in addition to formation defects, in a limited fashion.[22]

Similar to unconscionability, one presumed function of public policy is that it should protect parties where asymmetry of information strips the "bargain" feature from transactions. Yet, it is doubtful that there is a need for another doctrine to protect the information of parties on their contractual payoff. There are ample theories and safeguards carved into the edifice of contract law aiming to protect symmetry of information between parties. Fraud, economic duress, and unconscionability, as well as mistake, are among the main theories designed to protect parties.

In other aspects of the public policy doctrine—for instance in the enforcement of arbitral awards—however, the courts have no choice but to employ the doctrine of public policy. If judgments and awards are based on a contract with serious asymmetry of information between parties, the only tool remaining in the courts' toolbox is public policy (since economic duress and unconscionability can be invoked only in the litigation phase of contractual disputes). In short, courts might consider serious and significant asymmetry of information between parties when enforcing awards and judgment based on the doctrine of public policy.

Yet, non-enforcement should not be a punishment for the less informed party because she is "less morally blameworthy."[23] The advantageous party cannot reap the benefits resulting from non-enforcement of contracts or

---

19 Alan Schwartz suggests four categories for non-substantive unconscionability: in the first instance, the poorer party cannot impose his or her preferences. In the second category, market dynamics limit the buyer's option. The third instance is where the buyer is too unsophisticated to be able to dictate his or her preferences. Lastly, lack of information creates a situation where a contracting party cannot make his or her preferences "either because the information is unavailable or because the cost of finding and absorbing it exceeds, at the margin, the value of the information." Schwartz argues that the three first instances do not provide a justification to invalidate the contract. Re the last category his article is silent, Alan Schwartz, *A Reexamination of Nonsubstantive Unconscionability*, 63 Va L. Rev. 1053, 1053–54 (1977).
20 Epstein, *supra* note 18 at 302.
21 His examples are add-on clauses, waiver-of-defense, exclusion of liability for consequential damages, due-on-sale clauses, and termination-at-will clauses. *Id.* at 306–15.
22 *Id.* at 315.
23 McIntosh v. Mills 121 Cal. App. 4th 333, 347, 17 Cal. Rptr. 3d 66 (2004), Medina v. Safe-Guard Products, 164 Cal. App. 4th 105, 111 (2008).

awards. In contract law this has been reflected in the doctrine of *in pari delicto*.[24] Under this theory the plaintiff can recover if she is not equally in wrong with the defendant, even if the contract is contrary to public policy. For instance in the case *Karpinski v. Collins*, plaintiff had to provide kickbacks to the defendant in order to receive grade A products. The market dynamics would not allow the plaintiff to obtain a similar product without paying the kickback. Notwithstanding the illegality of kickbacks, the court enforced the contract.[25] In this case the plaintiff knew about the illegality of kickbacks. But it is similarly applicable, *mutatis mutandis*, to situation where the plaintiff does not have information about the illegality involved in transactions.

2. Protecting third parties

The second function of public policy in law and economics mandates that negative externalities be avoided in contract law. Negative externalities or external diseconomies refer to situations where the production of a product (in economics) or exercise of a right (in law) incurs costs that outweigh the benefits it gives to society. A classic example is pollution. A plant in the middle of a city would incur costs (by polluting the city) that are greater than the benefits it confers on the welfare of society. In contrast, pollution by cars is tolerated because of the benefits of such transportation. The prevention of negative externalities is one economic rationale for the involvement of governments in economics and law.[26] In other words, states intervene by enacting laws and enforcing various standards to prevent the negative externalities as much as possible.[27] [28]

---

24 On the doctrine of *in pari delicto*, see generally T.S. Ellis III, *In Defense of In Pari Delicto*, 56 A.B.A. J. 346 (1970).
25 Kappriski v. Collins, 252 Cal. App. 2d. 711, 715 (1967).
26 Alfred Marshall coined the notion of externalities and his pupil, Arthur C. Pigou developed Marshall's theory and based his welfare economics on the notion of externalities, ALFRED MARSHALL, PRINCIPLE OF ECONOMICS (1890); A.C. PIGOU, THE ECONOMICS OF WELFARE (1920). Pigou favors taxing the activities which create negative externalities and tax breaks for activities such as education, which result in positive externalities, JOHN E. ANDERSON, PUBLIC FINANCE 110–15 (2011). Ronald Coase disagrees. He believes we can reduce externalities by reducing transaction costs, which allow the people creating the externalities and those affected to bargain, Robert Coase, *The Problem of Social Cost*. 3 J. L. & ECON. 1, 1–2 (1960). There is also strong skepticism as to functionality of governments in reducing externalities from public choice school of economics. *See generally* KENNETH J. ARROW, SOCIAL CHOICE AND INDIVIDUAL VALUES. (2d ed., 1951); DUNCAN BLACK, THE THEORY OF COMMITTEES AND ELECTIONS (1958); JAMES M. BUCHANAN & GORDON TULLOCK, THE CALCULUS OF CONSENT: LOGICAL FOUNDATIONS OF CONSTITUTIONAL DEMOCRACY (1962); ANTHONY DOWNS, AN ECONOMIC THEORY OF DEMOCRACY (2003); WILLIAM A. NISKANEN, BUREAUCRACY AND REPRESENTATIVE GOVERNMENT (2007); MANCUR OLSON, THE LOGIC OF COLLECTIVE ACTION: PUBLIC GOODS AND THE THEORY OF GROUPS (1965); WILLIAM H. RIKER, THE THEORY OF POLITICAL COALITIONS (1962).
27 JOHN B. TAYLOR, ECONOMICS 399 (5th ed., 2007).
28 Economists worry about positive externalities as well. Positive externality happens when a product or right has a positive spill over, yet the costs are not efficiently distributed.

40 *Economics of the public policy doctrine*

The courts should engage in balancing various interests in order to ascertain the best possible outcome when negative externalities are at issue. Laws protecting against unfair competition serve as an illuminating example. Companies should not engage in tying arrangements that minimize total welfare by reducing competition in the market. The *Microsoft* decision brought before the D.C. Circuit established the balancing test in in which the burden of proof was divided between plaintiff and defendant in the area of antitrust.[29] In this case, the United States brought a case against Microsoft for violation of the Sherman Act on multiple grounds: Microsoft maintained a monopoly in the market for Intel compatible PC systems, it attempted to gain a monopoly in the Internet Explorer market, and it tied its two products—Windows and Internet Explorer—together illegally. On the latter issue (the alleged tying arrangement), the court delegated to the parties the balancing task of evaluating whether the anticompetitive harm of the Java design was outweighed by the efficiencies that resulted to society.[30] Following the *Jefferson Parish* case, the court declared that tying arrangements should not be subject to *per se* analysis because they do not necessarily stifle competition.[31] Central to the tying issue was whether the Microsoft's action harmed or benefited the public and whether the public interest was better or worse served by Microsoft's action. The court aptly applied a balancing test to weigh the different interests at stake.

Stifling competition is an example of a negative externality that should be avoided in contracts and in the enforcement of awards. Courts ought to take a similar approach in regards to other negative externalities. The *Microsoft* case provides us with a valuable precedent for similar cases that might arise under the rubric of the public policy doctrine. When dealing with public interest matters, the doctrine of public policy allows courts to weigh the interest of the parties (or one party) in enforcing the contract or award against the interest of society in non-enforcement. Protecting society in this sense is the principal mandate of the public policy doctrine under the law and economics approach.

    For instance, a neighbor who renovates the lobby out of pocket is benefiting the other neighbors. Yet, the marketplace has failed in equally distributing the costs among all stakeholders, in our example, the neighbors, Ugo Mattei, Basic Principles of Property Law: A Comparative Legal and Economic Introduction 60 (2000).

29 Sangin Park, *Market Power Revisited* in Research in Law and economics 8–9 (Richard O. Zerbe & John B. Kirwood eds., 2012); William H. Page & John E. Lopatka, The Microsoft Case: Antitrust, High Technology, and Consumer Welfare 195–96 (2007).

30 United States v. Microsoft Corporation, 253 F.3d 34, 96 (2001) ("...plaintiff must show that Microsoft's conduct was, on balance, anticompetitive. Microsoft may of course offer precompetitive justifications, and it is plaintiff's burden to show the anticompetitive effect of the conduct outweighs its benefits.")

31 Jefferson Parish, 466 U.S. at 9, 104 S. Ct. 1551 ("it is far too late in the history of our antitrust jurisprudence to question the proposition that certain tying arrangements pose an unacceptable risk of stifling competition and therefore are unreasonable 'per se'.")

3. Protecting redistributive justice

Lastly, and most controversially, public policy might serve to promote the redistributive feature of law. Generally speaking, in the law and economics camp the basic idea centers on contracts producing efficient results that subsequently result in a surplus.[32] This surplus could be redistributed throughout society. Thus, in a nutshell, there should be no redistribution concerns at the contract level. Courts should not render any contracts unenforceable simply due to distributive concerns. Fried, one of the proponents of this approach, maintains that "redistribution is not a burden to be borne in a random, ad hoc way by those who happen to cross paths with persons poorer than themselves."[33] Similar views have been expressed to buttress the idea that redistribution is a business of the state, through the tax and welfare system, and not the courts.[34]

Although Posner certainly shares Fried's general claim that the courts ought not to be the locus of the redistributive policy, he does argue that in the area of usury law judicial intervention to limit private choice will have a beneficial redistributive effect. He believes over-reliance on the welfare system prompts risky borrowing behavior, which racks up the costs of the welfare system. He believes that states are committed both to promoting the free market and to ameliorating poverty through welfare systems. He argues that a "hands-off" approach to the first function, i.e. free market promotion, will incur heavy costs on the second function, which is redistribution, because it incentivizes suboptimal risk-taking.[35] The long-held ban on usury in common law is a good example of how the courts can limit reliance on welfare. Usury is a practice in which the creditor imposes higher than market interest rates on the debtor. Chancellor Kent in the case *Dunham v. Gould* expresses a very strong and brief justification for usury:

> Lord Redesdale said, in 1803 (1. Sch. and Lef. 95, 312), many years after Jeremy Bentham, to whom the learned counsel referred for an able defense of usury, had first published his letters, that the statue of usury was founded on great principles of public policy. It was intended, he said, to protect distressed men, by facilitating the means of procuring money on reasonable terms, and by refusing to men who sit idle

---

32 Louis Kaplow & Steven Shavell, *Why the Legal System Is Less Efficient than the Income Tax in Redistributing Income*, 23 J. LEGAL STUD. 667, 674 (1994) (arguing that efficient legal rule leaves all individuals equally well off and leaves the government with a surplus).

33 CHARLES FRIED, CONTRACT AS PROMISE: A THEORY OF CONTRACTUAL OBLIGATION 106 (1981).

34 *See e.g.*, Charles J. Goetz & Robert E. Scott, *Enforcing Promises: An Examination of the Basis of Contract*, 89 YALE L.J. 1261, 1321 (1980). Louis Kaplow & Steven Shavell, *supra* note 33 at 674–75.

35 Eric Posner, *Contract Law in the Welfare State: A Defense of the Unconscionability Doctrine, Usury Laws, and Related Limitations on the Freedom to Contract*, 24 J. LEGAL STUD. 283, 285 (1995).

as high as rate of interest, without hazard, as those can procure who employ money in hazardous undertakings of trade and manufactures. I trust that theoretic reformers have not yet attained, on this subject any decided victory over public opinion.... The stature of usury is constantly interposing its warning voice between the creditor and the debtor, even in their most secret and dangerous negotiations, and teaches a lesson of moderation to the one, and offers its protecting arm to the other. I am not willing to withdraw such a sentinel.[36]

High-risk creditors—mainly impoverished people, according to Posner[37]—tend to take loans with high interest rates. The chances of their default are high, eventually subjecting them to the welfare system. Usury law aims to protect this risky behavior and ultimately to help with the retributive function of the state.[38] Posner's idea adds a new wrinkle to the underlying policies courts should take into account when adjudicating contractual issues. He reintroduced usury law as a modern theory justifiable from the perspective of law and economics.

However, it is not clear whether redistributive justice requires a separate consideration besides that we discussed for negative externalities. The redistributive concerns are related to the costs society has to pay if careless individuals engage in risky behaviors. It is linked to balancing societal interests in the benefits and costs of enforcing a certain risky contract or risky award. If enforcing a certain type of risky contracts ultimately results in unbearably high costs on the redistributive mechanism of a particular state, it could be barred from enforcement under the doctrine of public policy. Certainly, one contract or an arbitral award can hardly incur such a high cost, but judicial enforcement of that type of contract or award could snowball the conclusions of similar contracts or the issuance of similar awards in future.

In summary, we have analyzed three underlying justification for the doctrine of public policy under the law and economics approach. The first justification, that of protecting the parties, aims to regulate informational defects between the parties at the time they conclude the agreement. In view of the other mechanisms and legal theories designed to protect parties in this regard, there is no need for the doctrine of public policy to engage itself with this matter. Protecting third parties is the most important function of the doctrine of public policy. It protects society from potential negative externalities derived from the enforcement of contracts or arbitral awards. The last category addresses an essential element of today's society, which is redistributive justice. However, as described, the concerns of redistribute justice could be addressed under the negative externality rubric, utilizing the balancing test as described.

---

36 James Avery Webb, A Treatise on the Law of Usury and incidentally of interest 12–13 (1899).
37 Posner, *supra* note 37 at 318.
38 *Id.* at 316–17.

C. The leading role of public policy

Thus far, we have reviewed the historical genesis of the doctrine of public policy and its development in the common law. In Chapter 2 we reviewed the impact of legal theory as well as the emergence of the welfare state on the metamorphosis of the public policy exception in the twentieth century. In the preceding section, we scrutinized the Law and Economics analysis of the doctrine of public policy in order to grasp the economic justifications for this doctrine. In this section, however, we will observe the insufficiency of the Law and Economics approach in dealing with all instances of the public policy exception. This section aims to show that there is more in the doctrine of public policy than a simple cost–benefit analysis of the interests of parties and society. I argue that policy arguments in courts are inevitable. The doctrine of public policy has a leading role, not a passive one, in our judicial system.

1. Incompleteness of the law and economics approach

Let's imagine the following scenario: an immigrant, who is on the brink of being deported by authorities, approaches an employer and requests that she sign a document certifying she is hiring the immigrant. The employer does not need the immigrant and his skills, yet signs the document because the immigrant is a minority in his home country and is likely to be persecuted upon his return to his homeland. After a short period, the relationship between them turns sour, and the immigrant asks the court to enforce the employment contract in order to reap the benefits of it. The employer attests that he lied because of likelihood of persecution of the immigrant in his home country. The court faces a dilemma: whether to enforce an inefficient contract that is contrary to public policy or prevent probable human rights violations by the immigrant's government. The law and economics approach and balancing test is not much help here. In fact, some law and economics scholars believe that immigration, *per se*, results in negative externalities, although that is not the common view.[39] However, would it be fair?

In an actual case, a Jewish man bribed an official in France to help him enter the United States. The official promised that, on payment, he would secure him a visa before the Nazi army reached France. The plaintiff provided $28,000 worth of jewelry to the official. The official absconded with the jewelry without fulfilling his promise. Later, upon meeting the defendant in New York, the plaintiff sued defendant for the return of the jewelry. The defendant claimed that the contract was void under the public policy doctrine. The court rejected the motion, declaring that: "there is no question of public policy involved in a case like this where a man is attempting to save

---

39 ORN BODVAR BODVARSSON & HENDRIK VAN DEN BERG, THE ECONOMICS OF IMMIGRATION: THEORY AND POLICY 178–79 (2009).

himself from an enemy who has violated all the laws of civilization."[40] [41] This case is rightly decided. Yet, scholars using the law and economics approach have trouble justifying this case.[42] Notwithstanding the court's statement, it was precisely the doctrine of public policy which guided it to reach this decision. It is the public morality strand of public policy that led the court to rule in favor of the plaintiff. For the purpose of this section, this case illuminates one aspect of judicial decision-making that is overlooked by the literature of law and economics. It goes to the heart of judicial activism.[43]

The law and economics movement cannot entirely capture all aspects of public policy. Its methodology is highly useful for dissecting various types of public policy in law. It also provides us with a balancing method in cases where negative impacts arise from contracts or their enforcement. However, law and economics cannot fully explain the reasons, say, why contracts against prostitution or even bribery are unenforceable. The approach lacks methodological tools to clarify the reason a profitable arms sale contract with North Korea should be barred from enforcement when it creates numerous jobs in a stagnant economy. There is more in the doctrine of public policy than merely balancing interests in the economics sense. Not all aspects of social living can be reduced to cost–benefit analysis. Moreover, the courts' role should not be restricted to a calculation of various interests.

This brings us to the other aspects of public policy, which are what I call "educative" and "protective." In respect of these, courts have a more active role and there is no need for balancing; indeed, judges have a crucial role where a basic moral norm of society is in jeopardy or there is a potential threat to public safety. It might be argued that even in these instances courts follow a balancing approach. Enforcing a morally egregious contract or award that will jeopardize public safety is clearly outweighed by societal interest in non-enforcement of the contract or the award. However, there is a fine distinction

---

40 Liebman v. Rosenthal, 57 N.Y.S.2d. 877 (Sup. Ct), aff'd, 59 N.Y.S.2d 148 (App. Div. 1945).
41 A similar case is *Holzer v. Deutsche Reichsbahngesellschaf*, in which an employee was dismissed pursuant to non-Aryan laws of 1933 before the expiration of his employment contract. Subsequently, the employee sued for indemnification in the US courts. The lower court invoked the doctrine of public policy to argue that non-Aryan laws are not applicable and the employee was entitled to compensation. The Court of Appeals of New York rejected the public policy argument because of lack of sufficient contract with the US jurisdiction, Holzer v. Deutsche Reichsbahngesellschaf, 277 N.Y. 474 (1938); *see also*, Arthur Nussbaum, *Public Policy and the Political Crisis in the Conflict of Laws*, 49 YALE L.J. 1027, 1030–31 (1940).
42 "[T]he result of the case seems institutively correct, but its underlying argument should be tightly constrained to its facts . . . it also injects uncertainty of non enforcement into what would otherwise have been clearly unenforceable contracts, which have negative welfare effects." Note *supra* note 4 at 1452–53.
43 For discussions on judicial activism, *see, e.g.*, Robert M. Cover, *The Origins of Judicial Activism in the Protection of Minorities*, 91 YALE L.J. 1287 (1982); Keenan D. Kmiec, *The Origin and Current Meanings of "Judicial Activism"*, 92 CALIF. L. REV. 1441 (2004); J. Skelly Wright, *The Role of the Supreme Court in a Democratic Society—Judicial Activism or Restraint?*, 54 CORNELL L. REV. 1 (1968); P.N. Bhagwati, *Judicial Activism and Public Interest Litigation*, 23 COLUM. J. TRANSNAT'L L. 561 (1984); Bradley C. Canon, *Defining the Dimensions of Judicial Activism*, 66 JUDICATURE 236 (1982).

between the two balancing approaches. The first one relies on an economic analysis (the cost–benefit approach) of the various interests at stake. In the case of a plant causing pollution to a neighborhood, data could be shown on the benefits the neighborhood receives from job creation versus the costs to the health of its residents as a result of pollution. The same analysis could not be done when issues of morality and security are at stake. Looking back at the *Liebman* case, it was absolutely impossible for the court to collect numerical data on the costs incurred as a result of the moral wrongdoing of the officer. Similar issues exist for cases involving public security, yet they are subtly different. Public security concerns are—and ought to be—taken seriously. The sensitivity of the matter requires that even a slight chance of threat to public safety overrides normal cost–benefit analysis. The logic of public morality and public safety is distinct from the prevailing cost–benefit logic associated with ascertaining the public interest.

2. Policy arguments in courts

Montesquieu famously said that a judge is "no more than the mouth that produces the words of law."[44] American legal thought, and in particular judicial philosophy, took a completely opposite trajectory from this approach to law. Inspired by pragmatism, Holmes was one of the first leading American legal thinkers to lay the basis for American realism. He believed that judges should not follow the law blindly. Recognizing "judicial legislation," Holmes posited that judges should take into "consideration of what is expedient for the community concerned." According to him, the "secret roots" of law form the core from which "law draws the juices of policy." Holmes suggests that judges extrapolate the underlying public policy of laws rather than applying them blindly without any intellectual endeavor. Judges are forming the law and not simply following it.[45] They could shape the public policy of their community:

> Judges as well as others should openly discuss the legislative principles upon which their decisions must always rest in the end, and should base their judgments upon broad considerations of policy to which the traditions of the bench would hardly have tolerated a reference fifty years ago.[46]

---

44 MONTESQUIEU, THE SPIRIT OF LAWS 209 (Thomas Nugent trans., Univ. Cal. Press 1977) (1750).
45 This tradition has influenced other legal systems as well. Justice Barak, the former president of the Supreme Court of Israel, posits "I reject the contention that the judge merely states the law and does not create it. It is a fictitious and even a childish approach." Aharon Barak, *A Judge on Judging: The Role of A Supreme Court in a Democracy*, 116 HARV. L. REV. 19, 23 (2002). Barack believes that a Supreme Court judge should take into consideration: "1. The coherence of the system in which he operates; 2. The powers and limitations of the institution of the judiciary as defined within that system; and 3. The way in which his role is perceived", *Id.* at 30.
46 DAVID M. RABBAN, LAW'S HISTORY: AMERICAN LEGAL THOUGHT AND THE TRANSATLANTIC TURN TO HISTORY 241 (2013).

This view reverberates with the claim that judges inevitably have to enter the area of political arguments.[47] Historically, Lord Hardwicke L.C. in 1750 realized this ramification of the doctrine of public policy, describing the judicial task as involving "political arguments, in the fullest sense of the word, as they concern the government of the nation."[48] However, with the empowerment of a democratic parliament, this view lost its appeal. As we observed in the history section, skepticism towards the doctrine of public policy became the prevailing paradigm. This skepticism reached its culmination when the House of Lords suggested that courts should no longer engage in creating new categories of public interest in situations in which they found the legislative policy undesirable.[49]

A recurrent objection to the doctrine of public policy is its interference with the legislative role of parliament. Yet, this argument does not seem to be conclusive in ruling out the possibility and desirability of judicial interference. After all, discovering the "legislative intent" seems to be highly difficult, if not impossible. As Posner mentions, it is more about knowledge by empathy rather than mindreading the legislator.[50]

John Bell suggests three models under which policy arguments in judicial decisions are justified:

1) *The Consensus Model*: under this theory, judges are voices for the communal values of the society and ought to articulate them.[51] This follows from a basic distinction between the judicial and legislative branch. The legislature could pass laws that do not reflect popular opinion, whereas the judicial branch is restrained to conform to the consensus of society at large. Judges should not enter areas that are contentious and no consensus exists on fundamental values.[52]

2) *The Rights Model*: This model is based on Ronald Dworkin's theory. Dworkin keenly observes that in practice it is impossible to rule out the possibility of judicial decision-making. Moreover he objects to the

---

47 Chief Justice Shaw gave a classic expression to this view in Norway Plains Co. v. Boston & Maine R.R. Co., 67 Mass. 263, 267 (1854): "It is one of the great merits and advantages of the common law, that, instead of a series of detailed practical rules, established by positive provisions, and adapted to the precise circumstances of particular cases, which would become obsolete and fail, when the practice and course of business, to which they apply, should cease or change, the common law consists of a few broad and comprehensive principles founded on reason, natural justice, and enlightened public policy modified and adapted to the circumstances of all the particular cases which fall within it."
48 Chesterfield v. Janssen (1750) 1 Atk., 339, 352.
49 Janson v. Drieftein Consolidated Mines [1902] A.C. 484; JOHN BELL, POLICY ARGUMENTS IN JUDICIAL DECISIONS 157 (1983).
50 Richard A. Posner, *The Jurisprudence of Skepticism*, 86 MICH. L. REV. 827, 851 (1987). Eric Posner has voiced his view on intention in other fields of law as well. In intentional torts, he believes intention does not play a role besides alluding to certain characteristics of tortious acts. WILLIAM M. LANDES & RICHARD A. POSNER, THE ECONOMIC STRUCTURE OF TORT LAW 149–150 (1987).
51 BELL, *supra* note 50 at 11.
52 *Id.* at 12.

mainstream idea that judicial law-making is "parasitic" on the legislative branch.[53] He distinguishes between policy and principle in order to portray the distinct role of the legislative branch compared to the judiciary. Policy arguments refer to a political decision that advances some collective goal of the community as a whole. On the other hand, arguments of principle vindicate a political decision by resorting to a group or individual right.[54] An argument for a tax increase on wealthy people is an argument of policy. In contrast, arguments centered on anti-discrimination belong to the category of arguments of principle. Dworkin posits that legislative programs—especially complex legislation—often have both aspects of policy and principle. In contrast, judicial decisions "characteristically are and should be generated by principle not policy."[55] Dworkin cleverly pinpoints a distinctive feature of the judiciary as a guardian of rights in respect of collective welfare. These rights could derive from constitution, statutes, or common law.[56]

3) *The Interstitial Legislator Model*: proponents of this model argue that judges essentially legislate when dealing with hard cases.[57] In hard cases judges confront a number of rules and standards that might run counter to the existing law. Taking into account the interest of society at large, judges adjudicate based on these rules and standards. Although inconsistent at times, these theories show that there is something distinctive about judicial policy-making.[58] It cannot and should not be eliminated. There is always an empty space in law that should be filled with judgments of ethics and policy by courts.[59]

The doctrine of public policy has remained one of the few avenues of judicial policy-making. Subordination of judicial policy-making to the legislature runs the risk of weakening the judicial branch.[60] From its early

---

53 RONALD DWORKIN, TAKING RIGHTS SERIOUSLY 106 (1997).
54 *Id.* at 107.
55 *Id.* at 108.
56 BELL, *supra* note 50 at 15.
57 Article I (2) of the Swiss Code of 1807 exemplifies this model: "if no rule can be derived from the statue, the judge should decide in accordance with the rule which he would promulgate if he were the legislator." Richard Posner strongly object to this model as both unedifying and misleading, RICHARD A. POSNER, THE PROBLEM OF JURISPRUDENCE 130–131 (1990). This view leads to ontological skepticism on the existence of intent and even objectivity. Posner, *id.* at 866–71.
58 Barak, *supra* note 46 at 116.
59 *Id.* at 891.
60 Justice Barack gives an illuminating example on the role the doctrine of public policy can play. In 1994 a dispute came before the Supreme Court of Israel in which two political parties of Israel signed a "coalition agreement." The agreement stipulated that when any Supreme Court statutory interpretation decision changed the status quo on religion and state, the two parties would vote to restore the status quo. The majority opinion was that the contract was not contrary to public policy. Justice Barak, in dissent, believed that this agreement reduced confidence in the judicial branch and therefore was against public policy. Barak, *supra* note 46 at 135.

history, the doctrine of public policy was viewed as a separate category of the law. In 1853, the House of Lords opined that "public policy" holds a different meaning from the "policy of the law." It rejected the majority view in *Egerton v. Brownlow*, which found public policy and the policy of the law to be equivalent notions—meaning both refer to the object and policy of a particular law.[61] An example will illuminate this fine distinction. In *Adams v. Howerton*, the issue was whether a same-sex couple could qualify under the Immigration and Nationality Act for legal permanent resident status. The couple in the case was married legally by a minister in Colorado. The court held that the marriage should be valid under both state law and the Immigration and Nationality Act (INA). After investigating the legislative history of the Act, the court found that Congress' intent was clearly not to recognize same-sex marriages.[62] The Ninth Circuit did a thorough and convincing investigation of the "intent" of the legislature and policy of the Act. Yet, it is not clear whether it was a sound public policy, especially since the court could resort to states' exclusive power to regulate domestic relations. In other words, the policy of law in this case overshadows the public policy, which resulted in a weak decision.

In summary, the judicial branch's endeavor cannot and should not simply be to investigate the intent of the law-makers. If so, it sacrifices its inherent distinctive feature. The doctrine of public policy should be seen in this light.

---

61 W.S.W. Knight, *Public Policy in English Law*, 38 L.Q.R. 207, 216 (1922). This view has been contested since then. *Id.* at 216–17.
62 Adams v. Howerton, 673 F.2d 1036, 1041–42 (1981).

4 Public policy in arbitration*

A. Why people arbitrate: three paradigms

The alternative dispute resolution literature is replete with suggestions as to techniques, strategies, and negotiation styles occasionally coupled with the game theory rationalization of the system. I posit that the current approach reduces the ADR system to a procedural alternative to the states' court system. Similar to experts on the Civil Procedure, ADR specialists aim to foster a discipline concentrated on the minutiae of the various techniques of the alternative procedure. This new discipline has been widely embraced by the business community as well as academia. The backlog of court cases, along with the business community's need for an alternative method, paved the way for the rapid growth of this discipline.[1]

Notwithstanding the increasing growth of the ADR system, one fundamental question has been widely neglected: What is "alternative" about alternative dispute resolution? Following the current literature, should we simply stop at the proposition that it only means alternative procedures and techniques? In pursuit of answering this vexing yet important question, we need to ask ourselves about the underlying reasons that drive people to resort to ADR (and arbitration) versus litigating at courts. This section endeavors to answer these complex questions. The general theoretical framework of ADR and arbitration directly shapes the theory of public policy in arbitration.

In summary, I argue that the "alternative" feature of ADR poses a threat to the monopoly of the justice distribution of modern states. Therefore, it is structurally in friction with the judicial system. This new approach to ADR has several implications, one of which is to explicate the erratic reaction of states worldwide to ADR. More importantly and relevant to our discussion,

---

* The content of the following chapter has appeared previously in Farshad Ghodoosi, *Arbitrating Public Policy: Why the Buck Should not Stop at National Courts*, 20 Lewis & Clark L. Rev. 237, 237–80 (2016).
1 In the United States, the ADR system has undergone three phases. In the first stage, during the 1960s, local justice centers and community-based alternatives emerged. In the second phase (the late 1970s), ADR came as a help to the so-called medical malpractice crisis through arbitration and screening panels. The last phase was the commercialization of ADR, in which ADR gradually covered a wide variety of disputes, Lucy V. Katz, *Compulsory Alternative Dispute Resolution and Voluntarism: Two-Headed Monster or Two Sides of the Coin?* 1993 J. Disp. Resol. 1, 3 (1993).

it guides us as to the best paradigm of the thorny issue of public policy in ADR. This section challenges the prevalent explanation of the ADR system via liberal and rational-based theories. It concludes that ADR has an element of resistance that incentivizes the disputants to continue utilizing it.

1. Structural tension

Alternative dispute resolution claims to share an area that modern states conquered a few centuries ago. Centralization of the judicial system had a crucial impact on creating modern statehood. By some accounts, modern statehood emerged out of the commitment of regents (republican or monarchical) in medieval Europe to providing judicial services. This process resulted in the homogenization of cross-border statutory codes, such as the standardization of evidence and punishments in penal cases.[2] This came at the expense of private judicial bodies including seigniorial courts and manor courts.[3]

The twelfth and thirteenth centuries witnessed the centralization of judicial services through the papal revolution as well as the development of bodies of royal law.[4][5] In the papacy, Gregory VII[6] for the first time established the authority of the Pope alone to create laws; royal institutions in every kingdom of the West followed this lead and enjoyed the power to legislate.[7] Expansion of royal law marked the consolidation and centralization of the legislative function. As a result of this, a professional group of lawyers and judges, as well as hierarchical courts with a uniform procedure, emerged.[8] Gradually, the judiciary become centralized and top-down.[9]

---

2 Chris Thornhill, *Public Law and the Emergence of the Political* in AFTER PUBLIC LAW 25, 30 (2013).
3 *Id.*
4 HAROLD JOSEPH BERMAN, LAW AND REVOLUTION: THE FORMATION OF THE WESTERN LEGAL TRADITION 535 (1983).
5 Various kingdoms in Europe established bodies of royal law with a similar approach to Roman law and canon law, consisting of an interlocking set of rules and institutions. *Id.* at 535–36.
6 According to Berman, after Gregory VII, the church system turned into an institution which can be seen as a predecessor to modern statehood: "After Gregory VII, however, the church took on most of the distinctive characteristics of the modern state. It claimed to be an independent, hierarchical, public authority. Its head, the pope, had the right to legislate, and in fact Pope Gregory's successors issued a steady stream of new laws, sometimes by their own authority, sometimes with the aid of church councils summoned by them." *Id.* at 113.
7 *Id.* at 535. ("As Gregory VII in 1075 declared for the first time the power of the pope alone to 'make new laws' (*condere novas leges*), so thereafter in every kingdom of the West the monarch came to be 'maker of laws' (*conditor legum*, as he was called in Normal Sicily in the mid-twelfth century.)")
8 *Id.* at 116.
9 BRUCE L. BENSON, THE ENTERPRISE OF LAW: JUSTICE WITHOUT THE STATE 46–77 (2013); for a Law and Economics criticism of the top-down judiciary approach *see* Robert D. Cooter, *Structural Adjudication and the New Law Merchant: A Model of Decentralized Law*, 14 INT'L REV. L. & ECON. 215, 227 (arguing that law should evolve from social norms, emerged out of appropriate incentive structures, rather than from judges who make laws in light of public policy.)

Systemization coupled with rationalization of law in Europe resulted in the creation of a new form of governance. Max Weber believed that no other societies in the world underwent such a transformation, which served to form the bedrock of today's bureaucracy as well as a capitalist structure.[10] Pursuant to Weber, the rational-based approach to law is a precondition to our modern political life and statehood. Bureaucracy—as a central component of modern statehood—cannot be achieved without a formal, rational, as well as systematized, law.[11] More importantly, formal rationalization of law fosters a form of legitimization for modern statehood, which allows it to legitimately exert domination over its citizens. This internal form of legitimization is in contrast with traditional and charismatic forms, which are externally shaped forms of authority. According to Weber there are three pure types of legitimate domination:

> 1. Rational grounds—resting on a belief in the legality of enacted rules and the right of those elevated to authority under such rules to issue commands (legal authority). 2. Traditional grounds—resting on an established belief in the sanctity of immemorial traditions and the legitimacy of those exercising authority under them (traditional authority; or finally, 3. Charismatic grounds—resting on devotion to the exceptional sanctity, heroism or exemplary character of an individual person, and of the normative patterns or order revealed or ordained by him (charismatic authority).[12]

Thus, modern statehood and governance is inextricably tied to a centralized top-down judiciary. As explained, this new form of domination has been shaped by the formalization and rationalization of law.

The alternative dispute resolution system challenges the modern paradigm of justice distribution on multiple grounds. First, ADR eschews the formal component of the legal rational ground in the Weberian sense. One of the main promises of ADR is to emancipate the parties from the

---

10 Weber seemed to link the factor of formal and rational administration of law to the calculability of economic activity. It other words, for him rationalization of law was a prerequisite to profit-making economy and capitalism. However, he was uneasy about the English common law, as it seemingly did not experience a robust systemization similar to other Western legal systems, *see* ANTHONY T. KRONMAN, MAX WEBER 120–22 (1983).
11 We should note that approach of Weber to the concept of law is rather simplistic and similar to the command theory of Austin. In his seminal work, Weber distinguishes between convention and law and defines law as follows: "An order will be called (a) convention ... (b) law if it is externally guaranteed by the probability that physical or psychological coercion will be applied by a staff of people in order to bring about compliance or avenge violation." MAX WEBER, ECONOMY AND SOCIETY: AN OUTLINE OF INTERPRETIVE SOCIOLOGY 34 (1978). For a critique of Weber's approach to the notion of law *see* David M. Trubek, *Max Weber on Law and the Rise of Capitalism* 1972 WIS. L. REV. 721, 725–27 (1972).
12 MAX WEBER, *Id.* at 215–16; *See also* David M. Trubek, *Id.* at 732.

entangling procedural elements of judicial bodies. This reduces the control of states, exercised routinely through formal procedures. Second, the idea of ADR partially rests on charismatic or traditional forms of legitimate domination, to borrow Weber's terminology. To some degree, all forms of ADR—with mediation being the highest—hinge on the "the exceptional sanctity, heroism or exemplary character of an individual person"[13] and his or her normative stance. To a lesser extent, most notably in the concept of customary international law, ADR still values "immemorial traditions and the legitimacy of those exercising authority under them"[14] more than other formal methods of dispute resolution. Lastly and more importantly, the idea of ADR runs counter to the centralized, top-down, judicial approach of modern statehood. ADR shapes a paradigm in which people can participate in shaping the notion of justice rather than being mere passive subjects of it. It also resembles the decentralized judicial mechanism prior to the appearance of the modern "Leviathan."[15] [16]

This section identifies three underpinning paradigms of ADR with a focus on arbitration in order to discern the best-fitting approach in light of the structural tension described above. It concludes that the resistance-based paradigm, although widely neglected, aptly describes the "alternative" feature of ADR and paves the way for a fresh look at a variety of crucial issues, including the public policy exception, that will be discussed in subsequent sections.

2. Consent-based

The consent-based paradigm remains the most prevailing narrative of ADR. It places the emphasis on the "consent" to ADR by parties and their "freedom" to resort to alternative methods for resolving their disputes.[17] It is directly linked to a liberal philosophy, believing that the idea of ADR is a product of parties' freedom.[18] Parties to a contract can adjust the contractual terms to their needs as long as there is no violation of any mandatory rules. Similarly, they enjoy the freedom to select the governing applicable

---

13 WEBER, *supra* note 11.
14 MAX WEBER, ECONOMY AND SOCIETY: AN OUTLINE OF INTERPRETIVE SOCIOLOGY 215–16 (1978).
15 Hobbes employs the metaphor Leviathan, a biblical creature with "greater stature and strength than the natural," to describe the modern sovereignty, THOMAS HOBBES, LEVIATHAN 7 (2009).
16 The tension is notable in some earlier courts' decisions. In *Tobey v. Country of Bristol*, 23 Fed. 1313 the Court clearly doubts the qualification of arbitration to administer justice: "[A] court of equity ought not to compel a party to submit the decision of his rights to a tribunal, which confessedly, does not possess full, adequate, and complete means, within itself, to investigate the merits of the case, and to administer justice."
17 ANDREA M. STEINGRUBER, CONSENT IN INTERNATIONAL ARBITRATION 2.04 (2012) (stating that the principal characterization of arbitration in the classical categorization of arbitration is that it is chosen by the parties).
18 JAN PAULSSON, THE IDEA OF ARBITRATION 23 (2013).

law and can opt to select a jurisdiction that is competent to hear their potential disputes. The same "philosophy" should apply if, instead of choosing a court, they insert an ADR/arbitration clause. Their "freedom" to opt out of the court system is seemingly and plausibly linked to a "liberal" paradigm stating that parties are free to choose their dispute resolution mechanism as much as they are free to select contractual terms. This view is rampant in the existing literature.[19]

The consensual approach to ADR became fortified as disappointment with court adjudication surged in the second half of the twentieth century. The dichotomy between consensual proceedings and adversarial adjudication shaped the prevailing narrative. Ultimately, ADR and the courts reached a similar qualitative theme: "both assume that dispositions based upon the consent of the parties are somehow better than those achieved by adjudication."[20] The decline of faith in adjudication, for a multitude of reasons,[21] resulted in widespread acceptance of the consensual approach.[22]

This paradigm depicts ADR as a technique shaped by the consent of parties.[23] It is "alternative" in the sense that the procedure deviates from the parliament-approved one. Parties can mold the procedure by agreement as long as they do not violate any mandatory rules of procedure.[24] Under this

---

19 For instance, most treatise on international commercial arbitration start off their analysis by laying the grounds of arbitration on consent, as well as the freedom of the parties *see, e.g.,* JULIAN D. M. LEW, COMPARATIVE INTERNATIONAL COMMERCIAL ARBITRATION 4 (2003) ("the principal characteristic of arbitration is that it is chosen by the parties. However, fulsome or simple the arbitration agreement, the parties have ultimate control of their dispute resolution system"); EMMANUEL GAILLARD & JOHN SAVAGE, FOUCHARD GAILLARD GOLDMAN ON INTERNATIONAL COMMERCIAL ARBITRATION 29–30 (1999) (stating that arbitration is contractual-based by its nature); GARY BORN, INTERNATIONAL COMMERCIAL ARBITRATION 97 (2014) ("international commercial arbitration is a fundamentally consensual means of dispute resolution: unless parties have agreed to arbitrate, there can be no valid arbitral determination of their rights.") ALAN REDFERN ET AL., REDFERN AND HUNTER ON INTERNATIONAL ARBITRATION 15 (2009) ("The foundation stone of modern international arbitration is (and remains) an agreement by the parties to submit to arbitration any disputes or differences between them").
20 Judith Resnik, *Failing Faith: Adjudicatory Procedure in Decline,* U. OF CHI. L. REV. 494, 537 (1986).
21 Some of the reasons are 1) the increased caseload; 2) the upsurge of disputes between powerful and non-privileged citizens; 3) the appearance of complex lawsuits, *Id.* at 526. For a criticism of this view on adjudication, *see* RICHARD A. POSNER, THE PROBLEMS OF JURISPRUDENCE 41 (1993).
22 *Id.* at 538.
23 *See e.g.,* U.S. Equal Employment Opportunity Commission, *Types of ADR Techniques* available at http://www.eeoc.gov/federal/adr/typesofadr.cfm (last visited, May 16, 2014). *See also* Judith Resnik, *Managerial Judges,* 96 HARV. LAW REV. 374, 376–380 (1982) (explaining and critiquing the ever increasing use of various methods including ADR by trial judges to manage their case load).
24 Carrie, Menkel-Meadow, *Trouble with the Adversary System in a Postmodern Multicultural World, The Teaching of Legal Ethics,* 38 WM. & MARY L. REV. 5, 42 (arguing that the adversarial system cannot be changed by simply modifying procedures but through true reform resulting from creating a opposite system to courts e.g., through ADR).

paradigm, the structural tension, as described above, translates into the friction between the consent of the parties and the public policy of the state. Alternative dispute resolution becomes suspect when dealing with public law and values, a concern that justifies limiting its scope.[25] Parties cannot derogate from fundamental norms of the state and society—so-called public policy—by resorting to the ADR mechanism.[26] [27]

Hence, following this paradigm, institutionalization of alternate methods of settling disputes serves as the most efficient way to resolve the above-mentioned tension.[28] This way, parties' consent is easily channeled into pre-existing institutions specializing in ADR techniques while governments can conveniently monitor the practice of ADR in order to assure its compliance with mandatory norms.[29] In summary, this paradigm leads

---

25 Harry T. Edwards, *Dispute Resolution: Panacea or Anathema?* 99 HARV. L. REV. 668, 676 (1986) ("If ADR is extended to resolve difficult issues of constitutional or public law—making use of nonlegal values to revolve important social issues or allowing those the law seeks to regulate to delimit public rights and duties—there is real reason for concern"; Owen Fiss, *Against Settlement*, 93 YALE L.J. 1073, 1085 (1984) (stating that unlike "strangers chosen by parties in the ADR methods, judges as public officials have the task "not to maximize the ends of private parties, not simply to secure the peace, but to explicate and give force to the values embodies in authoritative texts such as the Constitution and statutes; to interpret those values and to bring reality in accord with them"); David Luban, *Settlements and the Erosion of the Public Realm*, 83 GEO L.J. 2619, 2637("in adjudication, the law—the residual of political action—receives elaboration and reasoned reconsideration in the light of subsequent cases and controversies that have revealed its weak points. This process is as much a part of political validity as free elections and legislative debate"). *See also* Resnik, *supra* note 23 at 380–86 (arguing that a managerial approach to adjudication has resulted in increased use of ADR which in turn has shifted the judiciary system from the adversarial model and justice endorsed by the U.S. Constitution).
26 The most important international instrument specifying the public policy exception is Section V (2)(b) of the 1958 New York Convention on the Recognition and Enforcement of Foreign Arbitral Awards (the so-called New York Convention). We will focus on this provision in the next section of this chapter.
27 Following this view is concern over the distinction between private and public disputes. Pursuant to this approach, ADR is merely equipped to tackle private claims, *see* Edwards, *supra* note 25, 671–72. This debate stretches today to international arbitration as well. *See generally* Julie A. Maupin, Public and Private in International Investment Law: An Integrated Systems Approach, 54(2) VIRGINIA J. INT'L L. 367 (2014).
28 In the existing literature, this phenomenon sometimes is referred to as "mandatory ADR" (*see e.g.*, Thomas Eisele, *The Case Against Mandatory Court-Annexed ADR Programs*, 75 JUDICATURE 34, 35 (1991); "nonconsensual ADR" (*see e.g.*, John R. Allison, *The Context, Properties, and Constitutionality of Nonconsensual Arbitration: A Study of Four Systems*, 1990 J. DISP. RESOL 1, 1 (1990) or institutionalization of ADR (see e.g., Douglas Yarn, *The Death of ADR: A Cautionary Tale of Isomorphism Through Institutionalization*, 108 PENN ST. L. REV. 929, 929 (2003). I prefer the term institutionalization because, *sub silentio*, it includes other terms as well.
29 Several authors have warned about the consequences of institutionalizing the ADR mechanism: Yarn, *supra* note 28 at 1012 (2003) (recounting the story of how arbitration shifted from a conciliatory process to an adjudicative (adversarial) process by the twentieth century "through legislation, commercial institutionalization, judicial decisions and the shifting processing priorities of a changing society"); Carrie Menkel-Meadow, *Pursuing Settlement*

to the institutionalization of ADR, which purportedly strikes the balance between "consent" and "public policy" and reaches a stable compromise.

The problems with the consent-based explanation of ADR are manifold: it is simplistic; it has led to the government-annexed ADR system; and, finally, it does not offer satisfactory responses to pervasive problems of ADR. This narrative does not satisfactorily explain the reason parties select various methods of ADR in the first place. Disputants do not select an alternative method because they are free to do so. The liberty to opt out of the court system is a necessary condition, yet not a sufficient one. This paradigm seems to furnish a normative stance—i.e., touting ADR because it advances liberty and freedom—rather than an explanation. However, as elaborated earlier, this normative stance has led to the institutionalization of ADR through boilerplates as well as government-annexed programs.[30] Since the focal point has been placed on "freedom," several schemes have been devised to obtain "consent" from disputants, either from the commercial community or congested courts. In the long term, therefore, the "alternative" method becomes part of the existing "litigation game," rendering it a mainstream method of dispute resolution.[31]

Additionally, the consent-based paradigm does not offer satisfactory solutions for the long-lasting problems associated with ADR. Most importantly, it does not offer any satisfactory explanation regarding the problem of public policy. It is widely believed that the ADR mechanism cannot adjudicate matters fundamental to state and public interest, giving courts an exclusive jurisdiction over these issues. Hence, ADR methods are not equipped to investigate, and should not enter into, matters related to public policy. ADR does not go beyond alternative techniques, making it an unsuitable venue for addressing the vital interests of state and society.

3. Interest-based

The interest-based theory probably offers the most convincing apolitical and ahistorical justification for the ADR system. It regards justice as a service

---

in an Adversary Culture: A Tale of Innovation Co-Opted or "the Law of ADR," 19 FLA ST. U. L. REV. 1, 15–17 (1991) (stating that ADR was taken over by the system instead of making new changes); Katz, *supra* note 1 at 41 ("compulsory ADR can evolve quickly into intense pressure to settle—or at least to negotiate. Yet both of these phenomena are highly questionable in terms of judicial ethics and basic litigants' rights"); *See also* Nancy A. Welsh, *The Current Transitional State of Court-Connected ADR*, MARQ. L. REV. 873, 874 (2011); Jacqueline Nolan-Haley, *Mediation: The "New Arbitration,"* 17 HARV. NEGOT. L. REV. 61, 63–66 (2012); Nancy A. Welsh, *The Thinning Vision of Self-Determination in Court-Connected Mediation: The Inevitable Price of Institutionalization?*, 6 HARV. NEGOT. L. REV. 23, 25–27 (2001).

30 For a glance at Federal Court-Annexed ADR program, *see* http://www.justice.gov/olp/adr/annexedkant.htm (last visited, May 16, 2014).
31 Judith Resnik, *Many Doors? Closing Doors? Alternative Resolution and Adjudication*, 10 OHIO ST. J. ON DISP. RESOL. 211, 264–65 (1995).

and courts as private vendors offering this service. Similar to other markets, if courts fail to meet market needs, participants will resort to other providers of justice.[32] This approach is not typically discussed in the literature on arbitration, yet it serves as an important ground for the literature on bargaining, negotiation, and settlement.[33] [34] As explained above, the main focus of this chapter is on arbitration as against other forms of ADR. Despite its importance, little attention has been paid to game theory in arbitration. This section aims to give a broad brush analysis of its main premises. A thorough discussion of the game theory of arbitration requires a separate book.

The interest-based approach views ADR as a profit-maximizing method. Judicial systems cannot offer a wide variety of options and remain largely a zero-sum game. ADR promises to increase parties' choices by creating a non-zero-sum game that adds more options to the table.[35] For example, in

---

32 William M. Landes & Richard A. Posner, *Adjudication as a Private Good*, 8 J. OF LEGAL STUD. 235 (stating that a court system has two functions: dispute resolution and rule formulation as a by-product of the dispute-settlement process. Alternative methods to the court system cannot deliver the second function as desired, and therefore the court system still offers the best service in the market.)

33 For instance in the context of negotiation *see e.g.*, JAY FOLBERG & DWIGHT GOLANN, LAWYER NEGOTIATION: THEORY, PRACTICE, AND LAW 34–36 (2011) (illustrating the game theory behind competitive or adversarial negotiation versus cooperative negotiation); Gary Goodpaster, *A Primer on Competitive Bargaining*, J. DISP. RESOL. 325, 342–46 (1996) (elaborating on the role of negotiator as a some who is doing an information game, aiming to obtain much information while disclosing little information); MAX H. BAZERMAN & MARGARET A. NEALE, NEGOTIATING RATIONALLY 67 (1994) (arguing that negotiator's task is to add value by understating integrative and distributive components of negotiations); DAVID A. LAX & JAMES K. SEBENIUS, THE MANAGER AS NEGOTIATOR 33 (1986) (arguing that arbitrators either claim value—distributive task—or add value—integrative task—); Russell Korobkin, *A Positive Theory of Legal Negotiation*, 88 GEO. L.J. 1789, 1791 (1999) (rejecting the integrative/distributive dichotomy in negotiation literature on the ground that all negotiations add value and suggesting zone definition/surplus allocation instead).

34 A relevant literature attempts to answer the underlying reason parties opt for litigation versus settlement while the former is clearly in their best interest. Scholar have proposed that parties opt for litigation because either one of them or both are unable to predict the outcome of litigation or because bargaining process has failed, *see e.g.*, William M. Landes, *An Economic Analysis of Courts*, 14 J. L. & ECON. 61, 98–101 (1971) (in the context of criminal courts); Richard A. Posner, *An Economic Approach to Legal Procedure and Judicial Administration*, 2 J. LEGAL STUD. 399, (1973) (in the context of administrative agencies); John P. Gould, *The Economics of Legal Conflicts* 2. J. LEGAL STUD. 279, 296–97 (1973) (in the context of labor-management disputes).

35 Menkel-Meadow argues that ADR allows parties to break free of what she calls "limited remedial imagination." By this terms she means that courts are restricted a few remedies including granting injunction and awarding damages, Carrie Menkel-Meadow, *Toward Another View of Legal Negotiation: The Structure of Problem Solving*, 31 UCLA L. REV. 754, 789–94 (1984). The ADR Local Rules of the Northern District Court of California find that "A hallmark of mediation is its capacity to expand traditional settlement discussion and broaden resolution options, often by exploring litigant needs and interests that may be formally independent of the legal issues in controversy," UNITED STATES DISTRICT COURT NORTHERN DISTRICT OF CALIFORNIA, ADR LOCAL RULES (2012) available at: http://www.cand.uscourts.gov/mediation.

an intellectual property dispute, courts are asked to adjudicate whether a copyright or patent has been infringed. Each side either loses or wins the case. However, upon referral to negotiation, it is conceivable that parties carve out a third solution which goes beyond the dichotomy of infringement/non-infringement. In other words, in the process of negotiation, with the help of the neutral person, parties are asked set aside the adversarial logic of litigation and devise new ways to resolve their disputes.[36]

The interest-based paradigm could also form an underlying logic for arbitration. In arbitration, parties litigate their disputes before an arbitrator or a panel of arbitrators instead of in front of a judge. Thus, from the outside, arbitration follows an adversarial logic—similar to litigation in courts. Yet, it does not tell the entire story. Since arbitrators are not bound by complex and rigid procedural and substantive rules, they can indirectly increase the options of litigants, for instance by employing other methods of assessing damages. This is sometimes referred to as "conventional interest arbitration," in which arbitrators craft an outcome to reach a compromise between parties.[37][38] The same approach applies to

---

36 Several articles have focused on the benefit of the ADR system, compared to the courts system, from an economic perspective. For instance, Steven Shavell argues that *ex-ante* agreement to ADR will 1) reduce the cost of dispute resolution for parties; 2) improve parties' incentives to implement good performance and 3) bring about optimal changes in the frequency of disputes brought by parties, Steven Shavell, *Alternative Dispute Resolution: An Economic Analysis*, 24 J. LEGAL STUD. 1, 5–7 (1995). He does not believe that *ex-post* ADR agreements can yield similar results. Furthermore, he argues that *ex-post* ADR agreements do not enhance social value, and therefore the public policy of requiring court-annexed ADR is flawed, *Id.* at 3–4. *See also* Richard A. Posner, *The Summary Jury Trial and Other Methods of Alternative Dispute Resolution: Some Cautionary Observations*, 53 U. CHI. L. REV. 366–93 (1986) (arguing that summary judgment will promote settlement but will increase the number of lawsuits as well); Lisa Bernstein, *Understanding the Limits of Court-Connected ADR: A Critique of Federal Court-Annexed Arbitration Programs*, 141 U. PA. L. REV. 2169, 2250–51 (1993) (showing that even though some of the benefits of resorting to ADR could be captured by *ex-post* ADR agreements, court-annexed mandatory non-binding ADR does not produce similar results).

37 "In general, there are three types of interest arbitration. The first, known as 'issue-by-issue, last best offer' arbitration, requires the arbitrator to select the final proposal of one of the parties on an issue-by-issue basis. The second type, known as 'total package, last best offer,' requires the arbitrator to choose between the parties' final offers on a total package basis. In this form of arbitration, an arbitrator may end up selecting the final offer of one party even though it contains proposals on specific issues that the arbitrator might not normally award. In the third type of interest arbitration, the arbitrator has the authority to fashion an award on an issue-by-issue basis without being limited by final proposals of parties," WILL AITCHISON, INTEREST ARBITRATION 3–4 (2000).

38 In some jurisdictions, the scope of arbitration was limited by introducing the final-offer arbitration method, in which the space of maneuver for arbitrators is much limited. Final offer arbitration is a procedure which attempts to increase the parties' incentives to bargain by retaining the first of these conditions while eliminating the second. Since the arbitrator will not be free to compromise between parties' positions, the parties will be induced to develop even more reasonable positions prior to the arbitrator's decision in the hope of winning the award." PETER FEUILLE, FINAL OFFER ARBITRATION: CONCEPTS, DEVELOPMENTS, TECHNIQUES 13 (1975).

international arbitration, in which arbitrators have significant discretion in assessing damages.[39]

Furthermore, even if one argues that arbitration cannot "increase the pie" by widening parties' options, the possibility of compromise is at the center of arbitration. Following "prisoner's dilemma" logic, parties opt for arbitration because, on average, each side gains more compared to litigation in courts. Let's say that the parties each have a 50/50 chance of winning in court. In arbitration there is a possibility that each gains 1/3 of what they have demanded. This possibility of compromise is the "Pareto efficiency"[40] of disputants' choices, in which each individual gains without necessarily making the other party lose. In other words, arbitration serves as an "alternative" option for the win-lose litigation game.[41][42][43] As Steven Brams observes, "arbitration need not be by fiat but may cede different kinds of choices to the disputants."[44]

Rationality lies at the core of the interest-based paradigm. Disputants choose the ADR system because it is in their best interest employing cost–benefit analysis. The focus of ADR, therefore, should rest on its

---

39 In international arbitration various valuation methods are employed to assess damages: the income-based approach (DCF method), the market-based approach, the asset-based approach, valuation by reference to amounts invested, and the hybrid approach. *See* SERGEY RIPINSKY, DAMAGES IN INTERNATIONAL INVESTMENT LAW 188–242 (2008).

40 "The efficient frontier—sometimes called the Pareto Optimal Frontier, after the economist Vilfredo Pareto—is defined as the locus of achievable joint evaluations from which no joint gains are possible." HOWARD RAIFFA, THE ART AND SCIENCE OF NEGOTIATION 139 (2003).

41 R. J. Aumann, *Game Engineering* in MATHEMATICAL PROGRAMMING AND GAME THEORY FOR DECISION MAKING 279, 282–283 (Sankar K Pal et al., 2008); *see also* STEVEN J. BRAMS, NEGOTIATION GAMES: APPLYING GAME THEORY TO BARGAINING AND ARBITRATION 98–99 ("one's faith in the perceived median as a compromise, versus one's faith in the arbitrator's judgment, will be the determinant of whether one regards Combined Arbitration, or either Two-Stage or Multistage FOA, as the better arbitration procedure(s) for settling disputes").

42 Furthermore, arbitration (especially international arbitration) sometimes is called upon to fill in the shortcomings of the pre-contract negotiation phase. For instance, in long-term gas supply contracts, parties resort to arbitration so that it adjust the contract in accordance with change of circumstances. This method differs from traditional arbitration, Kyriaki Karadelis, *Is Arbitration Suitable for Resolving Gas Price Disputes?* Available at http://globalarbitrationreview.com/news/article/32591/is-arbitration-suitable-resolving-gas-price-disputes/?utm_medium=email&utm_source=Law+Business+Research&utm_campaign=4027182_GAR+Briefing&dm_i=1KSF,2EBE6,9GPI9R,8PH0R,1

43 Some authors believe that ascribing the term win-win to alternative dispute resolution is inaccurate and will lead to false expectations, Carrie Menkel-Meadow, *When Disputes Resolution Begets Disputes of Its Own: Conflicts Among Dispute Professionals*, 44 UCLA L. Rev. 1871, 1872 (1997) (fn. 4).

44 BRAMS, *supra* note 41 at 263. Brams believes that arbitrators should have judgments independent of the two sides, *id.* at 65. He furnishes Kissinger's "shuttle diplomacy" in the Middle East as an example of how arbitrators (and negotiators) should be able to fashion settlement to provide the best outcome, *id.* at 94–66.

option-maximizing feature. The "alternative" feature of ADR hinges on its delivery of new rational options that courts are incapable of or unwilling to offer. The interest-based paradigm provides a satisfactory non-historical non-political narrative of the ADR system. However, it fails to envisage ADR as an autonomous institution with its own distinct philosophy. Furthermore, it is not clear whether all disputants opt for ADR simply because it offers more options; not all ADR proceedings result in profit-maximization and not all parties are aware of it.

4. Resistance-based

A critical approach to the ADR system is rarely discussed. Under this paradigm parties neither opt for alternative methods because they are "free" to do so, nor because they are "rational."[45] Parties instead prefer ADR methods because they feel they can "participate" in the process of shaping justice. The impression that parties have more control over the procedure is of paramount importance in this paradigm. The recent literature demonstrates that participation in the adjudicative process is the most important factor that parties value; this in turn result in compliance with law and judgments.[46] Furthermore, I argue that parties, by participating in a parallel justice system, challenge the monopoly of government over the dissemination of justice.

Unlike the interest-based approach, this paradigm views ADR diachronically and within a socio-political context. The structural tension between the formal judiciary and ADR, as described in section A1, lies behind the viability of ADR. Hence, ADR should not submit itself to any forms of institutionalism since it withers the very essence of it. Ad hoc and individualized dispute resolutions best serve the interest of parties, as well

---

45 Some authors adhered to an approach which could be classified under the resistance paradigm. For instance, Jerold S. Auerbach suggests that alternative dispute settlement should derive its sources form communal values instead of law. JEROLD S. AUERBACH, JUSTICE WITHOUT LAW? RESOLVING DISPUTES WITHOUT LAWYERS 138–47 (1983).

46 TOM R. TYLER, WHY PEOPLE OBEY THE LAW 163–66 (2006) (showing that people's participation in the procedural justice and decision-making is directly linked to obedience of law); E. ALLEN LIND & TOM R. TYLER, THE SOCIAL PSYCHOLOGY OF PROCEDURAL JUSTICE 176–77 (1988) (" . . . one of the most potent determinants of the procedural fairness of a social decision-making procedure is the extent to which those affected by the decision are allowed to participate in the decision-making process . . . satisfaction is one of the principal consequences of procedural fairness"). Other scholars point to the fact that the effect of litigation on non-parties through its mainly rule-making function has a crucial impact on the parties' decision to pursue litigation, *see e.g.*, Bruce H. Kobayashi, *Case Selection, External Effects, and the Trial/Settlement Decision* in DISPUTE RESOLUTION: BRIDGING THE SETTLEMENT GAP 17, 18 (David A. Anderson ed., 1996) (refuting the argument that litigation is a result of failure of bargaining but instead is due to external incentives, mainly its rule-making function); Paul Rubin, *Why is Common Law Efficient?* 6 J. OF LEGAL STUD. 51, 61 (1977) (showing parties will litigate inefficient rules than efficient rules).

as society. Creating a subordinate ADR mechanism would attenuate the overall systemic implication desired under this paradigm. The structural tension should subsist by maintaining a robust alternative mechanism, aiming to crack the edifice of a top-down and exclusive justice system.

The resistance to integration with the formal judiciary forms a basis of this paradigm. Contrary to the interest-based approach, ADR is viewed as being part of a larger picture with necessary systemic implications. It is not a mechanism for creating more options within the existing system. It has the potential to revolutionize the very game itself. Borrowing Wittgenstein's terminology, pursuant to the interest-based paradigm, ADR operates under the same "language game," yet offers more options.[47] ADR, according to the resistance-based approach, aims to define a new language game parallel to the formal judicial system.

Some authors have attempted to depart from the previous paradigms of ADR and shape what could be aptly called the "post ADR-movement."[48] A notable example is Bush and Folger's book on *The Promise of Mediation*. After discussing other views on ADR—the satisfaction story,[49] the social justice story,[50] and the oppression story[51]—they endorse what they call the transformation story

---

[47] *See generally* LUDWIG WITTGENSTEIN, PHILOSOPHICAL INVESTIGATIONS (Trans. G.E.M. Anscombe et al., 2010).

[48] There was an upsurge in the utilization of ADR starting from the 1970s and 1980s, which is often referred to as the "ADR Movement." *See generally* Laird C. Kirkpatrick, *Scholarly and Institutional Challenges to the Law of Evidence from Bentham to the ADR Movement* 25 LOY. L. A. L. REV. 837 (1992); Robben W. Fleming, *Reflection on the ADR Movement* 34 CLEV. ST. L. REV. 519 (1985).

[49] ROBER A. BARUCH BUSH & JOSEPH P. FOLGER, THE PROMISE OF MEDIATION, 16–18 (1994). The satisfaction narrative refers to a similar paradigm to what is described here as an interest-based paradigm. Under this narrative, endorsed by the post-World War II ADR movement, the ultimate purpose of mediation is to attain parties' satisfaction by providing a win-win situation to their disputes, *Id.* at 16. This story centers on efficiency, which brings about the parties' satisfaction, *Id.* at 17. The followings scholarship falls under this category: ROGER FISHER & WILLIAM L. URY, GETTING TO YES: NEGOTIATING AGREEMENT WITHOUT GIVING IN (1981); ROGER FISHER & SCOTT BROWN, GETTING TOGETHER: BUILDING RELATIONSHIP AS WE NEGOTIATE (1989); JEFFREY CRUIKSHANK & LAWRENCE SUSSKIND, BREAKING THE IMPASSE: CONSENSUAL APPROACHES TO RESOLVING PUBLIC DISPUTES (1987); WARREN E. BURGER, DELIVERY OF JUSTICE: PROPOSAL FOR CHANGES TO IMPROVE THE ADMINISTRATION OF JUSTICE (1990).

[50] This approach mainly narrates the function of mediation in community disputes. Mediation diverts the attentions of parties from their disputes to the bigger picture in which communal interest is best served in the settlement of their dispute. This way parties recognize the larger picture and their mutual enemy, *Id.* at 18. For example, in disputes between co-tenants, block residents, victims of environmental disaster, and consumers, mediation helps them to focus on communal adversary which, respectively, could be landlords, city agencies, land developers, and manufacturers, *Id.* at 19. Wahrhaftig's work on community mediation (Paul Wahrhaftig, *An Overview of Community-Oriented Citizen Dispute Resolution Programs in the United States*, THE POLITICS OF INFORMAL JUSTICE 1 (1982) and Shonholtz's piece (Raymond Shonholtz, *The Citizen's Role in Justice: Building a Primary Justice and Prevention System at the Neighborhood Level*, 494 THE ANNALS OF THE AM. ACAD. OF POLITICAL & SOC. SCI. 42 (1987)) pioneer this approach.

[51] The oppression narrative reveals the structural shortcomings of the mediation movement. It believes that stronger party can and will take advantage of the mediation proceeding

of mediation. By this, they mean that the goal of mediation should not simply be to reach an agreement but to transform people as well as situations.[52] Mediation should be the opposite of adjudication and arbitration, which disempowers parties by "taking control of outcome out of parties' hands and by necessitating reliance on professional representatives."[53] Mediation promises that its goal is "engendering moral growth and transforming human character, towards both greater strength and greater compassions."[54] [55] This way, the goal of mediation is not solely placed on "settlement" but on "empowerment and recognition" between parties, as well.[56]

Similar to other critical theories, the resistance-based theory runs the risk of being utopian, with far-fetched ideals. Furthermore, in the present system ADR cannot be independent from the judicial system since it depends on it for the enforcement of awards.[57] However, one should bear in mind that paradigmatic thoughts shape the way we approach each phenomenon. They do not necessarily lead to immediate concrete results. In

---

because of the informality as well as its consensual nature. In addition, the mediator's role remains limited, preventing him/her from intervening in the process to produce more just results. Furthermore, public interest will be harmed since mediation is a private mechanism, producing individualized results without paying due attention to their consequences. Landlords, manufacturers, employers, and land developers employ the mediation to cut deals with the weaker party behind closed doors, without any information needing to come to light. *Id.* at 22–23.

52 *Id.* at 29.
53 *Id.* at 30.
54 *Id.* at 27.
55 In practice, the authors identify elements that mediators could do to follow the transformative approach: the mediator should avoid taking any overarching evaluation of what the dispute is about and should concentrate on each party's contributions, *Id.* at 192. The mediator should encourage parties' deliberation and choice-making by allowing them to reflect on their demands and clarify them, *Id.* at 194–95. The mediator also should look out for opportunities in which parties consider each other's positions by having a more sympathetic and positive view, *Id.* at 196. The mediation as such has strong critics including Richard Abel (RICHARD ABEL, POLITICS OF INFORMAL JUSTICE: THE AMERICAN EXPERIENCE (1982); Christine Harrington (CHRISTINE HARRINGTON, SHADOW JUSTICE: THE IDEOLOGY AND INSTITUTIONALIZATION OF ALTERNATIVE TO COURTS (1985); Richard Delgado (Richard Delgado et al., *Fairness and Formality: Minimizing the Risk of Prejudice in Alternative Dispute Resolution* 1985 WIS. L. REV. 1359 (1985), Martha Fineman (Martha Fineman, *Dominant Discourse, Professional Language, and Legal Change in Child Custody Decisionmaking,* 101 HARV. L. REV. 727 (1988) along with Own Fiss (Owen Fiss, *Against Settlement,* 93 YALE L.J. 1073 (1983) and Laura Nader (Laura Nader, *Disputing Without the Force of Law,* 88 YALE L.J. 998 (1979).
56 *Id.* at 200.
57 For instance, in the context of enforcing arbitral awards, several courts have emphasized its discretionary nature: *see e.g.*, Karaha Bodas v. Perusahaan Pertambangan Minyak Dan Gas Bumi Negara, 335 F.3d 357, 368 (5th Cir. 2003) ("Under the Convention, a court maintains the discretion to enforce an arbitral award even when nullification proceedings are occurring in the country where the award was rendered"); Chromalloy Aeroservices v. Arab Republic of Egypt, 939 F. Supp. 907, 910 (1996) ("In the present case, the award was made in Egypt, under the laws of Egypt, and has been nullified by the court designated by Egypt to review arbitral awards. Thus, the Court may, at its discretion, decline to enforce the award").

the ADR discussion, the resistance-based paradigm, however, will affect the way arbitrators as well as policy-makers and judges view arbitration, especially since the system is relatively nascent.

B. The doctrine of public policy in arbitration

1. Role of the public policy exception

The legal scene is undoubtedly changing, both domestically and internationally. This is largely due to unprecedented growth in alternative dispute resolution, a mechanism that aims to resolve disputes outside of courts and through private legal institutions and arrangements. Domestically, the United States Supreme Court expanded the application of the Federal Arbitration Act to cover almost all disputes with limited court supervision.[58] Boilerplate contracts along with legislation prescribing arbitration leave, in many instances, no "alternative" for parties apart from the mechanisms of alternative dispute resolution. Internationally, with the staggering increase in treaties and transnational contracts referring to arbitration, institutionalized international courts or national courts rarely adjudicate important transnational disputes.

Against this backdrop, it is only at the enforcement stage that arbitration and the court system meet. Therefore, as discussed, a tension arises out of the "private" nature of arbitration with "public" law and policy. One of the old yet largely marginalized concepts in law is the doctrine of public policy.[59] This doctrine grants discretion to courts to set aside private legal arrangements, including arbitral awards, which harm the "public" and endanger the legal order and society. This is among a very few control mechanisms available for courts to monitor arbitral proceedings and arbitral awards.

Yet, over time, courts have limited the scope and applicability of the public policy doctrine.[60] In the famous labor law case, *Misco*,[61] the Supreme Court declared that the Court of Appeals erred in setting aside the award on public policy grounds. For the Supreme Court, the public policy exception can be invoked only in situations where it is explicit, meaning that it is "well-defined and dominant, and is to be ascertained by reference to the laws and legal precedents and not from general considerations of supposed public interests." This statement was a reiteration of the approach in *Grace v. Rubber Workers*,[62] later reaffirmed in *Eastern Association Coal Corporation*

---

58 *See generally* Judith Resnik, *The Public in the Private of Arbitration, the Private in Courts, and the Erasure of Rights*, 124 YALE L.J. 2808 (2015).

59 *See generally* Farshad Ghodoosi, *The Concept of Public Policy in Law: Revisiting the Role of the Public Policy Doctrine in the Enforcement of Private Legal Arrangements*, 94 NEB. L. REV. 685 (2016).

60 *See generally* David M. Glanstein, *A Hail May Pass: Public Policy Review of Arbitration Awards*, 16 OHIO ST. J. DISP. RESOL. 297 (2000).

61 United Paperworkers Int'l Union v. Misco, 484 U.S. 29 (1987).

62 W. R. Grace & Co. v. Rubber Workers, 461 U.S. 757, 766.

*v. UMWA.*⁶³ The discussion in the preceding section also sheds light on the tendency towards limited application of the public policy exception.

Two approaches are noticeable in instances where courts are dealing with the issue of public policy and enforcement of arbitral awards. The first approach, which is reflected in Justice Scalia's concurring opinion in the *Eastern Association case*, can be called the objective approach. Under this viewpoint, an award is not enforceable in cases where it is evidently and unmistakably contrary to "actual prohibition of the law."⁶⁴ The other approach takes a subjective view of the doctrine of public policy. As declared in the *Eastern Association* case, "the public policy exception is not limited solely to instances where the arbitration award itself violates positive law."⁶⁵ These two ostensibly distinct approaches in fact result in the use of similar legal techniques. Discovering the "actual prohibition of the law" which constitutes the public policy exception is an interpretive and judicial task. In order to find out whether an award violates antitrust law, a judge has to dig out the underlying public policy of the statutes related to antitrust. By no means is it clear which prohibitions in each statute constitute a mandatory and public policy related provision that the arbitral award cannot violate. Therefore, probing into instances where an arbitral award violates public policy is inevitably a judicial and interpretive task and might in fact result in "flaccid" public policy, the term used derogatorily by Justice Scalia.⁶⁶

2. Courts' approach to public policy exceptions

Courts in various parts of the world have reacted differently to the public policy exception enshrined in the New York Convention. Numerous judgments attempt to shape jurisprudence on public policy in the context of international arbitration. The reaction of courts in the area serves as an indispensable platform to understand the doctrine of public policy in arbitration. As mentioned in the first section, the public policy exception goes to the heart of the structural tension described earlier. The close examination of the courts' reactions leads us to better comprehend the ADR system in its totality.

There are two ways of approaching the national courts' reactions. One is simply to address them country by country as law firms and academicians have done in the past.⁶⁷ As much as this method is helpful for those

---

63 E. Associated Coal Corp. v. UMWA, Dist. 17, 121 S. Ct. 462 (2000).
64 *Id.* at 470 (Scalia, concurring).
65 *Id.* at 469.
66 Whether the courts can gauge the terms of an award and its reasoning against the public policy exception remains unresolved in the US courts, David M. Glanstein, *supra* note 60 at 297–301.
67 *See e.g.*, United Nations UNCITRAL, Shearman & Sterling LLP, and Columbia Law School, 1958 NEW YORK CONVENTION GUIDE available at: http://www.newyorkconvention1958.org/index.php?lvl=more_results&look_ALL=1&user_query=*&autolevel1=1&provision=64.

in the practice of arbitration, it does not let us go far into envisaging a general picture of arbitration and the doctrine of public policy. The second method, which I prefer, is to categorize the various courts' reactions by the subject matter of disputes and the definition put forward in connection with the public policy exception. I found that courts have followed at least four paradigms in implementing the public policy exception. Please note that some national courts might adopt a mix of different paradigms. It is also important to keep in mind that the following paradigms have been harnessed from the approach of the courts, not the actual outcome of cases.

a. Social and economic life

This holistic approach considers the needs of the state as a whole while not restraining itself with juridical analysis of the public policy exception. Under this view, public policy is a pervasive matter, running through the entire critical socio-economic dimensions of a country. Alternative methods of settlement, including arbitration, should not interfere with and disrupt any public aspects. This is in line with political definitions put forward regarding the notion of public policy. In this approach, public policy encompasses a "projected programs of goals, values, and practices"[68] permeating various sectors of socio-economic life. In short, it includes all (re)actions of state towards the problems and concerns of society and the economy.[69]

A paramount example, falling under this category, is Russia. In a 1998 decision the Supreme Court of the Russian Federation defined the term "public policy" in Russian law:

> [U]nder the term "public policy" of the Russian Federation one should understand the basics of the social formation of the Russian state. The public policy reservation is possible only in specific cases when the application of foreign law create results inadmissible from the point of the Russian legal mentality.[70]

The Russian courts did not stop here. In a case before the *Arbitrazh* Court of the Moscow District the term "public policy" was further elaborated. The

---

68 This is a definition suggested by Harold Lasswell; *see* GROVER STARLING, THE POLITICS AND ECONOMICS OF PUBLIC POLICY 4 (1979).
69 Public policy is a "purposive course of action or inaction followed by an actor or set of actors in dealing with a problem or matter of concern," JAMES E. ANDERSON, PUBLIC POLICY MAKING 7 (2011). *See also* JOSEPH STEWART ET AL., PUBLIC POLICY: AN EVOLUTIONARY APPROACH 6 (2008).
70 ANTON G. MAURER, THE PUBLIC POLICY EXCEPTION UNDER THE NEW YORK CONVENTION 210 (2012).

court declared that enforcement of arbitral awards violates Russian public policy when it results in acts:

- that are directly prohibited by law or harm the sovereignty or the security of the state;
- that affect the interests of a large social group;
- that are incompatible with principles of constructing the economic, political and legal systems of the State;
- that are against the basic principles of the civil State, such as the equality of the its members, the inviolability of property and freedom of contract . . . [71]

This approach equates public policy with the public sphere, i.e., every instance in which "public" life is affected. Not surprisingly, Russian courts have lumped a wide variety of issues under the rubric of public policy, from misapplication of law[72] to the "impact of [the] social and economic situation"[73] of a neighborhood.

China has adopted similar language in its legal system. Article 213(3) of the Civil Procedure of 2008 stipulates that the enforcement of arbitral awards will be refused if they violate "the social and public interest" of the Republic of China.[74] However, the picture of the enforcement of awards in China in light of the public policy defense is not clear yet. Some SPC judges provided a very political interpretation of this standard of public policy.[75] Others have narrowed it down by limiting its scope: for instance, a mere breach of mandatory laws does not necessarily violate the social and public interest; a mere unfairness or injustice in the process does not amount to violation of public policy; any kind of fraud does not mean that China's public policy has been violated; the substantive fairness of the outcome is not pertinent to the discussion of public policy.[76] However, China has shifted from emphasizing the public policy ground for non-enforcement

---

71 *Id.* at 211.
72 Boris Karabelnikov & Dominik Pellew, *Enforcement of International Arbitral Awards—Still a Mixed Picture*, 19 ICC INT'L COMMERCIAL ICC COURT OF ARBITRATION BULLETIN 65, 72 (2008) 72 fn. 25.
73 In 2003, the *Arbitrazh* Court refused to enforced an ICC Award on the public policy ground because it would "negatively impact on the social and economic situation in Nizhny Novgorod," MAURER, *supra* note 70 at 221.
74 CLARISSE VON WUNSCHHEIM, ENFORCEMENT OF COMMERCIAL ARBITRAL AWARDS IN CHINA 282–83 (2011).
75 Violation of public policy occurs where the award "(i) is in violation of the basic principles reflected/regulated in the Constitution or the Four Fundamental Principles of China; (ii) will damage the sovereignty or State security of China; (iii) is in violation of the fundamental rules of Chinese law; (iv) is against the obligations that China undertook in the international treaties that China concluded, or against the public[ly]-recognized principle of fairness or justice in international law", *Id.* at 283.
76 *Id.* at 284–85.

to refusal of enforcement based on procedural irregularity. Yet, courts in China have broadly interpreted the scope of procedural irregularity, practically disguising the social and public interest narrative under the rubric of procedural irregularity.[77][78]

b. Basic notions of morality and justice

Under this discourse, morality, as defined by the government, shapes the thrust of public policy. It does not necessarily concern itself with governmental policies or the welfare of society. The center of gravity rests on the idea of protecting morality and justice, which are mainly defined by resorting to a constitution or bill of rights, due process, and society's morals. The scope of this approach remains fuzzy and imprecise as concepts of morality and justice are elusive notions. However, the benefit of this discourse is that the only way governmental policies, as well as societal concerns, might fit into the public policy exception is if they are interpreted to constitute basic notions of morality and justice, a matter which is highly unlikely in most instances.

The United States' approach to public policy serves as an example that falls under this discourse. Before discussing it in depth, it is noteworthy to mention that the US has experienced three phases in its approach to arbitration. In the beginning phase—from the mid-1700s to the mid 1800s—the commercial community used arbitration to resolve commercial disputes based on trade practice and common law principles. The courts looked favorably at this development, yet would refrain from ordering specific performance of future arbitral clauses.[79] The second phase, which commenced at the beginning of twentieth century, culminated in the enactment of the Arbitration Act of 1925. This phase is marked by its espousal of less formalism by courts in dealing with arbitration and its endorsement of arbitration as an inexpensive and expedited method of resolving disputes.[80] The last phase, beginning in the 1970s, was a new

---

77 ALYSSA KING, PROCEDURAL PERILS: CHINA'S SUPREME PEOPLE'S COURT ON THE ENFORCEMENT OF AWARDS IN INTERNATIONAL ARBITRATION [manuscript is with the author], Friven Yeoh & Yu Fu, *The People's Courts and Arbitration: A Snapshot of Recent Judicial Attitude on Arbitrability and Enforcement*, 24 J. OF INT'L ARB. 635, 646 (2007) ("the Mitsui decision is seen to confirm a prevailing view among many Chinese legal practitioners that the SPC is loath to permit non-enforcement on this ground save where the offense in question blatantly and obviously violates state sovereignty and security, or base moral decency").
78 In 1971, the *Bundesgerichtshof* Court in Germany adopted a similarly broad language in defining public policy: "recognition of a foreign arbitral award can only be refused if the arbitral proceeding suffered a grave defect which is intolerably at odds with *the fundamental principles of state and economic life*" [emphasis added]. MAURER, *supra* note 70 at 106.
79 Mette H. Kurth, *The Dawning of Arbitration Techniques* in DISPUTE RESOLUTION: BRIDGING THE SETTLEMENT GAP 193, 194 (David A. Anderson ed., 1996)
80 *Id.*

movement towards relieving arbitration of the burdensome formalism of courts on a wide range of issues including arbitrability and public policy exceptions. Kurth believes that the Supreme Court responded negatively to this new surge of demands by requiring strict and unyielding enforcement of arbitration agreements.[81]

The US courts generally took a more moral and ethical approach to arbitration. In a very early case, *Underhill v. Van Cortlandt*, the Court for the Correction of Errors of New York declared that judges "should be *eagle-eyed* in looking into the proceedings and conduct of the arbitrators, and the acts of parties, to see that everything has been conducted fairly, impartially, and honestly."[82]

In 1974 a seminal case set the approach to the doctrine of public policy in alternative dispute resolution. The case was brought pursuant to Chapter 2 of Title 9 of the United States Code (Federal Arbitration Act), which is the US codification of the New York Convention. Société Générale de l'Industries du papier (RAKTA), an Egyptian corporation, sought to enforce an arbitral award against the US corporation Parsons & Whittemore Overseas. The dispute arose out of a contract between the two corporations, in which Overseas promised to construct, start up, and for a year manage a paperboard mill in Egypt. Due to the intense political conditions in the region at the time—which eventually culminated in the Six-Day War—the Egyptian government terminated its relationship with the United States, ordering Americans to leave the country unless they obtained a special visa. Consequently, Overseas invoked the "force majeure" clause in the contract, claiming change of circumstances made the contract's performance impossible. RAKTA initiated an arbitral proceeding for contract violation and damages. The arbitral panel declared that the "force majeure" condition existed only for a short period (May 28 to June 30, 1967) and did not justify unilateral revocation of the contract. Subsequently, RAKTA sought to enforce the award in the United States, but faced multiple legal challenges by Overseas. One argument set forth by Overseas—relevant to our discussion—was that the enforcement would violate the public policy of the United States. The Second Circuit responded by stating that public policy should be construed narrowly and that "Enforcement of foreign arbitral awards may be denied on this basis only where enforcement would violate the forum state's most basic notions of morality and justice."[83]

---

81 *Id.*
82 Phillip Van Cortlandt et al. v. Abraham I. Underhill & Joshua Underhill, 17 Johns 405, 424 (N.Y. Ct. Corr. of Errors 1819); *See also* Jackson, Van Alen & Van Alen v. Ambler, 14 Johns. 96, 104 (N.Y. Sup. Ct. 1817) (stating that arbitration should be maintained because even though it does not have technical accuracy, "the ends are mainly honest, and tend to terminate intricate disputes with very little expenses to the parties ... ").
83 Parsons & Whittemore Overseas Co., Inc. v. Société Générale de l'Industries du papier (RAKTA), 508 F.2d 969, 975 (1974).

68 *Public policy in arbitration*

The Second Circuit's framework of the public policy exception under the New York Convention has set the precedent for subsequent courts' interpretation in the third phase of the arbitration movement in the US.[84] This paradigm keenly distinguishes between national policy and public policy while endeavoring to keep the latter out of the public policy equation.[85] This way, governmental policies, foreign policies, and national policies can only bar awards and judgments from enforcement if they fit in the box of countering the "most basic notions of morality and justice." As courts have shown, even in the context of arbitration involving countries with strained relationships with the US, hostile foreign policies in place by the US government do not reach the level of public policy.[86]

Several other countries have adopted a similar paradigm. Canada defined public policy as "fundamentally offensive to Canadian principles of justice and fairness." In *Beals v. Saldanha*, the Canadian Supreme Court declared, in the context of conflict of laws, that foreign laws should not be applied if against the fundamental morality of the Canadian legal system.[87] The Court of Queen's Bench of Alberta in Canada held in the case of *Yugraneft Corporation v. Rexx Management Corporation* that "the concept of imposing our public policy on foreign awards is to guard against enforcement of an award which offends our local principles of justice and fairness in a fundamental way."[88] English courts have built the notion of public policy on the morality paradigm. New Zealand codified this view on public policy in its Arbitration Act of 1996, adopting the UNCITRAL Model Law on International Commercial Arbitration. It declared that the award is contrary to public policy if "a breach of the rules of *natural justice* occurred (i) during the arbitral proceedings, or (ii) in connection with the making of the award" [emphasis added].[89] Hong Kong courts have adopted

---

84 *See e.g.*, Admart AG v. Stephen and Mary Birch Foundation Inc., 457 F.3d 302, 309 (2005); Brandeis Intsel Limited v. Calabrian Chemicals Corporation, 656 F. Supp. 160, 167 (1987); Karaha Bodas Co., LLC v. Perusahaan Pertambangan Minyak Dan Gas Bumi Negara, 364 F.3d 274, 307 (2004); Changzhou Amec Eastern Tools and Equipment Co. Ltd. v. Eastern Tools & Equipment Inc., 2012 WL 3106620, 12 (2012); Chevron Corporation v. Republic of Ecuador, 949 F. Supp. 2d 57, 71 (2013).

85 The Court astutely distinguishes between "national policy" and "public policy": "In equating 'national' policy with United States 'public' policy, the appellant quite plainly misses the mark. To read the public policy defense as a parochial device protective of national political interests would seriously undermine the Convention's utility. This provision was not meant to enshrine the vagaries of international politics under the rubric of 'public policy,'" *Id.* at 975.

86 *See e.g.* National Oil Corporation v. Libyan Sun Oil Company, 733 F. Supp. 800, 820–21 (1990); Ministry of Defense and Support for the Armed Forces of the Islamic Republic of Iran v. Cubic Defense Systems, 665 F.3d 1091, 1100-1101 (2011).

87 Beals v. Saldanha [2003] S.C.J. No. 77.

88 ALBERT JAN VAN DEN BERG, YEARBOOK OF COMMERCIAL ARBITRATION, VOL. XXXIII 443–45 (2008).

89 Amokura Kawharu, *The Public Policy Ground for Setting Aside and Refusing Enforcement of Arbitral Awards—Comments on the New Zealand Approach*, 5 J. OF INT'L ARB. 491, 493–94 (2007).

an identical view to that of *Parsons & Whittemore Overseas v. RAKTA* and state that enforcement of awards is denied when they violate the forum state's most basic notions of morality and justice.[90]

c. Fundamental principles of law

Unlike the holistic approach of the first paradigm, the "fundamental principles of law" discourse adopts a juridical and positivistic approach to public policy. For an issue to fall under the rubric of public policy, it should have a strong basis in laws, regulations, and/or precedents of the state. The courts cannot resort to non-juridical factors, such as the insolvency of a neighborhood, to set aside awards based on public policy. Instead, the courts not only have to justify their stance on public policy pursuant to laws, but they also have to make sure it deserves to be denominated as a fundamental principle.

Austria could serve as an illuminating example that links the notion of public policy to the existing positive laws. The Supreme Court of Austria in a 2005 decision held that the standard for review regarding the public policy exception is whether an arbitral award "is irreconcilable with the fundamental principles of the Austrian legal system."[91] The Court carefully crafted the doctrine of public policy in a way that differs from the moralistic approach of the US legal system, on the one hand, and the internationalist approach of the French legal system on the other hand. First, it focused on the "enforcement" feature of public policy by holding that the enforcement of awards—not "the law or legal relation itself"—should be intolerable to the domestic legal system. Subsequently, it enumerated the sources of public policy, deriving from various codes: "the fundamental principles concerned by public policy are especially the basic principles of the federal constitution, but also [basic principles] of criminal, private, and procedural law."[92] Lastly, the Court keenly separated its approach from that of the holistic and teleological view of countries such as Russia by rejecting the importance of the trajectory, reasons, and end goals of awards: "it is not the path followed or the reasons given to but the outcome of the arbitral award that is decisive to determine whether the award is compatible [with public policy]."[93]

This paradigm of public policy attempts to avoid the natural law stance of the "basic notions of morality and justice" approach. Instead, it creates the doctrine of public policy pursuant to the existing laws with the main focus on the "enforcement" of awards versus their objectives or legal merits.

---

90 ALBERT JAN VAN DEN BERG, YEARBOOK OF COMMERCIAL ARBITRATION, VOL. XXIII 680 (1998) (*Polytek Engineering Company Limited v. Hebei Import & Export Corporation*).
91 Buyer (Austria) v. Seller (Serbia and Montenegro), Oberster Gerichtshof [Supreme Court], 30b221/04b, January 26, 2005 in ALBERT JAN VAN DEN BERG, YEARBOOK OF COMMERCIAL ARBITRATION, VOL. XXX 428–29 (2005).
92 *Id.*
93 *Id.*

Thus, this paradigm could be called a "synchronic" view of public policy, versus the historical or "diachronic" approach of other models. Although this paradigm offers a more clear-cut conceptualization of public policy, it fails to provide a theoretical guide to what could constitute fundamental principles by culling from various, occasionally incongruent, statutes and provisions.

d. International public policy

A few countries, pioneered by France, have attempted to frame a new paradigm of public policy in the context of ADR and especially international arbitration. This aims to differentiate between "domestic public policy" and "international public policy" depending on whether courts are dealing with domestic matters or international awards. Pursuant to this paradigm, international awards should not be subject to the vagaries of domestic public policy as they are derived from a different legal order.[94][95]

The French Code of Civil Procedure explicitly separates the two concepts: under article 1502(5) a court decision granting recognition or enforcement is only available based on a few grounds, one of which is that "if recognition or enforcement is contrary to international public policy." This stands in contrast to Article 1488 of the same Code regarding domestic awards, which stipulates, "no enforcement order may be granted where an award is manifestly contrary to public policy." The aim is to restrict the unnecessary intervention of domestic public policy in the scene of international arbitration. Not all aspects of domestic public policy can constitute international public policy. In the language of the Federal Supreme Court in Civil Matters of Germany—another country that endorses this paradigm—international public policy "comprises only such parts of the mandatory applicable law which will successfully dominate any conflict with applicable foreign law."[96]

Several other jurisdictions have espoused this paradigm by differentiating between national and international public policy. The Swiss Supreme Court delineated the international public policy by stipulating that international public policy "consists of fundamental and generally recognized principles" the "non-application" of which "would be contrary to the basic

---

[94] Emmanuel Gaillard, a proponent of the paradigm of international public policy, calls it the arbitral legal order, EMMANUEL GAILLARD, LEGAL THEORY OF INTERNATIONAL ARBITRATION 35–66 (2010).

[95] Several courts have emphasized the "universal" character of this international public policy. For example, the Court of Appeals of Milan declared a: "body of universal principles shared by nations of similar civilization, aiming at the protection of fundamental human rights, often embodied in international declarations or conventions," Allsop Automatic v. Tecnoski, Corte di Appello, Milan, 4 December 1992 in ALBERT JAN VAN DEN BERG, YEARBOOK OF COMMERCIAL ARBITRATION VOL. XXII 726 (1997).

[96] MAURER, *supra* note 70 at 104. The Supreme Court of Germany indirectly confirmed this approach, *Id.* at 104–05.

values common to all civilized nation."[97] Italy serves as another example. The Court of Appeals of Milan embraced a similar doctrine and defined international public policy as a "body of universal principles shared by nations of similar civilization, aiming at the protection of fundamental human rights, often embodied in international declaration or conventions."[98] Spain is another jurisdiction which adopted this doctrine, but provided a clearer definition, limiting it to its Constitution and basic procedural irregularities in the arbitral proceeding: "Hence, on an international level [public policy] essentially corresponds with the rights and guarantees enshrined in the Constitution in respect of the prohibition to violate due process [*indefensión*] provided in Art. 24(2) [of the] Constitution."[99] [100]

Analyzing the international public policy paradigm requires a separate book as it has not remained in the area of international commercial arbitration and has crept into other areas including the jurisprudence of state-investor arbitration.[101] However, it is necessary here to briefly look at it. Pierre Lalive was among the first scholars who noticed a trend towards this paradigm and endeavored to formulate it. He posited that the concept of public policy in international private law differs from municipal public policy because of necessity and the different purposes of each legal order.[102] For him, the concept of international public policy "is made up of a series of rules or principles concerning a variety of domains, having a varying

---

97 MAURER, *supra* note 70 at 177. The Supreme Court confirmed this approach in the subsequent decisions, *Id.* at 177–81.
98 ALBERT JAN VAN DEN BERG, YEARBOOK OF COMMERCIAL ARBITRATION, VOL. XXII 725–26 (1997).
99 ALBERT JAN VAN DEN BERG, YEARBOOK OF COMMERCIAL ARBITRATION, VOL. XXII 578 (2003).
100 The *Bundesgerichtshof*, the Swiss Federal Supreme Court in Civil Law, has also differentiated between internal public policy or international public policy: "*ordre public intern* means mandatorily applicable law (*ius cogens*) which is not at disposal of the parties but will be legally effective. Such law is not necessarily part of the *ordre public international*. *Ordre public international* comprises only such parts of the mandatory applicable law which will successfully dominate any conflict with applicable foreign law." MAURER, *supra* note 70 at 104.
101 *See, e.g.*, Inceysa v. El Salvad., ICSID Case No. ARB/03/26, Award, ¶ 245–46 (Aug. 2, 2006) ("International Public Policy consists of a series of fundamental principles that constitute the very essence of the State and its essential function is to preserve the values of the international legal system against actions contrary to it" (footnote omitted)); World Duty v. Kenya, ICSID Case No. ARB/00/7, Award, ¶ 138–57 (Oct. 4, 2006) (holding that committing bribery and corruption is a breach of international public policy).
102 Pierre Lalive, *Transnational (or Truly International) Public Policy and International Arbitration* in COMPARATIVE ARBITRATION PRACTICE AND PUBLIC POLICY IN ARBITRATION 258, 259 (Pieter Sanders ed., 1986). Lalive maintains that public policy has both "positive" and "negative" functions. The negative function of public policy occurs when a judgment or an otherwise applicable foreign act is declined to be recognized and be enforced in a dispute. In its positive capacity, public policy imposes application of *lex fori* (law of the forum) by means of "unilateral conflict of rules." Lalive bundles the two functions under the title of "international public policy," *Id.* at 263–64.

strength of intensity, which form or express a kind of 'hard core' of legal or moral values . . . "[103] Lalive argues that the international public policy of states should not apply to the cases involving international matters. He refers to the *Zapata*,[104] *Scherk*,[105] and *Mitsubishi*[106] cases in the Supreme Court of the US as examples of limitation of domestic public policy as well as the positive impact of international public policy in international relations. In his view, international public policy is truly international (i.e., transnational) only if it has supernational purposes.[107] According to Lalive, examples of transnational public policy could be the doctrine of competence-competence in arbitral proceedings,[108] autonomy of the will, the criterion of the closest connection, and the legitimate expectation of the parties.[109] [110]

The formula of international public policy has stirred controversy among scholars—principally those from the common law tradition. Some found it to be too vague and not rigorous enough to be able to create a robust approach to public policy.[111] Others point out that this paradigm is just a façade and

---

103 *Id.*
104 M/S Bremen v. Zapata Off-Shore Company, 92 S.Ct. 1907 (1972) at 1913: "We cannot have trade and commerce in world markets and international waters exclusively on our terms, governed by our laws, and resolved in our courts."
105 Scherk v. Alberto Culver Company, 94 S.Ct. 2449 (1974) at 2456: "A parochial refusal by the courts of one country to enforce an international arbitration agreement would not only frustrate these purposes, but would invite unseemly and mutually destructive jockeying by the parties to secure tactical litigation advantages."
106 Mitsubishi Motors Corp. v. Soler Chrysler-Plymouth, Inc., 105 S.Ct. 3346, (July 2, 1985) at 629: "We conclude that concerns of international comity, respect for the capacities of foreign and transnational tribunals, and sensitivity to the need of the international commercial system for predictability in the resolution of disputes require that we enforce the parties' agreement, even assuming that a contrary result would be forthcoming in a domestic context."
107 Pierre Lalive posits three factors that shape the content of transnational public policy. Public policy might stem from private international law, the laws of *lex fori*, and the needs for international trade. *Supra* note 102 at 273.
108 *Id.* at 300.
109 *Id.* at 301–08.
110 Other scholars have also taken a stab at formulating the concept of international (or transnational public policy). For instance, Yves Derains approaches it from a private international law perspective, i.e., in choosing the applicable law. In his theory, transnational public policy determines whether parties can contract around mandatory rules, Yves Derains, *Public Policy and the Law Applicable to the Dispute in International Arbitration* in COMPARATIVE ARBITRATION PRACTICE AND PUBLIC POLICY, 227. Pierre Mayer takes this discussion to a radical level. He maintains that transnational public policy norms are not imposed on by arbitrators, but rather are created by them, Pierre Mayer, *Effect of International Public Policy in International Arbitration?* in Pervasive Problems in International Arbitration 61, 65–66 (Loukas A. Mistelis & Julian D.M. Lew eds., 2006).
111 W. Michael Reisman, *Law, International Public Policy (So-Called) and Arbitral Choice in International Commercial Arbitration* in ICCA CONGRESS SERIES 13/2007, 850, 850–52 (pointing out that, unlike domestic legislation in which competing views about public policies are represented in the law-making process, there is no such body in international law. In other words, public policies are the result of a legislative mechanism that enjoys transparent participation of a wide-range of groups representing diverse opinions).

that, at the end of the day, the public policy remains "French," "German," "Italian," etc.—definitely not "international."[112] The objection comes mainly from those who believe that public policy is inextricably linked to statehood and, therefore, a trans-state public policy is hardly conceivable.

However, I find that the main problem with this paradigm rests in its lack of a rigorous theoretical delineation of domestic and international public policy. As I will sketch out in the next section, a distinction between public interest from public morality and security is far more helpful.

3. Concluding remarks

Table 4.1 Four approaches of courts to the public policy exception

Paradigm	Ontology	Methodology	Epistemology
Social and economic life	Public policy exists above the law	Political	Interest of states and society
Basic notions of morality and justice	Public policy exists above the law	Natural law	Moral and ethics of society
Fundamental principles of law	Public policy exists at the core of the law	Positivistic	Basic and well-established principles in laws
International public policy	Public policy exists at the international aspect of law	Internationalist	Basic principles of law applicable to the international sphere

As surveyed and discussed, courts around the world have adopted various dispositions to interpret the public policy exception enshrined in the New York Convention. Neither of the paradigms has completely captured the intricacy of the public policy exception, leaving it, advertently or inadvertently, a Pandora's box. Among the four paradigms, the fundamental principle of law remains the most clear-cut with relatively clarified boundaries. Yet the language employed by courts under each of the paradigms, still far from being transparent, partially results from a lack of robust theory of arbitration as against court adjudication.

C. The United States Supreme Court

The stance of the US Supreme Court in the *Mitsubishi* case will serve to summarize our discussion and illuminate the most suitable approach to the thorny issue of public policy. Mitsubishi brought a suit against an automobile

---

112 JAN PAULSSON, THE IDEA OF ARBITRATION (2013).

dealer to compel arbitration of a dispute in Japan, in order to collect, *inter alia*, contractual damages and damages related to Soler's failure to fulfill the terms of the manufacturer's warranty.[113] Soler counterclaimed for a violation of the Sherman Act, the main antitrust statute in the United States.[114] The Court had to decide whether a properly constituted arbitral body pursuant to a valid arbitration clause under the auspices of the New York Convention could adjudicate matters related to competition and antitrust law. The Court eventually answered this question in the affirmative,[115] yet in reaching this decision it laid out a theoretical ground pertinent to our discussion.

The Supreme Court's opinion does not limit itself to the consensual approach, as it acknowledges the independence and necessity of international arbitration. The Court keenly observed that courts should be willing to "cede jurisdiction of a claim arising under domestic law" to resolve disputes arising out of an international commercial relationship.[116] It continued by boldly stating that national courts should "subordinate domestic notions of arbitrability to the international policy favoring commercial arbitration."[117] This view of international arbitration largely corresponds to the resistance-based paradigm, as it recognizes arbitration as a parallel justice system not subordinate to national courts.

Contrary to what has been claimed,[118] *Mitsubishi* does not take the internationalist approach but rather, I argue, a positivistic one. A careful look at the decision shows that the Court is not committed to the internationalist view on public policy. In other words, the Court does not seem to be primarily concerned about whether the arbitral proceeding in question is international or domestic. In reaching the decision, the Court clearly investigates the legislative history of the Sherman Act as well as the international obligations of the United States emanating from the New York Convention.[119] Only in this respect and in reconciling the two does the Court hold that "the international character of the controversy makes it arbitrable."[120] This is what Judith Resnik calls "effective vindication" of statutory rights in arbitration.[121] Arbitration can adjudicate matters of public law

---

113 Mitsubishi Motors Corp. v. Soler Chrysler-Plymouth, Inc., 473 U.S. 614, 618–19, 618 fn.2 (1985).
114 *Id.* at 619–20.
115 *See id.* at 628–29.
116 *Id.* at 638.
117 *Id.* at 639.
118 *See* Lalive, *supra* note 102 at 275: "The famous *Mitsubishi* decision accepts the argument, developed, inter alia, in the amicus curiae brief of the American Arbitration Association and decides that, in antitrust matters, the principle of non-arbitrability does not extend to international contracts."
119 *See* Mitsubishi, 473 U.S. at 636–38.
120 *Id.* at 659 (Stevens, J., dissenting) (describing the majority's holding).
121 Resnik, *supra* note 58 at 2811. She discusses the matter in depth in Part IV of her Article. *Id.* at 2874–2931. Resnik ultimately concludes that this approach fails to effectively vindicate rights. *See id.* at 2939.

and policy so long as it is effective in vindicating the rights stipulated in the statutes.[122] In establishing this approach the Court states that "in the event the choice-of-forum and choice-of-law clauses operated in tandem as a prospective waiver of a party's right to pursue statutory remedies for antitrust violations, we would have little hesitation in condemning the agreement as against public policy."[123]

The most critical part of the decision is where the Court stipulates that arbitral tribunals serve as qualified venues to vindicate the statutory cause of action. As the dissent notes, the Court had previously recognized the "weighty public interests" underlying the Sherman Act,[124] yet, contrary to its precedent, here held that (international) arbitral tribunals provide "an adequate mechanism" to resolve matters related to public interests.[125] The only requirement is that "the prospective litigant effectively may vindicate its statutory cause of action in the arbitral forum."[126]

The *Mitsubishi* approach provides one of the most delicately crafted theories of public policy in arbitration. Its stance on arbitration does not restrict itself to the consensual or interest-based approaches, and acknowledges the independence of the institution of arbitration, at least at the international level.[127] Furthermore, it takes a more positivistic approach than a political or ethical one. Lastly, the Court duly notes that the public interest category, which mainly involves an economic methodology, could be decided by arbitral tribunals as long as parties litigate the matter effectively.[128]

---

122 Justice Stevens argued in his dissent that arbitration clauses should not normally be read to cover statutory remedies. *Mitsubishi*, 473 U.S. at 641.
123 *Id.* at 637 n.19 (majority opinion). For the ramifications of the decision on subsequent cases related to international commercial arbitration, see Donald Francis Donovan, *International Commercial Arbitration and Public Policy*, 27 N.Y.U. J. INT'L L. & POL. 645, 655–57 (1995).
124 *See Mitsubishi*, 473 U.S. at 651 (Stevens, J., dissenting) (quoting United States v. Topco Assoc., Inc., 405 U.S. 596, 610 (1972)) ("Antitrust laws in general, and the Sherman Act in particular, are the Magna Carta of free enterprise. They are as important to the preservation of economic freedom and our free-enterprise system as the Bill of Rights is to the protection of our fundamental personal freedoms. And the freedom guaranteed each and every business, no matter how small, is the freedom to compete—to assert with vigor, imagination, devotion, and ingenuity whatever economic muscle it can muster. Implicit in such freedom is the notion that it cannot be foreclosed with respect to one sector of the economy because certain private citizens or groups believe that such foreclosure might promote greater competition in a more important sector of the economy").
125 *Id.* at 636 (majority opinion).
126 *Id.* at 637.
127 I agree with Donald Donovan that "if international commercial arbitration is to play the critical role in the international economy of which it is capable, arbitrators cannot shy away from, and courts must be prepared to refer to arbitration, both private and public law claims encompassed by a valid agreement to arbitrate." Donovan, *supra* note 123 at 657. As Donovan notes, this follows from the *Mitsubishi* decision. However, in order to balance this approach, courts need to be more active reviewing awards at the enforcement stage.
128 *See* Mitsubishi, 473 U.S. at 634.

On the other hand, the Court notes that courts retain the authority at the enforcement stage to "ensure that the legitimate interest in the enforcement of the antitrust laws has been addressed."[129] However, as discussed earlier, the problem is that the Supreme Court construed the scope of the reviewability of awards quite narrowly.[130] For instance, in the context of enforcement of labor arbitration, awards violate public policy only if the policies are "well defined and dominant," and are to be "ascertained by reference to the laws and legal precedents and not from general considerations of supposed public interests."[131] As a result it is not clear whether the public policy exception could truly serve as an avenue for courts to properly review the awards based on their impact on public interest. In other words, the bold move of the *Mitsubishi* decision towards delegating more authority to arbitration was jeopardized by that fact that courts have practically relinquished the authority to review awards based on the public policy exception.[132] This development is reflected in the *Hall Street Associates* decision in which the Supreme Court limited the reviewability of awards to grounds enumerated in the Federal Arbitration Act.[133] This ruling called into question the viability of judicially-created avenues for the review of arbitral awards that included, for instance, "a manifest disregard of law or violation of public policy."[134] Since then, in order to balance the Supreme Court decision, some state courts have argued that common law and state

---

129 *Id.* at 638.
130 The Supreme Court ruled in *Hall St. Assocs., LLC v. Mattel, Inc.*, 552 U.S. 576, 578 (2008), that arbitral awards may only be reviewed based on the grounds listed in the Federal Arbitration Act. *See also* Jonathan A. Marcantel, *The Crumbled Difference Between Legal and Illegal Arbitration Awards:* Hall Street Associates *and the Waning Public Policy*, 14 FORDHAM J. CORP. & FIN. L. 579, 599 (2009) ("While the *Hall Street Associates* holding did not specifically mention the public policy exception, the Court's reasoning invariably questions its continued existence in the context of arbitration awards, as the FAA does not include a 'void against public policy' standard").
131 Eastern Associated Coal Corp. v. United Mine Workers of America, 121 S.Ct 462, 464 (2000); W.R. Grace & Co. v. Rubber Workers, 461 U.S. 757, 766 (1995); United Paperworkers Int'l Union, AFL-CIO v. Misco, 484 U.S. 29, 43 (1987).
132 Originally, some scholars expressed doubts about the scope of this ruling especially in matters of punitive damages over which courts claimed exclusive authority. *See, e.g.*, Leo Kanowitz, *Alternative Dispute Resolution and the Public Interest: The Arbitration Experience*, 38 HASTINGS L.J. 239, 264 (1987). However, later the Supreme Court in the *Mastrobuono* decision declared that an arbitral panel had the authority to award compensatory and punitive damages even though the applicable law (New York law, in this case) prohibited arbitrators from awarding punitive damages. Mastrobuono v. Shearson Lehman Hutton, Inc., 514 U.S. 52, 63–64 (1995) ("[T]he best way to harmonize the choice-of-law provision with the arbitration provision is to read 'the laws of the State of New York' to encompass substantive principles that New York courts would apply, but not to include special rules limiting the authority of arbitrators").
133 *See* Hall St. Assocs., 552 U.S. at 578.
134 Maureen A. Weston, *The Other Avenues of* Hall Street *and Prospects for Judicial Review of Arbitral Awards*, 14 LEWIS & CLARK L. REV. 929, 932 (2010).

statutory grounds for review remain open to parties.[135] In summary, the scope of reviewability of arbitral awards has become extremely narrow.[136]

Yet, even after the *Hall Street Associates* decision, the public policy exception should remain a ground for reviewability of awards. For international awards, the New York Convention explicitly enumerates the public policy exception as a ground for refusal to enforce awards.[137] The Convention was codified as the second Chapter of the Federal Arbitration Act.[138] Regarding the public policy exception in the enforcement of domestic awards, the 1996 decision of the Supreme Court is relevant. In *Doctor's Associates, Inc. v. Casarotto*, the Supreme Court declared that the defenses applicable in contract law "such as fraud, duress, or unconscionability, may be applied to invalidate arbitration agreements without contravening § 2."[139] Section 2 of the Federal Arbitration Act declares that arbitration clauses are valid "save upon such grounds as exist at law or in equity for the revocation of any contract."[140] Undoubtedly, the public policy exception is an ingrained common law defense against enforcement of contracts. Thus, even if the *Hall Street Associates* decision negates all non-explicit FAA review grounds (contractually and judicially created), the public policy exception defense exists as a common law defense in contract law.

---

135 James E. Berger & Charlene Sun, *The Evolution of Judicial Review Under the Federal Arbitration Act*, 5 N.Y.U. J.L. & Bus. 745, 781–85 (2009) (citing Cable Connection, Inc. v. DIRECTV, Inc., 190 P.3d 586, 605 (Cal. 2008) (holding that, in California, parties could contract for judicial review of arbitration awards for legal error).

136 *See* Michael H. LeRoy, *Are Arbitrators Above the Law? The "Manifest Disregard of the Law" Standard*, 52 B.C. L. Rev. 137, 137–43 (2011).

137 Convention on the Recognition and Enforcement of Foreign Arbitral Awards art. V(2)(b), June 10, 1958, 21 U.S.T. 2517, 330 U.N.T.S. 38 ("[E]nforcement of an arbitral award may also be refused if . . . [t]he recognition or enforcement of the award would be contrary to the public policy of that country").

138 9 U.S.C. §§ 201–08 (2012).

139 517 U.S. 681, 687 (1996) (citing 9 U.S.C. § 2).

140 9 U.S.C. § 2.

5 The trajectory of international dispute resolution

A. Pre-modern developments

The history of international relations shows us that international dispute resolution has been a part of the international arena from ancient times. For instance, the Greeks and Spartans ended a thirty-year war—commonly called The First Peloponnesian War—by a treaty in which they stipulated an arbitration clause. The treaty was signed in 446/445 BC. However, Sparta did not adhere to the terms of the treaty, including the arbitration clause, when tensions grew again between two nations a few years later. Sparta declare that the problem was too important and too much of "vital interest" to be left for arbitrators to decide. They were concerned about the qualification and suitability of the arbitrators as well.[1]

The ancient Greek civilization employed arbitration between its several city-states to resolve disputes in lieu of resorting to wars. By one account, there were around eighty arbitrations between Greek city-states.[2] This astounding number shows the value that the Greeks attributed to resolving disputes through arbitration.[3] The disputes were mainly related to frontiers and borders; however, other issues including deprivation of property by another Grecian town or inappropriate treatment of a neighboring village became the subject of arbitration.[4]

---

1 SHEILA L. AGER, INTERSTATE ARBITRATIONS IN THE GREEK WORLD, 337–90 BC 20–21 (1996).
2 JACKSON H. RALSTON, INTERNATIONAL ARBITRATION FROM ATHENS TO LOCARNO 154 (2004).
3 "Thucydides praised the words of Archidamus, a king of Sparta, who declared that it was impossible to attack as an enemy him who offered to answer for his deeds before a tribunal of arbitration," *Id.* at 155.
4 "... differences did not always relate to frontiers. Thus, for instance, there were the attack upon Argos through the Achaean strategus, Aratus, in the midst of peace; the expedition of Athens against Oropus; the lack of proper treatment by another Greek town of a neighboring village, the citizens of which were deprived unceremoniously of their property; the disagreement between Athens and Delos on the subject of the right to administer the Sanctuary of Apollo at Delos; the difference between the town of Lebedos in Asia Minor and a neighboring village with reference to the priest of Zeus; and the question whether Lepreum was always obliged to pay rent to the Temple of Zeus at Olympia." *Id.* at 158.

With the decline of the ancient Greek civilization, the practice of arbitration dwindled as well. The Roman Empire dominated large parts of the world, making it an unrivaled power with no competitors. The centralized form of governing would not allow for arbitration between polities within the Roman Empire. Over the centuries, in the instances where disputes were referred to arbitration, it was popes, monarchs, emperors and lords who took on the task of arbitrator.[5] In a well-known example, Pope Alexander VI arbitrated the dispute between Spain and Portugal on the discovered lands in the new world. He famously drew a line and ruled that the lands to the west of the line belonged to Spain and to the east were to be Portuguese property.[6] As the spiritual authority and power of the popes declined, the tendency to appoint kings as arbitrators increased.[7] In most of the cases, neither kings nor popes acted as adjudicators; instead their counsel and aides managed the cases while the popes and the kings would merely sign off the final awards.

The emergence of the Westphalian international system[8] paved the way for international disputes to be resolved through arbitration. The Westphalian system refers to a period in history in which political units in Europe recognized each other's independence and submitted to the idea that only one regulatory entity—meaning state—had the exclusive authority

---

5 For instance the arbitration clause incorporated in a treaty of alliance concluded between Genoa and Venice in 1235 designate the Pope as the arbitrator: "If there should arise between the said cities any differences which cannot be easily settled between them, it will be determined by the arbitration of the Sovereign Pontiff." *Id.* at 177.

6 BARRY E. CARTER, PHILIP R. TRIMBLE, INTERNATIONAL LAW 354 (1995).

7 Examples are rampant: in 1263 Louis IX of France was chosen as an arbitrator for the dispute between Henry III, the King of England, and his barons. Louis IX of France also acted as an arbitrator between the Counts of Luxemburg and of Bar. In another instance, in a conflict between the King of Bohemia, the princes of Germany and the Duke of Brabant in 1334, Philip of Valois arbitrated the dispute. In 1444, Charles VII adjudicated a dispute between the Duke of Anjou and Count Antoine de Vaudemont. Louis XI also acted as an arbitrator in several disputes, including in 1463 between the kings of Castile and Aragon, and in 1475 between the Duke of Austria and the Helvetian Republic, RALSTON, *supra* note 2 at 182–83.

8 The Westphalia Treaties of 1648 are widely considered to be a landmark in history which created modern statehood as well as international law. As noted by scholars, the treaties did not bring about this radical change in international relations. In fact, it was the process of negotiation that helped these political entities to be recognized as independent and autonomous, THOMAS SCHULTZ, TRANSNATIONAL LEGALITY: STATELESS LAW AND INTERNATIONAL ARBITRATION, 50 (2014) (fn. 1). *See also* Nico Schriverm, *The Changing Nature of State Sovereignty*, 70 BRIT. Y.B. INT'L LAW 65, 68–69 (1999); ANTONIO CASSESE, INTERNATIONAL LAW 19 (2001); DAVID BOUCHER, POLITICAL THEORIES OF INTERNATIONAL RELATIONS 224-25 (1998); Stephen Neff, *A Short History of International Law in International Law in* INTERNATIONAL LAW 33, 42 (Malcolm Evans ed., 2001); John M. Gillroy, *Justice-as-Sovereignty: David Hume and the Origins of International Law*, 78 BRIT. Y. B. INT'L L. 429, 447–50 (2007); John M. Kelley, A Short History of Western Legal Theory 158, 175 (1992); MALCOLM N. SHAW, INTERNATIONAL LAW 21–25 (2003). James Crawford believes that a law of nations existed before the emergence of Westphalian international order, JAMES CRAWFORD, THE CREATION OF STATES IN INTERNATIONAL LAW 10 (2007).

80   *Trajectory of international dispute resolution*

to set laws and regulations for that specific entity.[9] Despite the emergence of nation-states, international arbitration was still rare in the seventeenth and eighteenth centuries.[10] The reason for this decline could be attributed to the fact that the nation-state system was in the process of establishment. Furthermore, as some scholars maintain, diplomacy, mediation, and other forms of alternative dispute resolution became the mainstream techniques for resolving disputes instead of arbitration.[11] In the eighteenth century, the Congress system in Europe fostered conflict resolution through diplomacy. This came into existence through the Vienna Settlement of 1814–1815 in order to keep peace in Europe following the defeat of Napoleon.[12]

B. Developments in the early modern era

The reemergence of arbitration in modern times occurred at the end of the eighteenth century with Jay Treaty arbitrations between the United States and United Kingdom.[13] Several scholars have cast doubt on the importance of Jay Treaty arbitrations in the resurgence of arbitration practice in modern era.[14] However, many authors still believe that such arbitrations initiated a new era of dispute resolution, creating a legacy that continues up until the present time.[15] This legacy does not simply relate to the fact that

---

9   THOMAS SCHULTZ, TRANSNATIONAL LEGALITY: STATELESS LAW AND INTERNATIONAL ARBITRATION 50 (2014). With the establishment of nation-states, the idea of international rule of law emerged as well: "In a system whose units are assumed to serve no higher purpose than their own interests and which assumes the perfect equality of those interests, the Rule of Law seems the sole thinkable principle of organization—short of the *bellum omnium*." Marti Koskenniemi, *The Politics of International Law*, 1 EUR. J. INT'L L. 4 (1990).

10 J.H.W. VERZIJL, INTERNATIONAL LAW IN HISTORICAL PERSPECTIVE, PART VIII: INTER-STATE DISPUTES AND THEIR SETTLEMENT 180–81 (1976).

11 Cornelis G. Roelofsen, *International Arbitration and Courts in* THE OXFORD HANDBOOK OF THE HISTORY OF INTERNATIONAL LAW 155–56 (2012).

12 Russia, Prussia, Austria and Britain created a mechanism (aka Congress) by which no major power should embark on policies and actions that might negatively impact other powers. This process was established following the Vienna Conference, COLIN S GRAY, WAR, PEACE, AND INTERNATIONAL RELATIONS: AN INTRODUCTION TO STRATEGIC HISTORY 267 (2007). The Congress System did not last long due to differences between Britain and the other major powers, *Id.* However, this system had an impact in the relatively long peace in Europe from 1815–1914, *Id.*

13 Treaty of Amity, Commerce, and Navigation, Nov. 19, 1794, between the US and Great Britain [hereinafter the "Jay Treaty"].

14 ROELOFSEN, *supra* note 11 at 160. ("The Jay Treaty became a landmark of the renaissance of arbitration only in the last quarter of the nineteenth century, after the emergence of a particular interest in international arbitration and its history"); *See also* C.G. Roelofsen, *The Jay Treaty and All That: Some Remarks on the Role of Arbitration in European Modern History and Its "Revival" in 1794* in INTERNATIONAL ARBITRATION: PAST AND PROSPECTS 201, 201–04 (A.H.A. Soons ed., 1990).

15 ALAN REDFERN & MARTIN HUNTER, LAW AND PRACTICE OF INTERNATIONAL COMMERCIAL ARBITRATION 60 (2004) ("The Jay Treaty of 1794 between the UK and the US is generally regarded as the new starting point for the development of arbitrations between

states opted to arbitrate their disputes, but rather that this method became systematized and ingrained in the international relations of the modern world.[16]

The Jay Treaty of 1794 between the United States and United Kingdom was signed in a historical context in which the United States was a capital importer and the United Kingdom was the economic superpower.[17] The Treaty aimed to foster economic ties with the UK[18] and resolve issues including US debts[19] and the boundary dispute[20] between the two countries that remained following the American Revolution. The Treaty established three commissions:[21] the Boundary Commission to resolve disputes regarding the St. Croix River boundary line;[22] the British Debts Commission to adjudicate on the debt claims of British merchants and subjects against Americans;[23] and the Maritime Claims Commission to resolve matters related to the free navigation

---

states . . . this system of mixed commissions became the usual method of settling claims by one government against another and by the nationals of one government against another") (footnotes omitted); CHRISTOPHER DUGAN ET AL., INVESTOR-STATE ARBITRATION 34 (2008) ("Perhaps the first use of special-purpose tribunals to resolve investment disputes was the 1794 Jay Treaty, concluded between the United States and Great Britain in the aftermath of the American Revolution") (footnotes omitted); Mark Feldman, *The United States as an International Litigant* in LITIGATING INTERNATIONAL LAW DISPUTES: WEIGHING THE OPTIONS 106, 108 (2014) ("There is a general agreement that modern international arbitration began with the 1794 Jay Treaty between Great Britain and the United States, which, following the War of Independence, settled unresolved issues between the two countries") (footnote omitted); Roger, P. Alford, *The American Influence on International Arbitration*, 19 OHIO ST. J ON DISP. RESOL. 69, 74–75 (2003–2004).

16 RALSTON, *supra* note 2 at 191 ("The modern era of arbitral or judicial settlement of international disputes, by common accord among all writers upon the subject, dates from the signing on November 19, 1794, of the Jay Treaty between Great Britain and the United States. Prior to this arbitrations were irregular and spasmodic").

17 Guillermo Aguilar Alvarez & William W. Park, *The New Face of Investment Arbitration: Capital Exporters as Host States under NAFTA Chapter 11* in ICCA CONGRESS SERIES No. 11: INTERNATIONAL ARBITRATION CONFERENCE LONDON, 12–15 MAY 2002, 392, 395 (A.J. Van Den Berg, 2003)

18 The rapprochement with the UK through the Jay Treaty stirred controversy in American politics. The Treaty had the support of President George Washington and Secretary of Treasury Alexander Hamilton and Federalists in general but it received harsh criticism from the Republican newspapers and supporters, TODD ESTES, THE JAY TREATY DEBATE, PUBLIC OPINION, AND THE EVOLUTION OF EARLY AMERICAN POLITICAL CULTURE 104–26 (2006).

19 Following the 1783 Peace of Paris between the UK and US, the British troops would not abide by the terms of the treaty to withdraw until the debts were paid, JAMES ROGER SHARP, AMERICAN POLITICS IN THE EARLY REPUBLIC: THE NEW NATION IN CRISIS 114 (1993).

20 The Paris Peace Treaty between the UK and the US "left a boundary gap of approximately 175 miles in an air line between the source of Mississippi and the northwesternmost corner of the Lake of the Woods," SAMUEL FLAGG BEMIS, JAY'S TREATY AND THE NORTHWEST BOUNDARY GAP 465 (1922).

21 For a detailed discussion of these three commissions, *see generally* Richard B. Lillich, *The Jay Treaty Commissions*, ST. JOHN'S L. REV. 260 (1962–1963).

22 Jay Treat, *supra* note 13, art. 5.

23 Jay Treat, *supra* note 13, art. 6.

of Americans who became subject to irregular capture by UK nationals.[24] The commissions comprised one or two commissioners appointed by each party and a final member selected by the drawing of lots.[25]

Not all commissions established under the Jay Treaty succeeded in the mission assigned to them. The Boundary Commission rendered its decisions in a timely manner[26] but the Debts Commission encountered major problems.[27] The Maritime Claims Commission was the most successful commission of all three,[28] and awarded a large amount of money to both British and American citizens.[29] The mixed commissions of the Jay Treaty became predecessors of the claims commissions that allow nationals of countries to bring claims directly against a sovereign state without their country's espousal.[30] Diplomatic protection or espousal refers to a customary rule in international law that states have the authority to turn private claims of their citizens into international claims.[31]

The Jay Treaty commissions caused a resurgence of international arbitration in the modern era. But it was the *Alabama* Claims arbitration that paved the way for systematization of the practice of international arbitration.[32] Although more than one hundred years after the Jay Treaty, once again, the *Alabama* Claims arbitration involved a dispute between the US and the UK. The arbitration arose as a result of UK interference in the American Civil War, in which the UK built warships (one of which bore the name *Alabama*),

---

24 Jay Treat, *supra* note 13, art. 7.
25 J. SIMPSON & H. FOX, INTERNATIONAL ARBITRATION LAW AND PRACTICE (1959) *reprinted in* BARRY E. CARTER & PHILIP R. TRIMBLE, INTERNATIONAL LAW 354, 355 (1995).
26 "The St. Croix River Commission, with a pedestrian problem to adjudicate, added little to the substantive law of international claims. It did, however, resolve a hotly contested boundary question . . . " Lillich, *supra* note 21 at 268.
27 The Debts Commission had to deal with many complex issues, some of which related to the poor drafting of Article 6 of the Jay Treaty, *Id.* at 275. The Commission eventually broke up in 1799, SIMPSON & FOX, *supra* note 25.
28 Lillich, *supra* note 21 at 276.
29 "When the commission concluded its business on February 24, 1804, it had awarded $11,650.00 to American claimants and $143,423.14 to British claimants," address by F.W. Anwar, Proceedings of the American Society of International Law, 3d annual meeting, Washington, D.C. (April 23 and 24, 1909). However, the Commission encountered some tensions and had to suspend its sittings between 1799 and 1802, SIMPSON & FOX, *supra* note 25.
30 Richard B. Lillich, *International Claims: Their Adjudication by National Commissions* (1962) *reprinted in* FOREIGN INVESTMENT DISPUTES: CASES, MATERIALS, AND COMMENTARY 478, 478–88 (Doak Bishop et al. eds, 2005). Lillich believes that the success of mixed commissions depends on the qualification and ability of commissioners, *id*; SIMPSON & FOX, *supra* note 25 at 355. The US and the UK engaged in further arbitration following the war of 1812 and conclusion of the Ghent Treaty. This Treaty also stipulated a Commission to determine the northeastern boundary of the United States from the source of the River St. Croix to the St. Lawrence River, RALSTON, *supra* note 2 at 194–95.
31 Nobuyuki Kato, *The Role of Diplomatic Protection in the Implementation Process of Public Interests* in PUBLIC INTEREST RULES OF INTERNATIONAL LAW: TOWARDS EFFECTIVE IMPLEMENTATION 189–91 (Teruo Komori & Karel Wellens eds., 2009).
32 SIMPSON & FOX, *supra* note 25 at 356.

for the Confederates seeking secession of the south of the US.[33] The tribunal was constituted pursuant to the Washington Treaty of 1871 and eventually rendered its decision, stating that the United Kingdom violated neutrality by interfering in the American Civil War.[34] The five-member tribunal consisted of an appointed arbitrator from each of the US and UK, as well as the King of Italy, the President of the Swiss Confederation, and the Emperor of Brazil.[35] The importance of the *Alabama* Claims arbitration rests also on the arbitral procedure innovations, which appeared as an annex to the Treaty of Washington.[36] These rules set standards for the conduct of arbitrators. Furthermore, the *Alabama* arbitration garnered support for arbitration in other nations as well, a matter that resulted in the increasing incorporation of arbitration clauses in bilateral and multilateral treaties.[37]

Thus, Jay Treaty arbitration brought arbitration back into the sphere of international relations. The *Alabama* Claims arbitration solidified the practice and prompted a momentum that resulted in popularity of arbitration. The first codification of arbitration at the international level occurred in 1899 with a groundbreaking Hague Convention "For Pacific Settlement of International Disputes."[38] Article 15 of the Convention for the first time attempts to define "the system of arbitration": "International arbitration has for its object the settlement of differences between States by judges of their own choice, and on the basis of respect for law."[39] The Convention also stipulated a court of arbitration, which remains active to this day:

> With the object of facilitating an immediate recourse to arbitration for international differences, which it has not been possible to settle by diplomacy, the Signatory Powers undertake to organize a Permanent Court of Arbitration, accessible at all times and operating, unless otherwise stipulated by the parties, in accordance with the Rules of Procedure inserted in the present Convention.[40]

The Hague Conference came about at the initiative of the Czar of Russia in 1899 and included twenty-six states.[41] The purpose of the Conference was to

---

33 THOMAS WILLING BLACH, THE ALABAMA ARBITRATION 4–5 (1900); MAURO RUBINO-SAMMARTANO, INTERNATIONAL ARBITRATION LAW AND PRACTICE 148–49 (2001).
34 RUBINO-SAMMARTANO, *supra* note 33.
35 WILLING BLACH, *supra* note 33 at 131.
36 SIMPSON & FOX, *supra* note 25 at 356.
37 BOB REINALDA, ROUTLEDGE HISTORY OF INTERNATIONAL ORGANIZATIONS 60 (2009).
38 Hague Convention I, Pacific Settlement of International Disputes, July 29, 1899, 32 Stat. 1779, 1 Bevans 230, 26 Martens Nouveau Recueil (ser. 2) 720, 187 Consol. T.S. 410, *entered into force* Sept. 4, 1900 [hereinafter the "Hague Convention"].
39 *Id.* at art. 15.
40 *Id.* at art. 20.
41 CHARLES EMANUEL MARTIN, THE PERMANENT COURT OF INTERNATIONAL JUSTICE AND QUESTION OF AMERICAN ADHESION 6–7 (1932).

eliminate or at least alleviate the potentially grave consequences of disputes between important powers. The drafters of the resulting Convention had a dispute between the US and Spain in mind; this arose from an incident involving a US ship, the *Maine*, which was allegedly destroyed by a Spanish submarine.[42] They aimed to reduce tensions in case of such incidents and opened a platform for fact-finding, inquiry, and the amicable resolution of disputes.[43] A few years later, in 1907, the Convention underwent a revision as a result of the efforts of President Roosevelt and the Czar of Russia.[44]

The Hague Convention defined a new paradigm in international law pertaining international adjudication and its limits. Following the Hague Convention, several international instruments were signed with explicit reference to arbitration. In 1928, the General Act of the Pacific Settlement for International Disputes dedicated a chapter to arbitration, from articles 21 to 28.[45] This Act was an attempt to provide a comprehensive dispute resolution mechanism under the auspices of the League of Nations.[46] A few years later, Article 33 of the UN Charter also stipulated arbitration as its method for resolving international disputes.[47] Subsequently, in the area of commercial arbitration, the International Law Commission drafted its first model law of arbitration in 1958,[48] [49] and ten countries signed a groundbreaking Convention on the Recognition and Enforcement of Foreign Arbitral

---

42 J.G. MERRILLS, INTERNATIONAL DISPUTE SETTLEMENT 41–42 (2011).
43 *Id.*
44 MARTIN, *supra* note 41 at 7–8.
45 General Act of the Pacific Settlement for International Disputes, 2123 League of Nations Series 345, 353–55 (September 26, 1929)
46 NII LANTE WALLACE-BRUCE, THE SETTLEMENT OF INTERNATIONAL DISPUTES: THE CONTRIBUTION OF AUSTRALIA AND NEW ZEALAND 45 (1998).
47 UN Charter, art. 33. ("1. The parties to any dispute, the continuance of which is likely to endanger the maintenance of international peace and security, shall, first of all, seek a solution by negotiation, enquiry, mediation, conciliation, arbitration, judicial settlement, resort to regional agencies or arrangements, or other peaceful means of their own choice.")
48 ILC Model Rules of Arbitral Procedure, II (12) Y.B. INT'L L. COMM. Later, the UN Commission on International Commission on International Trade Law (UNCITRAL) came with its own arbitral rules in 1985, amended in 2006, UNCITRAL MODEL LAW ON INTERNATIONAL COMMERCIAL ARBITRATION 1985: WITH AMENDMENTS AS ADOPTED IN 2006, UNCITRAL 23 (2008).
49 The snowball effect of the arbitration procedure was not only limited to the International Law Commission and the UN bodies. Here are some other examples: European Convention for Peaceful Settlement of Disputes, April 29, 1957, 320 U.N.T.S. 243; Convention on Conciliation and Arbitration of the Organization for Security and Cooperation in Europe, December 15, 1992, 32 I.L.M. 55 (1992); Rules of the International Center for the Settlement of Investment Disputes, April 2006, at https://icsid.worldbank.org/ICSID/StaticFiles/basicdoc/CRR_English-final.pdf; Permanent Court of Arbitration Optional Rules for Arbitrating Disputes Between Two States, October 20, 1992, 32 I.L.M. 572 (1993); Permanent Court of Arbitration Optional Rules for Arbitration of Disputes Relating to Natural Resources and/or the Environment of 2001, June 19, 2001, 41 I.L.M. 202 (2002).

Awards (the New York Convention), which has 149 signatories as of 2013.[50] In parallel, states started to sign bilateral investment treaties containing arbitration clauses, beginning with Germany and Pakistan in 1959.[51] Soon, around forty states established the International Center for Settlement of Investment Disputes (ICSID) by signing the Washington Convention in 1965.[52] Arbitration has become one of the main methods of resolving international disputes. In fact, today there are far more arbitration cases than there are cases that appear before the International Court of Justice as the principal judicial body of the United Nations.[53]

C. Emergence of the notion of public policy

With a systemic—albeit nascent—use of international dispute resolution, thanks to the Hague Convention, came the idea that arbitration and other similar methods cannot adjudicate matters that are of essential interest to states. The signatories to the Convention refer to this matter explicitly in Article 9 of Title III, which deals with international commissions of inquiry:

> [I]n differences of an international nature involving neither honor nor vital interests, and arising from a difference of opinion on points of fact, the Signatory Powers recommend that parties . . . institute an International Commission of Inquiry . . .[54]

The signatory states were afraid that fact-finding and inquiry of dispute resolution mechanism would open a door for foreign intervention.[55]

The exclusion of disputes involving vital interests or honor should be seen in light of the bifurcation of disputes into what Lauterpacht calls justiciable and non-justiciable disputes.[56] This distinction has had a lasting effect on international law to this day. It was a memorandum by Russian delegates which elaborately justified the necessity of distinguishing between legal and

---

50 Convention on the Recognition and Enforcement for Foreign Arbitral Awards, June 1958, 330 U.N.T.S. 3 [hereinafter "New York Convention"]
51 KENNETH J. VANDEVELDE, BILATERAL INVESTMENT TREATIES: HISTORY, POLICY, AND INTERPRETATION 1 (2010).
52 Convention on the Settlement of Investment Disputes Between States and Nationals of Other States, Mar. 18, 1965, 575 U.N.T.S. 159, 4 I.L.M. 524 (1965).
53 Dapo Akande, *The Peace Palace Heats up Again: But Is Inter-State Arbitration Overtaking the ICJ?* EJIL: TALK, Feb. 17, 2014, available at http://www.ejiltalk.org/the-peace-palace-heats-up-again-but-is-inter-state-arbitration-overtaking-the-icj/ ("However, it may be that inter-state arbitration is now eclipsing, or, is perhaps now as popular as, judicial settlement, even by the International Court of Justice.")
54 Hague Convention, *supra* note 38, art. 9.
55 MERRILLS, *supra* note 42 at 42.
56 HERSCH LAUTERPACHT, THE FUNCTION OF LAW IN THE INTERNATIONAL COMMUNITY 27 (1933).

political disputes.[57] The idea behind such a distinction rested on the fact that arbitration cannot adjudicate matters relate to sovereign authority and, hence, cannot oblige a state to exercise matters that fall under the inherent powers of sovereignty.[58] As a result, a paradigm emerged that staunchly believed that political disputes were beyond the purview of international adjudication.[59] [60] This distinction can easily be traced in the major international documents that followed, and in contemporary international law.[61]

The public policy exception arguably emerged out of this paradigm at the international level. The doctrine of public policy or the public policy exception had existed in domestic national orders for a long time.[62] However, at the international level, the bifurcation of disputes paved the way for a strong public policy exception to be built into the fabric of international law. In almost all areas of international law, states crafted a public policy exception in order to protect their political orders under various and highly ambiguous categories such as fundamental principles of law, basic notion of justice, etc.[63]

In the area of private international law and conflict of laws, public policy remained omnipresent. Interestingly enough, the Hague Conferences on Private International Law, which date back to 1893, did not stipulate a public policy exception.[64] The exception grew increasingly as international law

---

57 *Id.* ("The reasons for introducing the distinction were ably stated in the elaborate Russian Memorandum, in which the distinction between legal and other disputes served the purpose of supporting a cautious proposal for a limited scheme of obligatory arbitration—a proposal which failed to secure acceptance [footnote omitted]. However, the passages of the Memorandum relating to legal and political disputes subsequently proved a source of inspiration for many a lawyer and statesman; they constitute an important contribution to the history of the doctrine of the inherent limitations of the international judicial process.")
58 *Id.* at 28.
59 Lauterpacht calls it a doctrine of "inherent limitations of justifiability of international disputes" that have shaped the contemporary philosophy of international law and can be traced back to Vattel, *id.* at 6.
60 Other international lawyers were also troubled by this distinction: *see e.g.*, Hans Kelsen, *Compulsory Adjudication of International Disputes*, Am. J. Int'l L. 397, 397–98 (1943).
61 Both the League of Nations and the Charter of United Nations, two foundational international instruments of our times, have adopted this paradigm. Article 13(2) of the Covenant of the League of Nations declares: "Disputes as to the interpretation of a treaty, as to any question of international law, as to the existence of any fact which if established would constitute a breach of any international obligation, or as to the extent and nature of the reparation to be made for any such breach, are declared to be among those which are generally suitable for submission to arbitration or judicial settlement." Article 36(3) of the UN Charter stipulates: "3. In making recommendations under this Article the Security Council should also take into consideration that *legal disputes* should as a general rule be referred by the parties to the International Court of Justice in accordance with the provisions of the Statute of the Court" [emphasis added].
62 Farshad Ghodoosi, *The Concept of Public Policy in Law: Revisiting the Role of the Public Policy Doctrine in the Enforcement of Private Legal Arrangements*, 94 Neb. L. Rev. 685 (2016).
63 Farshad Ghodoosi, *Arbitrating Public Policy: Why the Buck Should not Stop at National Courts*, 20 Lewis & Clark L. Rev. 237, 237–80 (2016).
64 286 U.N.T.S. 265; *see generally* Friedrich Meili, The Four Hague Conferences on Private International Law: The Object of the Conferences and Probable Results (1905).

developed in the twentieth century. It can be found in various documents such as the UNIDROIT Principles of International Commercial Contracts[65] and the UNCITRAL Model Law on Procurement of Goods, Construction, and Services,[66] [67] as well as regional documents such as the Brussels Convention,[68] the Lugano Conventions,[69] and the Rome Convention.[70] The issue of public policy soon became the subject of many academic pieces.[71]

It is now a well-ingrained rule in conflict of laws that the forum court has the ability to refuse to recognize and enforce foreign laws that it deems to be contrary to its public policy.[72] *Lex fori*, or the law of the forum, has enough connection to a dispute to check the laws against its public policy.[73] In other words, the public policy exception ceases the normal application of conflict of laws, imposes the *lex fori* rules on disputes and, in a nutshell, runs against "the spirit and the whole idea of private international law."[74] Many

---

65 UNIDROIT (International Institute for the Unification of Private Law) Principles (2010) art. 1.4., available at http://www.unidroit.org/english/principles/contracts/principles2010/integralversionprinciples2010-e.pdf
66 Art. 29.
67 For the issue of public policy and United Nations Convention on Contracts for the International Sale of Goods (1980) *see* BRUNO ZELLER, CISG AND THE UNIFICATION OF INTERNATIONAL TRADE LAW 74–75 (2007).
68 Convention on Jurisdiction and the Enforcement of Judgments in Civil and Commercial Matters, art. 27, September 27, 1968, 1262 U.N.T.S 153, 8 I.L.M. 229 (1969).
69 Convention on Jurisdiction and the Enforcement of Judgments in Civil and Commercial Matters, art. 28., September 16, 1988, [1988] O. J. L319/9.
70 Convention on the Law Applicable to Contractual Obligations, art. 16, June 19, 1980, (80/934/EEC) O. J. L266.
71 *See e.g.*, Herbert F. Goodrich, *Public Policy in the Conflict of Laws*, 36 W. VA. L. Q. 156 (1930); Ernest G. Lorenzen, *Territoriality, Public Policy and the Conflict of Laws*, 33 YALE L. J. 736 (1924); Arthur Nussbaum, *Public Policy and the Political Crisis in the Conflict of Laws*, 49 YALE L. J. 1027 (1940); Charles B. Nutting, *Suggested Limitations of the Public Policy Doctrine*, 19 MINN. L. REV. 196 (1935); John Corr, *Modern Choice of Law and Public Policy: The Emperor Has the Same Old Clothes*, 39 U. MIAMI L. REV. 647 (1985); Conrad G. Paulsen & Michael I. Sovren, *"Public Policy" in Conflict of Laws*, 56 COLUM. L. REV. 969 (1956); Herbert W. Greenber, *Extrastate Enforcement of Tax Claims and Administrative Tax Determinations under the Full Faith and Credit Clause*, 43 BROOK L. REV. 630 (1977); Robert A. Leflar, *Extrastate Enforcement of Penal and Government Claims*, 46 HARV. L. REV. 193 (1932); Willis L. M. Reese, *Full Faith and Credit to Statutes: The Defense of Public Policy*, 19 U. CHI, L. REV. 339 (1952); for more recent discussions, *see e.g.*, Thomas G. Guedj, *The theory of the Lois de Police: A Functional Trend in Continental Private International Law—A Comparative Analysis with Modern American Theories*, 39 AM. J. COMP. L. 661 (1991); Barbara Cox, *Same-Sex Marriage and the Public Policy Exception in Choice of Law: Does it Really Exist?* 16 QUINNIPIAC L. REV. 61 (1996); Todd C. Hilbig, *Will New York Recognize Same-Sex Marriage?: An Analysis of the Conflict-of-Laws' Public Policy Exception*, 12 U. J. PUB. L. 333 (1998); Lynn L. Hogue, *State Common-Law Choice of Law Doctrine in Same Sex Marriage: How Will States Enforce the Public Policy Exception?* 32 CREIGHTON L. REV. 29 (1998).
72 MICHAEL BOGDAN, PRIVATE INTERNATIONAL LAW AS COMPONENT OF THE LAW OF FORUM 215 (2012).
73 *Id.*
74 *Id.* at 222.

courts have resorted to this notion on occasions in which they believed the foreign law would violate fundamental principles of justice, public morality, or public security.[75] However, as noted by some scholars, with the modern approach to the conflict of laws—at least in the US—a refusal to recognize foreign laws as against public policy decreased.[76] The modern approach retreats from a formalistic analysis and focuses on the law that has the most connections with disputes.[77][78] The New York jurisdiction was the pioneer in

---

[75] Judge Cardozo's opinion in the US case of Loucks v. Standard Oil Co., 120 NE 198, 202 (1918), best summarizes the court's approach even today: "The courts are not free to refuse to enforce a foreign right at the pleasure of the judges, to suit the individual notion of expediency or fairness. They do not close their doors, unless help would violate some fundamental principle of justice, some prevalent conception of good morals, some deep-rooted tradition of the common weal"; *see also* Nedlloyd Lines B.V. v. Superior Court, (1992) 3 C.4th 459, 465 ("The law of the state chosen by the parties to govern their contractual rights and duties will be applied . . . unless . . . application of the law of the chosen state would be contrary to a fundamental policy of a state which has a materially greater interest than the chosen state in the determination of the particular issue and which, under the rule of § 188, would be the state of the applicable law in the absence of an effective choice of law by the parties") (quoting the Second Restatement of Conflict of Laws § 187(2)) (emphasis added); Stoot v. Fluor Drilling Services, Inc., 851 F.2d 1514, 1517 (5th Cir. 1988) ("under admiralty law, where the parties have included a choice-of-law clause, that state's law will govern unless . . . the state's law conflicts with the fundamental purposes of maritime law"); Hale v. Co-Mar Offshore Corp., 588 F. Supp. 1212, 1215 (W.D.La. 1984) (when deciding whether to enforce a choice-of-law agreement in admiralty, the court must look to "public policy considerations . . . underlying admiralty law because maritime rules of decision would apply in the absence of a choice of [state] law"); *see also* Paulsen & Sovern, *supra* note 71 at 969–70.

[76] ROBERT L. FELIX, RALPH U. WHITTEN, AMERICAN CONFLICTS OF LAW: CASES AND MATERIALS 298–99 (2010).

[77] The modern approach is best reflected in the Second Restatement of Conflict of Laws, especially section 6(2): "When there is no such directive, the factors relevant to the choice of the applicable rule of law include (a) the needs of the interstate and international systems, (b) the relevant policies of the forum, (c) the relevant policies of other interested states and the relative interests of those states in the determination of the particular issue, (d) the protection of justified expectations, (e) the basic policies underlying the particular field of law, (f) certainty, predictability and uniformity of result, and (g) ease in the determination and application of the law to be applied. The Third Restatement of the Foreign Relations Law of the United States takes a similar approach for international cases in section 402; *see also* Lea Brilmayer & Raechel Anglin, *Choice of Law Theory and the Metaphysics of the Stand-Alone Trigger*, 95 IOWA L. REV. 1125 1131–132 (2009); Andrew T Guzman, *Choice of Law: New Foundations*, 90 GEO. L. J. 883, 891 (2002).

[78] The traditional choice of law approach in America was based on a vested right approach that would focus on the time and place of the cause of action and it was codified in the First Restatement of Conflict of laws, *see generally* Lea Brilmayer, *Rights, Fairness, and Choice of Law*, 98 YALE L. J. 1277 (1989); Perry Dane, *Vested Rights, "Vestedness," and Choice of Law*, 96 YALE L. J. 1191 (1987). Professor Joseph Beale was the chief crafter of the edifice of the traditional and systemized approach to conflict of laws in America, SYMEON SYMEONIDES, AMERICAN PRIVATE INTERNATIONAL LAW 110–11 (2008). For, him a single event, such as conclusion of a contract or an injury triggers and solidifies a right, which should be recognized as a vested right in the other jurisdiction. According to him, "when a right has been

embracing a multi-faceted approach to conflict of laws rather than the rigid single-factor analysis of traditional conflict of laws.[79] In the case *Bacock v. Jackson*, a New York court declared that in a car injury accident, where both parties were domiciled in New York and the car was registered and insured there, the relevance of the law of the place of injury (in this case, Ontario) was only accidental, and thus New York law should apply.[80][81]

International arbitration jurisprudence also includes a solidified and well-ingrained rule of public policy exception.[82] In the current manifestation of international arbitration, national courts have the final say in recognizing and enforcing arbitral awards. In 1927 the Geneva Convention on the Execution of Foreign Arbitral Awards, a convention under the auspices the League of Nations, marked the first comprehensive arbitral awards enforcement convention.[83] Article I(e) of the Geneva Convention enumerated, as a precondition for the recognition and enforcement of an award, that the award was not "contrary to public policy or to the principles of the law of the country in which it is sought to be relied upon."[84] The subsequent convention, the so-called New York Convention,[85] however, stipulates violation of public policy as a ground for refusal.[86] Therefore, the public policy doctrine became an integral control mechanism of international arbitration.

Yet, it is worth noting that the concept of public policy serves different purposes and functions in each sub-field of international law. The differences are very subtle, yet are crucial in interpreting and approaching the public policy exception in each sub-field. For instance, in private international law,

---

created by law, this right itself becomes a fact ... [T]he existing right should everywhere be recognized." JOSEPH HENRY BEALE, A TREATISE ON THE CONFLICT OF LAWS Vol. 3 1969 (1935). Beale's theory of vested right in conflict of laws was preceded by Joseph Story's theory of comity, which was not as widely accepted as Beale's theory, SYMEONIDES, 114–16.

79 *See* Austen v. Austen, 124 N.E. 2d 99 (1954); Babock v. Jackson, 191 N.E. 2d 279 (1963).
80 "Comparison of the relative 'contacts' and 'interests' of New York and Ontario in this litigation, vis-à-vis the issue here presented, makes it clear that the concern of New York is unquestionably the greater and more direct and that the interest of Ontario is at best minimal," Babock v. Jackson, *supra* note 79 at 284.
81 For a criticism of the modern approach as yet another single factor analysis *see* Lea Brilmayer & Raechel Anglin, *supra* note 77 at 1167.
82 "Almost all states refuse to recognize foreign judgments that violate local public policy or mandatory laws." GARY BORN, INTERNATIONAL ARBITRATION AND FORUM SELECTION AGREEMENTS: DRAFTING AND ENFORCING 134 (2010).
83 ANTON G. MAURER, PUBLIC POLICY EXCEPTION UNDER THE NEW YORK CONVENTION 12 (2013).
84 Convention on the Execution of Foreign Arbitral Awards, September 26, 1927, 91 L.N.T.S. 301.
85 Convention on the Recognition and Enforcement for Foreign Arbitral Awards, June 1958, 330 U.N.T.S. 3.
86 "2. Recognition and enforcement for an arbitral award may also be refused if the competent authority in the country where recognition and enforcement is sought finds that ... (b) the Recognition or enforcement of the award would be contrary to the public policy of that country," New York Convention, art. V (2)(b).

courts have leveraged the public policy exception to avoid the undesirable consequences of conflict of laws,[87] a trend that could decrease, and has decreased, due to the adoption of a theory of conflict of laws that is premised on a "most connection" criterion/interest-based analysis, and the like.[88] In the international arbitration context, as it is designed today, the public policy exception comes at the very tail end of a dispute, i.e., enforcement. At this stage, the stakes are high and courts, even if they set aside an award, cannot adjudicate the dispute, a matter that plausibly has had an essential impact on the way public policy is viewed and applied worldwide.[89]

In summary, international law today has been developed on a hard line between political and legal disputes. This fact arguably has contributed to the emergence and increasing importance of the notion of public policy. The public policy doctrine empowers national courts to set aside foreign legal elements, be it in the form of applicable foreign law, or an arbitral award, or other forms.

---

87 "In short, 'public policy' is one way to avoid the application of a choice of law rule which the forum wishes to avoid. The objection of the forum, thus, is not to the content of the foreign law but to its own choice of law." Paulsen & Sovern, *supra* note 71 at 981.
88 In the context of American law *see* ROBERT L. FELIX, RALPH U. WHITTEN, *supra* note 76.
89 *See generally,* Farshad Ghodoosi, *Arbitrating Public Policy: Why the Buck Should not Stop at National Courts,* 20 LEWIS & CLARK L. REV. 237, 237–80 (2016).

6 Theorizing international arbitration

A. Judicialization and state power

The traditional view in international relations, the so-called *realist* view, emphasizes the importance of the hard power of states in the anarchical setting of international relations.[1] In a nutshell, in an international setting with no centralized government, survival becomes the main objective of states, a concern that could merely be alleviated by having strong, hard, and militarized power.[2] For realists, therefore, no real legal constrains exist at the international level and states do not hesitate to break their legal arrangements if counter to their interests.[3]

Yet, the increasing judicialization of international relations as well as the unprecedented level of legal arrangements in bilateral or multilateral forms between states poses serious questions to the viability of the realist model. For those who believe in anarchic international politics in which states only pursue self-help, it is still baffling to observe that states commit to certain legal arrangements and often abide by them.[4] Regime theory

---

1 The founding fathers of classical realism in international relations are E.H. Carr and Hans Morgenthau. *See generally* HANS MORGENTHAU AND KENNETH THOMPSON, POLITICS AMONG NATIONS (6th ed. McGraw-Hill 1985) (1948); E.H. CARR, THE TWENTY YEARS' CRISIS 1919–1939, 166 (Palgrave 2001) (1964); Realism has brought into a new level and has been structuralized by Kenneth Waltz: KENNETH WALTZ, MAN, THE STATE, AND THE WAR (Columbia University Press, 2001) (1959).
2 With the increasing criticism of realism, its proponents developed a theory of protection using the game theory. They posited that in a world with no central authority, cooperation emerges out of rational "tit-for-tat" logic created out of long-term exposures and interactions of states, ROBERT M. AXELROD, THE EVOLUTION OF COOPERATION 60–63 (1984).
3 E.H. Carr famously stated that the quality of law rests in its capability to bring stability without which no political and social life is possible. Law's special stature in today's society is not due to its subject-matter or its ethical dimension. However, society cannot survive with law alone. He continues to stress the superiority of politics over law: "the ultimate authority of law derives from politics." E.H. CARR, *supra* note 1 at 166.
4 Judith Goldstein et al., *Introduction: Legalization and World Politics*, 54 INT'L ORG. 385, 391 (2000). On the other hand some scholars have tried to show that the role of realism in international law has been downplayed and realism indeed served as a theoretical base for several of development in international law, Richard H. Steinberg, *Wanted—Dead or Alive: Realism in International Law* in INTERDISCIPLINARY PERSPECTIVE ON INTERNATIONAL LAW AND INTERNATIONAL RELATIONS 146, 146–48 (2013).

emerged as one of the first theoretical responses to this phenomenon. According to this theory, states' behavior is shaped and changed pursuant to legal regimes.[5] Stephen Krasner suggested a definition of regimes that now serves as the classical approach for regimes: "regimes can be defined as sets of implicit or explicit principles, norms, rules, and decision-making procedures around which actors' expectations converge in a given area of international relations."[6] These regimes morph actors' expectations and behaviors independently from the power dynamics of international relations.[7] Robert Keohane, another prominent regime theorist, noted that international regimes perform valuable functions including reducing transaction costs, facilitating negotiations, and attaining mutual agreements between states through allowing certain types of bargaining.[8]

Yet, the rational and functional account of international cooperation suffers from two main shortcomings: it is highly difficult to measure the costs incurred by states as a result of cooperation and the benefits they gain from it. International investment law serves as an illuminating example, as studies deliver contradictory results on the benefits states receive from participating in the investment regime. Furthermore, it fails to entirely account for situations where states continue to partake in regimes even after they cease to benefit them. The NPT regime serves as a good example; countries such as Iran never left the regime, even after the costs seemed to surpass its benefits.

Another explanation follows a transnational approach and is commonly referred to as the liberal school of thought.[9] Through the scholarly works of Moravcsik, Slaughter, Keohane, and others, a transnational explanation of states' behavior has been put forward.[10] Briefly, this school emphasizes domestic actors and politics and their influence on the international behavior of states. Unlike other international relations theories, as Moravcsik argues, the liberal theory endeavors to furnish a systemic account of international cooperation, which includes the dynamics of domestic politics.[11]

---

5 Stephen Krasner, *Structural Causes and Regime Consequences: Regimes as Intervening Variables* in INTERNATIONAL REGIMES 1, 1 (1983).
6 *Id.* at 2.
7 *Id.* at 10.
8 ROBERT KEOHANE, AFTER HEGEMONY: COOPERATION AND DISCORD IN THE WORLD POLITICAL ECONOMY 107 (1984). For a similar functional account on the way international organizations work through centralization and independence, *see* Kenneth Abbott & Duncan Snidal, *Why States Act through Formal International Organizations* 42 J. CONFLICT RESOL. 3, 9–23 (1998).
9 Judith Goldstein et al., *supra* note 4 at 392.
10 *Id.*
11 Andrew Moravcsik, *Integrating International and Domestic Theories of International Bargaining* in DOUBLE-EDGE DIPLOMACY: INTERNATIONAL BARGAINING AND DOMESTIC POLITICS 3, 7–9 (Peter Evans et al. eds., 1993). Moravcsik provides examples of north–south relationship to buttress his view point: 1) Carter's human rights policy in Argentina and Guatemala, 2) US policies towards Panama and Nicaragua, 3) International Monetary Fund stabilization agreements in Jamaica and Somalia, *Id.* at 20.

This approach has its roots in Peter Hass' theory of "epistemic community," Robert Keohane and Joseph Nye's theory of "complex interdependence," as well as Robert Putnam's idea of a "two-level game," among others. All of these theories attempt to inject elements such as transnationalism and institutionalism, as well as the systemic implications of domestic politics. Recent theories have tended to deliver what could be called a "network account" of regulations and norms and their effects on states' behavior and international relations.[12]

A critical point seems to remain under the radar of scholars in the fields of international law and international relations. Growing state involvement in the use of law in international relations partially results from a new perspective that views international law as continuation of "foreign policy." In other words, states have become more skillful in utilizing international law in order to further their domestic or international agenda. Legitimacy, economic interest, systemic pressure, and other factors suggested by scholars undoubtedly play important roles in states' behavior. Yet, a paradigm shift is noticeable, whereby use of law is becoming a tool in states' toolbox next to the use of force. The use of law has proven to be less costly and more legitimate, allowing the states to be hands-off when dealing with thorny and difficult foreign policy issues. In today's world, civil society demands the state perform multiple tasks, many of which were not even conceivable at the genesis of the idea of modern statehood. States, therefore, seems to *outsource* some of their tasks through international law, endeavoring to bear minimal political costs in case things go awry.[13] I would like to call this the "outsourcing" theory of international law. I will return to this point in the concluding remarks to this chapter.

B. Two schools of international arbitration

I have identified two main approaches to international dispute resolution. This intellectual map could guide us in understanding positions taken by scholars and practitioners on various issues of international arbitration including transnational public policy. Many existing differences in today's

---

12 ANNE-MARIE SLAUGHTER, A NEW WORLD ORDER 48–51 (2004); DAVID GREWAL, NETWORK POWER: THE SOCIAL DYNAMICS OF GLOBALIZATION 247–58 (2008).
13 It requires another discussion, but this phenomenon also shows the reason states still prefer bilateral legal arrangements compared to multilateral arrangement even though the latter seem to suit their interests better. I believe this could be partially explained by the fact that the political costs of bilateral treaties remains low while states can outsource some of their functions through these legal arrangements. States tend to shun multilateral legal arrangements while creating international organizations, and this has baffled many scholars: "many states, notably the United States, now resist the creation of IOs [international organizations] and hesitate to support those already in operation, citing the shortcomings of international bureaucracy, the costs of formal organization, and the irritations of IO autonomy," Kenneth Abbott & Duncan Snidal, *supra* 8 note at 4.

international arbitration can also be traced back to the conceptualization of international law, as well as arbitration, by both sides of the debate. The first section fleshes out the theories put forward by notable European scholars in this field, mostly from France, who advocate for transnationalism in arbitration. The second section digs into the statist (or American) approach.

1. The transnationalist approach

Surprisingly enough, despite the multitude of academic and practice guides on international arbitration, only a very few notable pieces have attempted to theorize it. Emmanuel Gaillard, an active arbitrator and lawyer, is among the first authors who ventured to theorize about the jurisprudence order (*ordre juridique*) of international arbitration. Gaillard attempts to answer a paramount question: where does the source of power and the legal nature of international arbitration stem from?[14] In other words, his aim is to excavate the source of juridicity in international arbitration. He analyzes the reality of international arbitration against existing legal theories including Holmes' pragmatism[15] and Hart's version of legal positivism.[16] He suggests that the *ordre juridique* of international arbitration can be perceived in three major approaches. The first approach is "Monolocal," which relegates arbitration to a single national legal order. He refers to F.A. Mann[17] and Roy Goode[18] as proponents of this approach. Mann maintains that only the legal system of the seat (*lex fori*) can, objectively, offer a structure within which arbitration can be established.[19] Goode also believes that when parties make a choice in their contract in regard to arbitration, they are in fact expressing their intent to subject themselves to a given national legal order.[20] In the first approach the concept of *lex arbitri*[21] is understood as the equivalent of the national judges' *lex fori*. Philosophically, Gaillard argues that the first approach derives from Hart and Kelsen's notion of state positivism.[22] In summary, Monolocalists believe that arbitrators' authority comes from a given national legal order.

The second approach tries to anchor international arbitration in a plurality of national legal orders. Gaillard calls it the Westphalian approach, referring to the Westphalia Treaty that (as commonly believed) established nation-state sovereignty. Since all sovereigns and legal orders are autonomous,

---

14 He bases his theory on Henri Batiffol's legal theory of private international law. EMMANUEL GAILLARD, LEGAL THEORY OF INTERNATIONAL ARBITRATION 1 (2010).
15 *See generally* Thomas Grey, *Holmes and Legal Pragmatism*, 41 STAN. L. REV. 787 (1989).
16 H.L.A. HART, THE CONCEPT OF LAW 214 (2012).
17 *See generally* F.A. Mann, *Where is an Award Made?* 1 ARB. INT'L 107–08 (1995).
18 *See generally* Roy Goode, *The Role of the Lex Loci Arbitri in International Commercial Arbitration* 17 ARB. INT'L 19–40 (2001).
19 GAILLARD, *supra* note 14 at 17–18 (Gaillard categorizes it as the objectivist view).
20 *Id.* at 19 (Gaillard categorizes it as the subjectivist view).
21 *Lex Arbitri* refers to the law which governs the arbitration.
22 For a discussion on legal positivism, *see* ROBERT GEORGE, THE AUTONOMY OF LAW (1999).

they have an equal say with regard to the validity of contracts and the ensuing awards. *L'ordre juridique* of international arbitration stems from the law of the state in which enforcement of the resulting award is sought. In the Wesphalian approach, within the confines of its legal order each state is entitled to impose its conception of what would constitute arbitration worthy of legal protection. This doctrine minimizes the role of law of the seat and characterizes awards as "international,"[23] not limited to a specific national order. Methodologically, Gaillard suggests that the difference arises when one focuses on the starting point of arbitration (Monolocal) versus its end result (Westphalian).[24] Simply put, the former focuses on the law of the seat of arbitration while the latter believes *lex loci executionis*[25] should prevail.[26]

The third approach, which Gaillard endorses, tries to detach arbitration from national legal orders and find it autonomous.[27] In other words, the *ordre juridique* of international arbitration is independent from national legal orders and stems from the collective normative activity of the community of states. Laws of various national legal orders, when considered collectively, make up the common rules of arbitration law in which the source of the arbitrators' power to adjudicate is rooted. This is a transnational approach. Since arbitral juridicity is independent from national legal orders, it has its own transnational rules as well as public policy:

> In situations where arbitrators, confronted with plurality of views, endeavors to identify rules that are generally endorsed at a given time by the international community and determine that they should prevail over those reflecting a State's isolated position, the question arises as to the transnational source of the arbitrators' power to adjudicate and that of the existence of an arbitral legal order. Here, the expression "transnational" is preferable to "a-national," which does not convey the notion that the rules thus identified find their roots in national laws.[28]

According to Gaillard, international arbitration should not be subject to national public policy since it has its own truly international public policy, which corresponds to the public international law concept of *jus cogens*. Transnational public policy includes the fundamental principles of law, which are to be complied with irrespective of the connections between the

---

23 GAILLARD, *supra* note 14 at 31 (Gaillard believes that the New York Convention follows this approach).
24 *Id.* at 25.
25 The law of the forum in which enforcement of the award is sought.
26 Gaillard criticizes this view partly because it directs arbitrators to make every effort to make their awards enforceable and even a "formal requirement to apply all national laws that could potentially come to be connected to the dispute." *Id.* at 33–34.
27 *See generally* Emmanuel Gaillard, *Transnational Law: A Legal System or a Method of Decision Making?* 13 ARB. INT'L 59 (2001).
28 *Id.* at 37.

dispute and a given country. International arbitrators should follow international norms pertaining to arbitration, as opposed to the Westphalian approach which binds arbitrators to consider different national laws. Gaillard maintains that this approach improves predictability in international arbitration.[29]

Gaillard attempts to base his theory on positivism rather than natural law. The normative activity of states through the choice of law process constitutes arbitral legal order. States' expectations of arbitration are broadly delineated, and thus the awards, i.e., the results of arbitral proceedings, are binding on states. Since the final decision as to the recognition of awards lies within the authority of states, Gaillard still considers the transnational approach within the boundaries of positivist thinking.[30] According to Gaillard, "legal order" exists where a structure, body of norms, or system "answers all of the questions arising as between its subjects and reflect of its sources and its relations with other legal orders."[31] [32] He continues that an arbitral legal order, similar to an international legal order, stems from the will of the states, while maintaining its autonomy:

> By conferring to the arbitrators the power to adjudicate international business disputes when the parties so wish, and by recognizing the result of the arbitral process, i.e. award, without reviewing the merits of the dispute, the international community has granted arbitration true autonomy.

Yet, the distinction between the Westphalian and transnational approach as proposed by Gaillard is far from clear. The categorization appears to lead to practical benefits rather than having strong theoretical grounds. It helps Gaillard to vest additional power and autonomy in arbitration awards in the case of challenges such as anti-suit injunctions, the issue of *lis pendens*, and enforcement of awards in the second for a.[33]

However, theoretically, it seems that for both of these approaches, it is the sovereignty that acts as a "constitutive structure." In other words, even in in the transnational approach, the arbitral order—as well as recognition and enforcement of awards—is shaped and constituted by the consent of

---

29 Gaillard, *supra* note 27 at 70–71 (" . . . contrary to common wisdom, transnational rules offer as much predictability, if not more predictability, than genuine legal systems").
30 *Id*. at 46.
31 *Id*. at 56.
32 Some authors believe that a legal system cannot exist without the ability to force its rules. In his short discussion of *Lex mercatoria*, Pierre Mayer rejects its existence as a legal system because of lack of a power of coercion. Pierre Mayer, *Effect of International Public Policy in International Arbitration?* in Pervasive Problems in International Arbitration 61, 64–65 (Loukas A. Mistelis & Julian D.M. Lew eds., 2006).
33 One of the principal differences, resulting from adopting each of the approaches, pertains to the enforcement of the awards in secondary fora, *see infra* section 3.

states. Consequently, Gaillard tries to buttress his transnational approach by resorting to *forced* recognition by national legal orders.[34] Gaillard has a clear objective. He wants to restrict the applicability of national laws and their respective public policy in international awards. He believes arbitrators adjudicate in a transnational order and, thus, should respect transnational public policy in their decisions. The pragmatic concerns about the practice of international arbitration outweigh the theoretical significance of Gaillard's theory. It seems that Gaillard endeavors to import paragraph 1(c) of Article 38 of the Statute of the International Court of Justice into arbitration jurisprudence. This chapter refers to the "general principle of law recognized by civilized nations" as one of the sources of international law. As much as this source looks appealing at first glance, it remains highly controversial and vague. A quick review of the literature on international law demonstrates that this source and its wording does little to help frame any substantive contribution to the vexing and complex legal problems of today's world.[35] Gaillard's attempt, along with other similar scholarship, fails to deliver the desired result for the same reason.

On the very issue of transnational public policy, it was Pierre Lalive who first endorsed it in a 1987 article.[36] Lalive argues that the international public policy of states is not, and should not be, applicable to cases involving international matters. He refers to the *Zapata*,[37] *Scherk*,[38] and *Mitsubishi*[39] cases from the US Supreme Court as examples of the limitation of domestic public policy as well as the positive impact of international public policy in international relations. In his view, international public policy is truly international (i.e., transnational) only if it has *supernational* purposes. Public policy, stemming from private international law such as mandatory rules,

---

34 *Id.* at 60–66.
35 Johan G. Lammers, *General Principles of Law Recognized by Civilized Nations* in ESSAYS ON THE DEVELOPMENT OF THE INTERNATIONAL LEGAL ORDER: IN MEMORY OF HARO F. VAN PANHUYS (Frits Kalshoven ed., 1980).
36 Pierre Lalive, *Transnational (or Truly International) Public Policy and International Arbitration* in COMPARATIVE ARBITRATION PRACTICE AND PUBLIC POLICY IN ARBITRATION, 258 (Pieter Sanders ed., 1987).
37 M/S Bremen v. Zapata Off-Shore Company, 92 S. Ct. 1907 (1972) at 1913: "We cannot have trade and commerce in world markets and international waters exclusively on our terms, governed by our laws, and resolved in our courts."
38 Scherk v. Alberto Culver Company, 94 S. Ct. 2449 (1974) at 2456: "A parochial refusal by the courts of one country to enforce an international arbitration agreement would not only frustrate these purposes, but would invite unseemly and mutually destructive jockeying by the parties to secure tactical litigation advantages."
39 Mitsubishi Motors Corp. v. Soler Chrysler-Plymouth, Inc., 105 S. Ct. 3346, (July 2, 1985) at 629: "We conclude that concerns of international comity, respect for the capacities of foreign and transnational tribunals, and sensitivity to the need of the international commercial system for +predictability in the resolution of +disputes require that we enforce the parties' agreement, even assuming that a contrary result would be forthcoming in a domestic context."

gradually forms transnational public policy as they are applied to international disputes. The laws of *lex fori* may also endorse the protection of the foreign public policy of one or several states. And, finally, the needs of international trade dictate the application of certain mandatory rules of *lex fori*.[40] Lalive has little doubt as to the existence (*ontology*) of transnational public policy because of courts' practices, the "common law of international arbitration,"[41] and, most importantly, the lack of a "valid theoretical reason"[42] to challenge its existence. Lalive posits that neither the mere vagueness of the concept nor the shortage of it being a "legal system" would negate its very existence.[43]

Another French scholar who has theorized about transnational public policy is Yves Derains. He approaches the issue of public policy in arbitration mainly from a private international law perspective, i.e., in choosing the applicable law. In his theory, transnational public policy determines whether parties can contract around mandatory rules. Generally speaking, either the parties select the applicable law for the contact or the arbitrator has the duty to find the applicable law. According to Derains, there are two circumstances in which arbitrators have to face the issue of public policy: "the domestic rules of *lex contractus* and mandatory rules from elsewhere."[44] Derains, however, believes in the interference of transnational public policy as well. If parties choose an applicable law (e.g., French law), they are bound to its public policy restrictions too. His example is a contract between a Norwegian ship-builder and a Peruvian ship-owner, under French law, which limits the liability of the seller for latent defects. This provision is against the public policy of French law. Derain believes that in this scenario the arbitrator should not enforce the provision unless he discovers that the parties intended to exclude this part of French law. This is true in a situation in which the arbitrator determines the applicable law of *lex contractus*. Mandatory rules, on the other hand, should be applied regardless of the choice of *lex contractus*. Per our present discussion, for Derains, transnational public policy plays an important role in the determination of mandatory rules. His example is a contract between German and Italian nationals who—in order to avoid competition laws—choose Swiss law as governing their contract. The challenge is whether they can contract around their national laws by selecting a national law with more relaxed

---

40 Lalive, *supra* note 36 at 273.
41 *Id.* at 295.
42 *Id.* at 311.
43 According to Lalive, examples of transnational public policy could be the doctrine of competence-competence in arbitral proceedings, autonomy of the will, the criterion of the closest connection, and the legitimate expectation of the parties, Lalive, *supra* note 36, at 301–08.
44 Yves Derains, *Public Policy and the Law Applicable to the Dispute in International Arbitration* in COMPARATIVE ARBITRATION PRACTICE AND PUBLIC POLICY IN ARBITRATION, 227, 254 (ICCA Congress Series, Pieter Sanders, ed., 1986).

antitrust provisions. Derains believes they can as long as it is not against the transnational (truly international) public policy of Swiss law:

> It seems that the only way of resolving this question is by recourse to the theory of "truly international public policy." First of all, it goes without saying that if the mandatory law excluded was considered to be contrary to truly international public policy by virtue of its content, an arbitrator would have to give effect to the parties' intention of excluding its application (e.g. a law establishing a racial discrimination). Likewise, if the object of that law is to guarantee the respect of principles considered by the arbitrator as forming part of truly international public policy, the arbitrator would have to make that law, or at least its principles, prevail over the will of the parties. But situations as clear cut as this are seldom met with in practice.[45]

Pierre Mayer takes this discussion to a radical level. He maintains that arbitrators do not impose transnational public policy norms, but rather create them. Mayer believes that arbitrators are free to invoke principles that they consider necessary for dispute resolution. As he asserts, this view leads to the conclusion that arbitrators' moral and even religious convictions play a role in the process of adjudication.[46] He posits that, in the absence of *lex fori* mandatory rules, arbitrators can apply moral rules based on their own consciences and do not have to follow the specific public policy of a nation. Yet, he ostensibly avoids any systemic and structured approach to moral values in arbitration. In other words, as Gaillard points out, "the existence of higher values is central to his thinking. Yet, their consistency and their organization as a system is negated."[47]

The transnationalist approach aims to foster an autonomous or semi-autonomous legal order for arbitration. It desires to break the arbitrators free from nuances of national public policies or legal orders. Yet, the vagueness of the theories coupled with the decline of normative discourse at the international level renders these efforts quite limited. Scholars might agree on occasions where, for instance, slavery is involved, as contrary to transnational public policy. However, this makes the scope of theory substantially narrow and of limited practical use.

2. The statist approach

The American approach to international arbitration remains state-centric, holding a skeptical view of the autonomy of international arbitration. Michael Reisman is among the first scholars to have voiced his

---

45 *Id.* at 251.
46 Pierre Mayer, *Effect of International Public Policy in International Arbitration?* in Pervasive Problems in International Arbitration 61, 65–66 (Loukas A. Mistelis & Julian D.M. Lew eds., 2006).
47 Gaillard, *supra* note 13, at 45.

opposition to the transnationalist approach. He is skeptical about the role of public policy in international litigation and in particular the existence of international public policy.[48] He believes that all laws are policies. Yet, in his view, it is beyond the responsibility and vocation of arbitrators to enter the area of policy-making.[49] The arbitration tribunal neither has the means nor the jurisdiction (unless with the explicit consent of the parties) to enter into the norm-making process. Governments and national courts have the opportunity to protect their public policy at the enforcement stage of the current arbitration regime.[50] Due to the "protean" nature of transnational public policy, Reisman believes that its application would cause great uncertainty. He maintains while international courts are extremely cautious in applying peremptory norms (*jus cogens*) against international agreements, it is not reasonable for private dispute settlement arbitrators to engage in such a volatile practice.[51] Furthermore, he asserts that transnational public policy may become a tool for some "to affect their own preferences without having to prove that they [the norms] have become customary international law."[52]

Although not conspicuous, Reisman's position on arbitration is linked to his general theory of international law—the so-called New Haven School of Law (NHSL), as it was dubbed by Richard Falk. This school of thought had a lasting effect on the study and practice of international law in the US. It was originally a reaction to the legal formalism and positivism of the time, because the prevailing narrative could hardly explain the dynamics of international law in the post-World War II era. NHSL was the result of the theory

---

48 The skepticism is mainly for international commercial arbitration cases, W. Michael Reisman, *Law, International Public Policy (So-called) and Arbitral Choice in International Commercial, Arbitration* in ICCA CONGRESS SERIES 13/2007, 849, 856 (fn. 2) ("Certainly international investment law, if it looks to public policy, should look to international public policy, if it is admissible. The law applied in investment arbitration is authentically international and not national as in commercial arbitration."). Similar doubts have been expressed in the area of international investment arbitration. Following the two cases of ICSID (*World Duty* and *Inceysa*) ruling on public policy grounds, some scholars have questioned its necessity even in international investment arbitration. For instance, Donald Francis Donovan argues that an investment arbitration tribunal should not impose an international norm on both the state and the investor of a particular dispute. He poses the question that if a state has not assumed any international obligation by ratifying a treaty, why would an investment arbitration tribunal impose it on that particular state? The tribunal has traditional legal principles such as good faith, fair dealing, or sanctions against fraud to rely on in cases involving corruption, bribery, and the like. He questions the need "to resort to international public policy, rather than simply to rely on the law of the treaty against the backdrop of general international law." Donald Francis Donovan, *Investment Treaty Arbitration*, in MANDATORY RULES IN INTERNATIONAL ARBITRATION 286, 286–90 (George A. Bermann & Loukas A. Mistelis eds., 2011).
49 The only exception is when the applicable law allows the arbitrator to act as a legislator. Reisman, *id.* 850.
50 *Id.* at 852–53.
51 *Id.* at 855.
52 *Id.* at 856.

of jurisprudence developed by Myres McDougal and Harold Lasswell. It is a policy-oriented jurisprudence theory which concentrates on the process of decision-making[53] rather than only on laws and decisions. For the NHSL, law—specifically international law—is not only and principally made through the official channel of a legislative body. Law is produced through a complex process of communication. As Lasswell suggests, in order to understand what constitutes law, a legal scholar should consider five inquiries: "who" "says what" "in which channel" "to whom" and "with what effect."[54]

For a message to be prescriptive, and thus law-making, it must contain three elements: policy content, an authority signal, and a control intention.[55] Policy content refers to the norm that specific prescription entails. The policy needs not to be explicit and clear for the law-making process. Nor do policies which incorporate expressed norms intend to be enforced as laws. The second prong, the authority signal, states that the communicator should unequivocally convey its authority to prescribe. As Reisman points out, the search for the authority signal is complex and empirical because, in most cases, it is the audience who "renders the communication prescription."[56] The third component of law-making communication is power, indicating that the prescription is controlling.[57]

If any communication lacks any of the mentioned components the law-making process is not complete. An example would be when naked force is used to command an order, e.g., the evacuation of a building, while the communication lacks policy content and/or the commander lacks authority. In the same example, if the commander is a university security guard (authority) who is trying to save people from a fire in the building (policy), the outcome is law. It is worth mentioning that the NHSL does not consider norms as outcomes of shared understanding in a given community. To the contrary:

> Norms are prescribed because they are policies which part of community does not voluntarily or spontaneously support. Norms become effective because some elites have enough interest to make them effective. They continue to be norms only so long as some are able and willing to make them effective. Norms are not the issue of an always benign process.[58]

---

53 Components of the decision-making process are as follows: 1. Intelligence (the function of gathering, evaluating, and disseminating information; 2. Promotion of policy; 3. Prescription of policy; 4. Invocation of decisions in case of violation of policy; 5. Application of policy; 6.Termination of existing norms; 7. Appraisal of the performance of the decision process. Myres S. McDougal, Harold D. Lasswell & Lung-chu Chen, *Human Rights and World Public Order: A Framework for Policy-Oriented Inquiry*, AM. J. OF INT'L L., 237, 260–74 (1969).
54 Michael Reisman, *International Law Making: A Process of Communication: The Harold D. Lasswell Memorial Lecture*, AM. J. OF INT'L L. 101, 108 (1981).
55 *Id.*
56 *Id.* at 110.
57 New Haven School of Law approach has significant similarities to the Speech Act Theory.
58 *Id.* at 111.

This sounds similar to the positions of legal realism as well as *realpolitik*. Norms are created and maintained by the power to serve the interests of those who have the power. NHSL, however, has a normative agenda which should not be overlooked. Its main objective is to promote public order of human dignity through supporting shared values among human beings. In this sense, the NHSL holds praxis: it aims to implement its ideas and values in practice, "which can increase the likelihood of their realization in future decision[s]."[59]

According to the NHSL, "public order" derives from the world constitutive process, which is "authoritative decision(s) which provide an institutional framework for decision and allocate indispensable functions in the making and application of law."[60] NHSL classifies the values which public order decisions purport to attain into eight categories: respect, power, enlightenment, well-being, wealth, skill, affection, and rectitude.[61] Decisions in the international setting should be valued based on their conformity with the fundamental goals of the international community.[62]

Harold Koh best summarizes the enduring themes of the NHSL. In his article, which aims to frame a "new" New Haven School of International Law, he enumerates five concepts as the bedrock of the New Haven theory of jurisprudence: it is an interdisciplinary approach as opposed to the pure legalism propounded by legal positivism; it studies law as a process by analyzing authoritative decision-making; it is committed to normative values by pursuing the "public order of human dignity"; it connects law and policy; and, lastly, the NHSL, according to Koh, is the first approach to recognize the importance of *transnational law*.[63]

Despite the normative commitment of the NHSL to human values and its transnational character, Reisman resists the idea of transnational public policy in arbitration. While for the NHSL the existence of a "communicator" is essential, in international arbitration it is hard to conceive of a body responsible for shaping transnational public policy. As Reisman points out, unlike domestic legislation in which competing views about public policies are represented in the law-making process, there is no such body in international law. In other words, public policies are the result of a legislative mechanism that enjoys the transparent participation of a wide-range of groups representing diverse opinions.[64] International arbitration,

---

59 Michael Reisman, *McDougal's Jurisprudence: Utility, Influence, Controversy*, AM. J. OF INT'L L. 266, 279 (1985).
60 McDougal et al., *supra* note 53 at 239.
61 *Id.* at 239.
62 This broad term and definition has become the subject of criticisms of the NHSL from scholars including Oscar Schachter. *See* Oscar Schachter, *McDougal's Jurisprudence: Utility, Influence, Controversy*, AM. J. INT'L L. 266, 270 (1985).
63 Harold Hongju Koh, *Is there a "New" New Haven School of International Law?* Faculty Scholarship Series. Paper 1683. http://digitalcommons.law.yale.edu/fss_papers/1683.
64 Reisman, *supra* note 48 at 852.

however, is mainly a non-public dispute resolution mechanism, which is limited to the views of the parties involved. For the same reason, Reisman is relatively more comfortable with the investment arbitration tribunals applying international public policy. International investment arbitration is a public procedure and the governing law, unlike almost all commercial arbitration cases, is international law. Furthermore, Reisman is concerned about *excès de pouvoir* and the lack of a control mechanism as the nemesis of international arbitration.[65] As a result, he seems to be more comfortable with international commercial arbitration and the New York Convention design whereby states promise to lend their legal apparatus for control and enforcement of awards.[66] [67]

In the American school of international arbitration there are some who would propound further discretion for arbitral tribunals to enter into matters of public policy. Jan Paulsson, a longtime practitioner and scholar, has

---

65 "But when modern transnational arbitration increased as a function of the increase in transnational commercial activity, the inadequacy of this classical control mechanism became apparent. Arbitration was in danger of being undermined by its own control mechanism." Reisman, *supra* note 48 at 746. Following the *Klöckner I* and *Amco I* decisions at ICSID in which the *ad hoc* annual committee entered into the merits of those cases, Reisman warned about the breakdown of the ICSID system while suggesting ways to reform it. *Id.* at 804–07.

66 W. MICHAEL REISMAN, SYSTEMS OF CONTROL IN INTERNATIONAL ADJUDICATION AND ARBITRATION 139–40 (1992). Reisman calls this "the public international infrastructure of arbitration" in which "private international commercial arbitration depends, for its effectiveness, on substantial and predictable governmental and intergovernmental support." *Id.* at 107.

67 Another reason rests on the "pragmatic" nature of the NHSL. It is not only transnational public policy but also *jus cogens*, an ingrained notion in international law, which is the subject of skepticism for Reisman. Based on the practice and *opinio juris* in international law, he shows that even heinous conduct in the international sphere, such as slavery, hardly reach the status of *jus cogens* (e.g., when it should be balanced against the principle of sovereignty). He maintains that concepts such as transnational public policy, with their volatile character, "give international law a bad name," *id.* at 856. This is in line with one of the main objectives of NHSL which is to prove that international law is distinct from domestic law, yet is a "system" of law. Tai-Heng Cheng, another scholar who has theorized about this issue, focuses on the pragmatic side of NHSL. Tai-Heng Cheng tries to expand on NHSL, especially its effectiveness concerns. He calls his theory the "justificatory theory of international law" (cf. configurative jurisprudence of McDougal). Cheng surveys different sectors of international law, including arbitration and ICJ rulings on self-defense, to emphasize the role of effectiveness in international law. In his view, calling international law a system of "law" is a political act rather than a legal endeavor, TAI-HENG CHENG, WHEN INTERNATIONAL LAW WORKS, REALISTIC IDEALISM AFTER 9/11 AND THE GLOBAL RECESSION, 22 (2012). According to him, decision-makers are the gate-keepers of international law whose decisions constitute international law. The aim of international law is to promote common values (through shared understandings) and it is attainable if it remains effective: "The justification for international law does not depend on whether it is a law. It depends on whether the international legal system is effective. International law works best when decision-makers interpret prescriptions to balance values and the common good." *Id.* at 32.

contemplated the issue of public policy, yet with a different approach.[68] [69] He distinguishes between matters of public policy that are subjective versus those that remain objective. Arbitral tribunals should enjoy the discretion of reviewing and ruling on matters of public policy that are less established, or in Paulsson's wording, subjective.[70] According to him, we should adopt a two-tiered approach to mandatory norms and public policy values: ordinary norms and overriding mandatory norms.[71] In overriding mandatory norms, stakes of public interest are so high that arbitral determination could be challenged in front of national courts.[72] As I have laid out in another piece, Paulsson's theory lacks a holistic and systemic approach to international arbitration.[73] Even though his theory of public policy is thought-provoking, his classification does not appear to guide us far. It would be a taxing task for tribunals to investigate the instances where the public interest stake is high or "objective."

3. Practical significance

As discussed, the transnationalist school believes in a semi-autonomous arbitral order which requires its own separate transnational public policy. It receives its legitimacy and power from the shared normativity between states and has minimal contact with national legal orders. The statist approach, however, is concerned about the ambiguity and effectiveness of this order. It fears that the introduction of protean concepts such as transnational public policy undermines the new, yet relatively robust, international dispute resolution.

These two approaches have direct practical implications. For instance, in cases in which local courts issue anti-suit injunctions, the reaction of the arbitral tribunal would differ depending on their approach to arbitration.[74] If the arbitral proceeding is part of a transnational order, their autonomous

---

68 Alison Ross, *Seoul Ponders Public Policy*, 7 GLOBAL ARBITRATION REVIEW (June 12, 2012) at http://globalarbitrationreview.com/journal/article/30626/seoul-paulsson-ponders-public-policy

69 Similar to the European approach, Paulsson seems to believe that "the binding force of an international award may be derived... without a specific legal system serving at its foundation," Jan Paulsson, *Arbitration Unbound: Award Detached from the Law of its Country of Origin*, 30 INT'L & COM. L. Q. 358, 368 (1981).

70 JAN PAULSSON, THE IDEA OF ARBITRATION 136–37 (2013).

71 *Id.* at 229.

72 *Id.*

73 Farshad Ghodoosi, Book Note, 39 YALE J. INT'L L. 301 (2014) (reviewing JAN PAULSSON, THE IDEA OF ARBITRATION (2013)).

74 For discussions on anti-suit injunctions in arbitration and various opinions on this topic *see e.g.*, George A. Bermann, *The Use of Anti-Suit Injunctions in International Litigation*, 28 COLUM. J. TRANSNAT'L L. 589 (1990); Gabrielle Kaufmann-Kohler, *How to Handle Parallel Proceedings*, 2 DISP. RESOL. INT'L 110 (2008); Geoffrey Fisher, *Anti-suit Injunctions to Restrain Foreign Proceedings in Breach of an Arbitration Agreement*, 22 BOND L. REV. i (2010).

status grants them the discretion to decide and reject anti-suit injunctions and proceed with the dispute. If, on the other hand, the juridical status of arbitral proceedings emanate from a national legal order—in cases where applicable law is a national law or the tribunal adopts a national law—anti-suit injunctions from the seat of arbitration or the applicable national law courts would be binding for the arbitral tribunal. For instance, in the ICC case no. 10623, the highest court of the seat of arbitration issued an injunction to stay the arbitral proceeding.[75] However, the arbitral tribunal refused to stay the proceeding, citing cases related to international public policy and its impact on the relevance of domestic laws.[76] The tribunal concluded:[77]

> The Arbitral Tribunal accords great respect to the courts of State X, both in their own right and as the courts of the seat. Nevertheless, in this case, we are of the view that it would be improper, in light of our primary duty to the parties, to observe the injunctions issued by those courts, which have already significantly delayed these proceedings, given that they have the effect of frustrating the parties' agreement to submit disputes to international arbitration.[78]

Anti-suit injunctions present an illuminating example of the extent to which theory and practice are intertwined in international arbitration.

Another instance where two theories of arbitration diverge is in enforcement proceedings in national courts. For arbitral awards that have been set aside in the country of origin, courts have adopted two distinct approaches. Courts in countries such as France and Belgium have adopted the approach that even the awards that have been set aside in the country of origin are still enforceable in other fora (if they do not violate the public policy of the secondary fora). The underlying justification for such practice rests on the idea that awards do not *belong* to any national legal order. Hence, if the award has been set aside by any jurisdiction, including the seat of arbitration, the beneficiary of an award can try its chance in other jurisdictions.

The famous French case *Hilmarton v. OTV* (1994) demonstrates the significance of this approach.[79] In this case, the seat of arbitration was in Switzerland and the governing law for the arbitration proceeding was also Swiss law. However, a Swiss appellate court later refused to enforce the

---

75 Case No. 10623 of 2001, 21 ASA Bulletin 82 (2003) (ICC Int'l Ct. Arb.). (The court issued an injunction to stay the arbitration based on Article 332 of the Civil Procedure Code, pending the determination of issues raised by respondent to the court.)
76 *Id.* at 93–95.
77 Interestingly enough, Emmanuel Gaillard was the chairman for the Tribunal.
78 *Id.* at 99.
79 Cour de cassation (Cass.) (Supreme Court for Judicial Matters), Paris, Mar. 23, 1994, 20 Y.B. COMM. ARB. 663 (1995), synopsis also available at http://www.newyorkconvention1958.org/index.php?lvl=notice_display&id=140&seule=1

award because it found the award's reasoning to be "arbitrary."[80] The winning party in the arbitration did not give up. It sought the enforcement of the award in France. The *Cour de cassation* in France did not find enforcing the award to be against Article V(1)(e) because its local laws provided a more favorable right for enforcement.[81] More importantly, and relevant to our discussion, the court argued:

> The award rendered in Switzerland is an *international award* which is not integrated in the legal system of that State, so that it remains in existence even if set aside and its recognition in France is not contrary to international public policy [emphasis added].[82]

In the United States, however, the courts approached the matter differently. In one of the early cases on this issue, *Chromalloy*, the US courts seemed to adopt the French approach.[83] In that case, which was a "first impression" case at the time, the DC District Court accepted the petition to recognize and enforce the award. This was despite the fact that parties chose Egyptian law to be applicable and the Egyptian Court of Appeals nullified the award.[84] Yet, soon afterwards, the courts in the US seemed to change gears. In cases such as *TermoRio*[85] and *Pemex*,[86] the courts shifted to a more territorialist approach by recognizing that the set-aside proceedings occurred in the country of origin. In *TemoRio*, the DC Circuit refused to enforce an award that had been set aside by a Columbian court. The arbitration seat was in Bogotá under the ICC rules. The DC court announced that no violation of due process had occurred in the Colombian court proceeding and therefore no fundamental US public policy was violated.[87] In applying Article V(1)(2), the Court thus credited the judgment of

---

80 Claudia Alfons, Recognition and Enforcement of Annulled Foreign Arbitral Awards 86 (2010).
81 Article V(1)(a) of the New York Convention declares "1. Recognition and enforcement of the award may be refused [if] . . . (a) The parties to the agreement referred to in article II were, under the law applicable to them, under some incapacity, or the said agreement is not valid under the law to which the parties have subjected it or, failing any indication thereon, under the law of the country where the award was made . . . " However, the Court refers to Article VII of the Convention which declares that contracting states should not "deprive any interested party of any right he may have to avail himself of an arbitral award." *Id.*
82 *Hilmarton* case, *supra* note 79; 10 Y.B. Comm. Arb. 663–65.
83 Chromalloy Aeroservices v. Division of Chromalloy Gas Turbine Co, 939 F. Supp. 907 (D. D.C. 1996).
84 *Id.* at 913–14.
85 TermoRio S.A. E.S.P. v. Electranta S.P., 487 F.3d 928 (D.C. Cir. 2007).
86 Corporacion Mexicana de Manenimento Integral, S. del R.L. de C.V. v. Pemex-Exploracion y Production, 962 F. Supp. 2d 642 (S.D.N.Y. 2013).
87 *TermoRio*, 487 F.3d 928, at 939.

the primary state vacating the arbitral award.[88] In other words, the Court believed the award was Columbian and, therefore, Columbian courts were the primary jurisdiction in which to address its validity.

In *Pemex*, the New York Court refused to recognize a nullification judgment of the Mexican Supreme Court. The arbitration seated in Mexico and involved a contractor and a Mexican state-owned energy company. The award was in favor of the contractor. Yet, during the proceedings the Mexican legislature withdrew the authorization granted to the state-owned company to enter into arbitration. The New York Court refused to give effect to the nullification judgment because of a narrow public policy gloss on Article V(1)(e) of the New York Convention.[89] In other words, the Court carved a "public policy exception" into Article V(1)(e) in order to declare that the Mexicans' retroactive application of law violated US public policy.[90] As a result, the Court granted the motion to confirm the award.[91] Therefore, the decision is premised primarily on the public policy of the US, rather than enforcing a nullified award.[92]

The nuances of the cases and opinions regarding anti-suit injunctions and primary fora set-aside decisions are beyond the purview of this piece. Yet, these two examples clearly show the significance and impact of the theory of arbitration on its practice. Another important diverging juncture for these two prevailing theories pertains to their stance on public policy in arbitral proceedings. In the next two chapters, we will closely investigate the issue of transnational public policy in contemporary international litigation. In summary, the transnationalist approach limits the supervening public policy concerns to only those with transnational character. On the other hand, the statist camp does not recognize policies beyond those that emanate from national legal orders. The only caveat for the statist relates to instances where the governing law refers to some form of transnational or international law. We will examine this issue in depth in the next two chapters.

---

88 *Id.* at 939.
89 This decision follows the *Baker Marine* decision (191 F.3d at 197 n. 3) and departs from the stance of the *TermoRio* case on the issue of public policy gloss on Article V(1)(e), *TermoRio*, 487 F.3d 928, at 938–39. For more on this issue, *see* C. Ryan Reetz, *Public Policy and International Construction Arbitration in* CONTEMPORARY ISSUES IN INTERNATIONAL ARBITRATION AND MEDIATION 209, 220–21 (Arthur W. Rovine ed., 2014).
90 *Pemex*, 962 F. Supp. 2d 642, at 656–57.
91 *Id.* at 661.
92 For an in-depth discussion of the US approach to this issue, *see* Marc J. Goldstein, *Annulled Awards in the US Courts: How Primary is "Primary Jurisdiction"?*, 25 AM. REV. INT'L ARB. 19 (2014).

7 Transnational public policy in contemporary international commercial arbitration

> *... it can be said that transnational public policy is jeopardized ... by a hostile behavior against principles which are generally held to be fundamental from an ethical-juridical point of view.*
>
> (Pierre Lalive[1])

> *Public policy changes as public convictions or beliefs change.... Transnational public policy ... is perhaps built on less shifting sands.*
>
> (Alan Redfern[2])

In contemporary international litigation, transnational public policy comes into play in various forms. It is quite a challenging task to understand the notion of transnational public policy and its function amidst a wide range of cases and opinions. This sections aims to prune the existing literature and case law in order to investigate the role of transnational public policy in contemporary international litigation.

The doctrine of public policy, as I discuss elsewhere,[3] deals with a foreign and exogenous element that imposes itself on the legal acts and proceedings and bars them from yielding legal consequences. For example, a court might refuse to enforce a contract that deals with kickbacks. Or, a legal marriage license might encounter enforcement problems in certain states due to its clash with their gay/lesbian public policy. Thus, public policy is distinct from sheer illegality, as the former has an interpretive, protean character while the latter usually can be readily inferred from the face of the law.[4]

---

1 Pierre Lalive, *Ordre public transnational (ou réellement international) et arbitrage international*, REVUE DE L'ARBITRAGE 327, 339 (1984).
2 Alan Redfern, *Comments on Commercial Arbitration and Transnational Public Policy*, ICCA CONGRESS SERIES No.13, 872 (2007).
3 Farshad Ghodoosi, *The Concept of Public Policy in Law: Revisiting the Role of the Public Policy Doctrine in the Enforcement of Private Legal Arrangements*, 94 NEB. L. REV. 685 (2016).
4 The public policy doctrine is concerned with harms to the interests of the public and not necessarily the private interests of parties involved, MAURO RUBINO-SAMMARTANO, INTERNATIONAL ARBITRATION: LAW AND PRACTICE 719 (3d ed., 2014). ("First a distinction

By the same token, transnational public policy refers to a foreign and exogenous element that affects cross-border arbitrations and enforcement of awards. Yet, despite states' public policy doctrines in arbitration and contract law, ambiguities exist regarding the scope, function, and relevance of transnational public policy.[5] As we discussed in the previous section, a group of scholars are dismissive of such a notion, which they believe adds nothing but uncertainty to arbitration. Others find it essential not only in protecting certain values but in making arbitration proceedings and enforcement speedy. In order to find the answer to these challenging issues we need to understand the context in which transnational public policy is used in cross-border litigations.

Any form of public policy inevitably should stem from a legal order. By "legal order," as we know it today, we refer to a coherent set of rules formed that result in converged expectations amongst actors with a certain level of predictability. Having that in mind, there are only two sources from which transnational public policy can emanate.[6] Either arbitral tribunals should consider norms of public policy from national laws or they should consider the international law norms of a mandatory nature. Hence, the discussion is inextricably tied to *what legal order* or *law* should be applicable in each arbitral proceeding. At the next level, the enquiry continues to discover whether superseding norms of another source, be it national or international law, can trump the applicable law of each arbitration proceeding. We will discuss this matter in the first section.

The second stage at which transnational public policy enters into contemporary international litigation is enforcement. Winning parties typically seek to enforce their awards in a specific jurisdiction, at least in the international commercial arbitration context. Relevant to our discussion, the question remains: *which disputes* and *awards* can be enforced in each jurisdiction? More importantly, the question is whether the courts should consider the public policy of the forum, or transnational public policy. This problem will be addressed in the second section.

---

must be made between statutory provisions that *cannot* be derogated from, because they protect private interests against a stronger contracting party, and those that *may not* be derogated from, because they protect the public interest. The latter only form part of public policy.")

5 Professor Catherine Kessedjian finds it "the most difficult part" of inquiry about transnational public policy, Catherine Kessedjian, *Transnational Public Policy* in INTERNATIONAL ARBITRATION 2006: BACK TO BASICS?, ICCA CONGRESS SERIES No. 13, 857, 866 (Albert Jan van den Berg ed., 2007).

6 Generally speaking, some scholars believe that there are in fact four scenarios in which public policy plays a role in international arbitration: "(1) the arbitration agreement may violate public policy; (2) the conduct of the arbitration may violate public policy; (3) the law the arbitrators apply may violate public policy; and (4) enforcement of the award may violate public policy." Hans Smit, *Comments in Public Policy in International Arbitration*, 13 AM. REV. INT'L ARB. 65, 65 (2002).

A. Public policy in international commercial arbitration

1. The complicated picture of choice of law

Choosing the applicable law in each arbitration proceeding is a difficult task. The hard and fast rule here is that a party's chosen law is indisputably applicable in the proceeding.[7] The US Supreme Court finds this rule to be an "indispensable precondition to achievement of the orderliness and predictability essential to any business transaction."[8] For instance, an English and French business partner can sign a contract stipulating New York law to be the applicable law for their contract. In the case of a dispute, and if the contract has an arbitration clause, the arbitrator(s) should apply the law chosen by parties, i.e. New York law.

However, this rather simple scenario might never happen in practice. For one, parties' choices might not be easily discoverable or the contract might be silent on the applicable law. Figure 7.1 shows the possible scenarios in this regard.

The parties either remain silent or specify an applicable law in the contracts. In cases where the parties remain silent, tribunals either search for an implied applicable law or apply the law of the seat of arbitration. In past cases, several tribunals and courts ruled that the law of the place of arbitration served as an implied choice of law for the parties in cases where they remained silent as to the applicable law.[9] In other words, the arbitral tribunals should apply the law of the place of arbitration on the substantive aspect of the dispute as well

---

[7] The UNCITRAL Model Law, adopted in the domestic laws of more than 60 jurisdictions, states: "The arbitral tribunal shall decide the dispute in accordance with such rules of law as are chosen by the parties as applicable to the substance of the dispute . . . ", UNCITRAL Model Law on International Commercial Arbitration, art 28(1) (2012). Similar language exists in article 21 of the ICC rules: "1. The parties shall be free to agree upon the rules of law to be applied by the arbitral tribunal to the merits of the dispute," ICC Arbitration Rules 2014. The same holds true for the international investment law. The ICSID Convention declares: "The Tribunal shall decide a dispute in accordance with such rules of law as may be agreed by the parties," International Center for Settlement of Investment Dispute Convention, art. 42(1); *see* JULIAN D. M. LEW ET AL., COMPARATIVE INTERNATIONAL COMMERCIAL ARBITRATION 414 (2003) ("Unquestionably, party autonomy is the most prominent and widely accepted international conflict of laws rule"); *see also* JULIAN D. M. LEW, APPLICABLE LAW IN INTERNATIONAL COMMERCIAL ARBITRATION 80 (1978); CHRISTOPHER DUGAN ET AL., INVESTOR-STATE ARBITRATION 201 (2008).

[8] Scherk v. Alberto-Culver Co., 417 U.S. 506, 516 (1974).

[9] *See e.g.*, Slovenian Company, Formerly Yugoslav State Enterprise v. Agent (Germany), XXII YBCA 707 (November 15, 1997) (Oberlandesgericht Hamm) (the law of Zurich should apply because the parties selected Zurich as the seat); *Multinational Group A v. State B.*, ICC Case no. 1434, 103 Clunet 978 (1976); *See also* Case No. 2735 of 1997, 104 Clunet 947 (ICC Int'l Ct. Arb.); also in investment law *see e.g.*, Asian Agricultural Products Ltd. (AAPL) v. Democratic Socialist Republic of Sri Lanka, ICSID Case No. ARB/87/3, Award, ¶ 19–24, 17 Y.B.C.A. 106 (1992); *See also* Lawrence Collins, *Arbitration Clauses and Forum Selecting Clauses in the Conflict of Laws: Some Recent Developments in England*, 2 J. MAR. L. & COM. 363, 380 (1971).

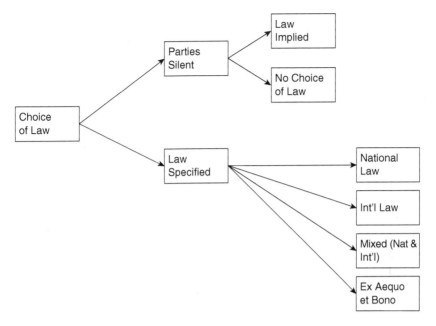

Figure 7.1 Choice of substantive law.

(*qui eligit judicem eligit jus*).[10] This approach does not seem to be prevailing in international arbitration.[11] As stated by an arbitral tribunal, the selection of the place of arbitration "may be influenced by a number of practical considerations that have no bearing on the issue of applicable law."[12]

Currently, two approaches are noticeable: objective and subjective.[13] Under the objective approach—mostly applied in common law jurisdictions—tribunals or courts will look into factors such as the place of performance or the place of enforcement of the contract in order to find the applicable law.[14] On the other hand, under the subjective approach—mostly applied in civil law jurisdictions—tribunals or courts endeavor to discover the true intent of parties regarding the applicable law.[15] As a continuation of the latter approach, several investment tribunals have ruled

---

10 Whoever chooses the forum chooses its law too.
11 D. M. LEW ET AL., *supra* note 7 at 416. ("Today it is no more than another general connecting factor which may be of relevance in the circumstance of the particular case.")
12 Case No. 117 of 1999, fn. 38 (ICC Int'l Ct. Arb.), cited in Sam Luttrell, *An Introduction to Conflict of Laws in International Commercial Arbitration*, 14 INT'L TRADE & BUS. L. REV. 404, 410 (2011) (fn. 27).
13 HEGE ELISABETH KJOS, APPLICABLE LAW IN INVESTOR-STATE ARBITRATION: THE INTERPLAY BETWEEN NATIONAL AND INTERNATIONAL LAW 72–73 (2013).
14 *Id.*
15 *Id.*

that international law should apply where parties do not specify any municipal laws.[16] This theory is called "implied negative choice" and refers to cases where parties deliberately refuse to refer to any national laws so that general principles of international law or some form of transnational law apply.[17]

In cases where parties opt for a clause specifying an applicable law, different scenarios might occur. Either the contract refers to a national law or the clause is a mix of national and international law.[18] International law here refers to any "amorphous bodies of law"[19] at the transnational level, which can be *lex mercatoria*, or international commercial law. Furthermore, it should be remembered that not all national laws and arbitral rules allow parties to opt for more than one legal system.[20] As an alternative to selecting a specific legal system, parties might also stipulate that the tribunal rules be based on fairness and justice following its own judgment.[21]

Moreover, in order to further complicate the picture we should remember that there are at least two laws applicable in each arbitral proceeding: *lex arbitri* and *lex causae*, as shown in Figure 7.2.

Lex arbitri refers to the law governing the procedural aspects of arbitration and the validity of the arbitration agreement. *Lex arbitri* might also be different from the law of situs of arbitration. The latter is sometimes referred to as *lex loci arbitri*, or the seat of arbitration. The New York Convention seems to allow this distinction.[22] *Lex causae* refers to the substantive law governing

---

16 Joseph Charles Lemire v. Ukraine, ICSID Case No. ARB/06/18, Decision on Jurisdiction and Liability, ¶ 111, January 14, 2010. ("Given the parties' implied negative choice of any municipal legal system, the Tribunal finds that the most appropriate decision is to submit the Settlement Agreement to the rules of international law, and within these, to have particular regard to the UNIDROIT Principles"); Case No. 7375 of 1996, 11 INT'L ARB. REP. A1 (ICC Int'l Ct. Arb.). (Ministry of Defense and Support for Armed Forces of the Islamic Republic of Iran v. Westinghouse Electric Corp., Section III.) (Parties' silence is interpreted as "implied negative choice of the Parties . . . in the sense that none of the Parties' national laws should be imposed on any of the Parties.")
17 KJOS, *supra* note 13 at 75.
18 D M LEW ET AL., *supra* note 96, at 418. In *Saudi Arabia v. Arabian American Oil Co.* the tribunal split the contract into parts since several laws governed the contract, Saudi Arabia v. Arabian American Oil Co. (ARAMCO), 27 ILR 117, 166 (1963).
19 D M LEW ET AL, *supra* note 96 at 417.
20 KJOS, *supra* note 13 at 70. The UNCITRAL Secretariat opined that if arbitration laws refer to "rules of law" rather than "law," parties could designate more than one legal system including international law in their contracts, *id*. Many investment treaties as well as the ICSID Convention allow for parties to select both national and international law and principles. For instance, the Tribunal in *Duke Energy v. Ecuador* recognizes that the choice of law is both Ecuadorian law and the principles of international law, Duke Energy Electroquil Partners & Electroquil S. A. v. Ecuador, ICSID Case No. ARB/04/19, Award, ¶ 196 (August 18, 2008), *see also id.* at 71.
21 *See e.g.*, International Centre for Settlement of Investment Disputes—Model Clauses, https://icsid.worldbank.org/ICSID/StaticFiles/model-clauses-en/13.htm#b.
22 Article V(1)(e): "The award has not yet become binding on the parties, or has been set aside or suspended by a competent authority of the country in which, or *under law of which*, the award was made." [Emphasis added.]

Transnational public policy in arbitration 113

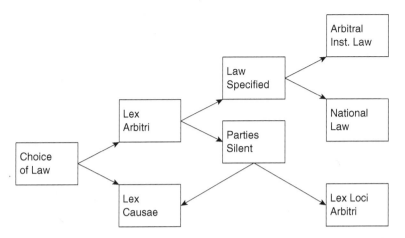

Figure 7.2 Choice of arbitral law.

the contract that includes the arbitration clause. This law governs the rights and obligations of each party and the substance of the dispute. For instance, a contract for the sale of goods between two merchants might include an arbitration clause and an applicable law clause. In this contact, the arbitration clause may refer to British law as the law governing the formation and procedural issues of arbitration, while the applicable law governing the contract may be New York law. The picture can be even more complicated where the parties, as occurs often, leave the law governing arbitration blank in their contracts. In these cases, for the law governing arbitration, the tribunals typically either apply the law of the seat (*lex loci arbitri*) or the law governing the substance of the contract.

2. *Empirical data on the success rate*

In order to build an understanding of arguments that have been based on the grounds of public policy, I surveyed published International Chamber of Commerce [ICC] International Court of Arbitration [ICCA] awards from 1985 to the present time. I used the Kluwer Arbitration database, which gathers its data from the Yearbook of Commercial Arbitration edited and complied b/y Albert Jan van den Berg and other sources.[23] I chose to analyze the ICC awards because of the significance and importance of ICCA in the area and its leading role in the market of resolution of cross-border commercial disputes. I predict that this analysis of ICC awards will provide

---

23 http://www.arbitration-icca.org/publications/yearbook_table_of_contents.html.

a proper representation of the trend in other arbitral institutions due to the leading role of the ICCA.

I conducted a comprehensive search for all issues and arguments which parties or arbitral tribunals (*ex officio*) refer to as "public policy" and which required a decision by the tribunals. In other words, the enquiry was "issue-based" and not "case-based." Normally, each case had one issue related to public policy, but in a couple of cases two public policy issues were raised. Issues raised ranged from constitutional challenges, anti-competition laws, limits on the arbitrability of disputes, anti-suit injunctions, corruption, bribery, trade in influence, state recognition, statute of limitation, agency laws, punitive damages, and so forth.[24] I limited the search from the date January 1, 1985 to January 1, 2015 in order to cover an approximate thirty year span. In the advanced search box, I input these terms in separate searches: "public policy," "*ordre public*," "mandatory rule," and "mandatory law."[25] Only seven cases referred to the terms "mandatory rule" and "mandatory law" and not "public policy."

I identified forty-two arguments and issues involving matters of public policy and I analyzed them based on their impact on the outcome of cases—whether the issue(s) partially or wholly influenced the result of the case.[26] I thoroughly analyzed each case to link the governing law with the public policy arguments and their effects on the outcome of each case. Each case was categorized based on the parties involved, its *lex arbitri* (if applicable), the governing law on the merits, the public policy issue, the result of the case, the reason(s) for acceptance or non-acceptance, and the source of the public policy argument. I used the code number 1 for cases where non-governing law public policy was raised and 2 for cases where governing law public policy was at stake. I assigned the number 3 to those cases in which arbitrators chose a law and made a decision about a public policy matter related to that law. In order to understand the outcomes of the case, I parsed each decision to make sure that the public policy argument was directly linked to the dispute, not simply a rhetorical and unrelated statement. With regard to the coding of the results, if public policy considerations did not affect the outcome of the case in any way I coded the case with the number 1, and if it did affect the case I assigned number 2. Public

---

24 The excel sheet containing a synopsis of all the awards is with the author and will be provided upon request.
25 Only six cases referred to the terms "mandatory rule" and "mandatory law" and not "public policy": 13610 (2006); 8528 (1996); 7047 (1994); 6998 (1994); 7528 (1993); 6379 (1990).
26 The reference numbers of cases that have been used are as follows: 16168 (2013); 13730 (2013); 16655/EC/ND (2011); 16655/EC/ND (2011); 16369 (2011); 13075/DK/RCH/JHN (2006); 11307 (2003); 10947/ESR/MS (2002); 10623 (2001); 9987 (2001); 10973 (2001); 13954 (2010); 14046 (2010); 14792 (2012); 8420 (1996); 8938 (1996); 6197 (1995); 7263 (1994); 8423 (1994); 8445 (1994); 7893 (1994); 7181 (1992); 6474 (1992); 6320 (1992); 6286 (1991); 6752 (1991); 6363 (1991); 5946 (1990); 6248 (1990); 6149 (1990); 5622 (1988); 5485 (1987); 5485 (1987).

Transnational public policy in arbitration 115

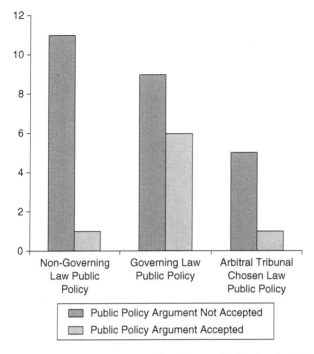

Figure 7.3 Statistics for cases showing applicable laws' public policy.

policy is broadly defined here and might be based on legislation, court decisions, or the general approach of a legal system. Also, this study only focuses on arbitral proceedings and not any ensuing or parallel court proceedings. Figures 7.3 and 7.4 show the outcomes of the analysis:

The main dividing line in each case is the source from which the public policy norm emanates. Parties have either stipulated a governing law for the substance of their dispute or they remain silent. As seen in Figures 7.3 and 7.34, in comparison to "non-governing" law public policy and "arbitral tribunal-chosen" law public policy, there were more cases where "governing law" public policy led to a result in which the public policy argument was accepted. In other words, of fifteen cases in which parties had determined the governing law, six of them successfully influenced the outcome invoking public policy arguments. This accounts for roughly 40% of the cases where governing law was determined and 75% of the instances where the public policy argument altered the outcome of the case partly or wholly. In cases where the governing law is left to the arbitral tribunal to decide, the tribunal accepted the public policy argument in only one case.[27] This

---

27 Case No. 13954 of 2010, 35 Y.B. Comm Arb. 218 (ICC Int'l Ct. Arb.). In the case the parties arranged a choice of law for their contract. Yet, the Tribunal argued that since the dispute

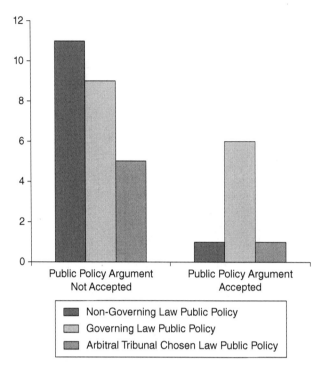

Figure 7.4 Statistics for cases showing public policy arguments in applicable laws.

category included cases where a party argued based on the governing law but the arbitral tribunal applied what it found to be the applicable law to the arbitration clause (*lex arbtiri*).[28] This might lead us to believe that arbitrators tend to avoid "laws" that may be applicable yet would prevent the arbitration proceedings due to their public policy restrictions. The last category belongs to issues raised based on other laws that have connections to the dispute. This could be the laws of countries where the entities are incorporated or contracts are to be performed, the seat of arbitration, etc. Interestingly enough, the success rate in this category is quite small too. In

concerned a party's capacity and power to contract, it lay within its discretion to determine the applicable law on this matter, *id.* at 228. Since the arbitration seat was in Paris and the parties had selected the ICC rules, the Tribunal decided that French law and in particular the French Code of Civil Procedure should be applicable, *id.* Consequently, the Tribunal declared that since the board of directors has not approved the letter of intent, it would be against French public policy to accept it as valid and enforceable, *id.* at 233, 238.

28 *See e.g.*, Case No. 14792 of 2012, 37 Y.B. Comm. Arb. 112. (ICC Int'l Ct. Arb.). In this case the defendant argues that Ukrainian law and public policy prohibited entities other than banks to issue payment guarantees, *id.* at 112. The Tribunal looked at the Swiss law as *lex arbitri* in order to address this issue. *Id.* at 113; Case No. 8420 of 1995, *infra* note 70.

fact, within the time period analyzed in my study, I only found one case in which the mandatory provision of a non-governing law affected the outcome.[29] Even in this case, the tribunal only went as far as accepting that the mandatory rule of the foreign law was relevant and applicable.[30] [31]

This qualitative research shows us the extent to which public policy arguments are effective in international commercial arbitration.[32] For matters involving public policy outside of the governing law, arbitral tribunals do not lend their hands to override governing law rules. It leaves us wondering whether the arguments related to public policy are "hail Mary" arguments, or whether public policy considerations remain largely and disproportionality under-litigated. In other words, this trend can be worrisome considering that the scope of disputes allowed in arbitration has expanded[33] while the success rate of public policy has remained substantially narrow.

The next section will look into how tribunals have employed the term "transnational public policy" to even further limit the relevance of mandatory provisions and public policy considerations.

B. Three approaches to transnational public policy

Finding the applicable law is a challenging process and sometimes is purely subjective. However, the process is even more complicated where supervening rules, so-called mandatory rules, and public policy concerns enter the picture. Unquestionably, the parties' autonomy in designating an

---

29 Case No. 8528 of 1996, 25 Y.B. Comm. Arb. 341 (2000). The case involved a mandatory provision of Turkish law that prohibits entities benefiting from export incentives sharing them with foreign partners, *id.* at 341–42. The applicable law to the merits of the case was Swiss law. Yet, the Tribunal accepted the mandatory nature of the law and that it had to apply the law, *id.* Yet, the Tribunal distinguishes between tax savings and tax benefits and declared that the former can be governed by private contracts such as the contract that is the subject of the dispute, *id.*
30 *Id.*
31 In the context of EU law it seems that some courts believe the arbitration agreement would be null and void if it circumvented mandatory principles of EU law by applying a foreign law, *see* Accenture Ltd v. ASIGRA Inc. [2009] EWHC 2655 and Fern Computer Consultancy Ltd v. Intergraph Cadworx & Analysis Solution Inc. [2014] EWHC 2908 (Ch), *cf.* Case C-126/07 Eco Swiss [1999] EC I-3055. For a discussion of these cases, *see* Kate Davies, Is an Arbitration Agreement "Null, Void" or "Inoperative" If It Applies a Foreign Law Which Does not Give Effect to Mandatory Principles of EU Law?, KLUWER ARB. BLOG, June 16, 2015 at http://kluwerarbitrationblog.com/blog/2015/06/16/is-an-arbitration-agreement-null-void-or-inoperative-if-it-applies-a-foreign-law-which-does-not-give-effect-to-mandatory-principles-of-eu-law/ .
32 This study can be replicated in other leading arbitral institutions cases. Most importantly, juxtaposition of the results here with the results from the ICSID awards—where the governing law is considered to be both international law and the host country's law—would be enlightening.
33 *See e.g.*, Karim Youssef, *The Death of Inarbitrability* in ARBITRABILITY: INTERNATIONAL & COMPARATIVE PERSPECTIVE 47 (Loukas A. Mistelis et al., 2009).

applicable law is not without limits. Considerations related to public life inevitably trump the choice of law by parties.[34] These supervening rules range from embargos, exchange control regulations, and antitrust laws, to corruption, bribery, and violation of public morality.[35] [36] For instance, Swiss law is renowned for its relaxed rules on antitrust matters.[37] Parties, however, cannot derogate their host countries' competition law simply by choosing Swiss law as the applicable law for their contracts.[38]

Yet, the sources from which these supervening elements emanate are scattered and hard to decipher, as is their scope. The application of mandatory rules also occurs frequently in transnational arbitration (in more than 50% of international arbitration cases, according to one study).[39] These trumping elements can derive from national or international law sources depending on the case (its facts, the contract at dispute, the context in which the parties signed the contract, etc.).[40] Tribunals also take into account the mandatory rules of the stipulated substantive law (if any), the place the contract was performed, the place the award will be enforced, the law of the seat of arbitration, the *lex arbitri*, and other potential rules that have connection to the dispute.[41] [42]

---

34 Farshad Ghodoosi, *The Concept of Public Policy in Law: Revisiting the Role of the Public Policy Doctrine in the Enforcement of Private Legal Arrangements*, 94 NEB. L. REV. 685 (2016).
35 CHRISTOPH BRUNNER, FORCE MAJEURE AND HARDSHIP UNDER GENERAL CONTRACT PRINCIPLES: EXCEPTION FOR NON-PERFORMANCE IN INTERNATIONAL ARBITRATION 267–79 (2009).
36 Some issues are typically discussed under the rubric of mandatory rules: embargos, exchange control regulations, competition laws, securities laws, US Racketeer Influenced and Corruption Organizations Act (RICO), carriage of goods by sea, and product liability, *id.* at 267. Some other issues are typically discussed under the category of public policy: "bribe or corrupt government officials, arrangements to smuggle goods in to or out of a particular country, assembling a mercenary army to support an insurrection against a legitimate government, agreement to transport children intended for slavery or under age labour, or to transport and smuggle individuals into another country, supplying armaments to a terrorist organization," D. M. LEW ET AL., *supra* note 7, at 423–24.
37 JEAN-FRANÇOIS POUDRET & SÉBASTIAN BESSON, COMPARATIVE LAW OF INTERNATIONAL ARBITRATION 607 (2007).
38 Several ICC awards recognize that EU competition law should be considered as mandatory rules from which parties cannot derogate, Gordon Blanke, *Antitrust Arbitration Under the ICC Rules* in EU AND US ANTITRUST ARBITRATION: A HANDBOOK FOR PRACTITIONERS 1840 (Gordon Blake & Philip Landoit eds., 2011).
39 Marc Blessing, *Mandatory Rules of Law versus Party Autonomy in International Arbitration*, 14 J. INT'L ARB. 23, 24 (1997).
40 Unlike the position of some scholars, the superseding elements (mandatory rules) of national law have critical consequences for international investment law, KJOS, *supra* note 13 at 262–69. For the supervening role of international law, *see* KJOS, *supra* note 13 at 195–06.
41 POUDRET & BESSON, *supra* note 37 at 609. D M LEW ET AL., *supra* note 7 at 421.
42 In order to identify rules of mandatory nature, some tribunals use the "Special Connection" theory: "(i) the rule in question must be norm of mandatory character; (ii) the rule must

Transnational public policy in arbitration 119

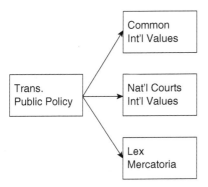

Figure 7.5 Types of transnational public policy.

The combination of the choice of law rules with the supervening elements (mandatory rules) shows the extent to which finding the applicable law is a strenuous task. This complexity, along with the need for predictability, seems to be the functional motive behind the development of the notion of transnational public policy in international arbitration. In summary, the theory behind transnational public policy rests on the proposition that tribunals should only apply supervening rules that bear a truly *transnational* nature.[43] However, I have identified three approaches to transnational public policy in the literature. Understanding these three approaches is critical to deciphering the role of transnational public policy in contemporary international litigation.

1. Common values among nations

The first approach to transnational public policy asserts that tribunals should only apply mandatory rules that are considered to be common international values.[44] In other words, tribunals should apply mandatory rules

---

be such as to impose itself irrespective of the applicable law (intention of application of the enacting state in international situations); (iii) the pre-condition regarding the application as per the particular mandatory rule must be given, considering that the scope of mandatory rules must be construed narrowly; (iv) there must be a close connection between the subject matter of the parties' contract and the jurisdiction or state that promulgated the mandatory rule; (v) examined under a functional analysis, the rule as such must stand a 'rule-of-reason test' (involving in particular the 'shared-valued-test'); (vi) the result must, in view of all circumstances, qualify as an 'appropriate result and (vii) the result must be satisfactory in view of the notion of 'truly international public policy'," BRUNNER, *supra* note 35 at 277 (2009).

43 Pierre Lalive, *supra* note 1 at 339.
44 Following several tribunals, some scholars call this a shared-values test, BRUNNER, *supra* note 35 at 274.

only if there is a "strong and legitimate interest to justify the application of such a law in international arbitration."[45] This means if a tribunal finds a mandatory rule to be only locally relevant, it can ignore the rule, as it does not reach the level of transnational public policy. By submitting their disputes to transnational fora, THE parties subject themselves to mandatory norms which have transnational character.[46]

An illuminating example pertains to cases involving the US Federal Racketeer Influenced and Corrupt Organization Act (RICO).[47] This Act aims to punish activities related to racketeering and corruption.[48] One of the remedies stipulated in the statute is that the injured party "shall recover threefold the damages he sustains and the cost of the suit, including a reasonable attorney's fee."[49] The treble damage remedy has been controversial in international arbitration and tribunals have shown hesitance in applying the Act, even when the applicable law is US law. In an ICC case,[50] the tribunal ignored the applicable law (New York) and denied the claimant the treble damages stipulated in RICO.[51] The tribunal decided it would be inappropriate to apply rules that are parochial and merely related to a specific state interest: "The application of international principles of law offers many advantages. They apply in a unique manner and they are independent of the particularities of any domestic legal system."[52][53] In a similar case, a non-US entity sued a US contractor,[54] alleging that that the defendant delivered steam generators knowing that they had serious corrosion

---

45 Case No. 6320 of 1992, 20 Y.B. Comm. Arb. 98–99 (ICC Int'l Ct. Arb.). In this case, a non-US party sought RICO damages from the defendant, a US party, because of the mandatory nature of the RICO statute and its trumping nature over *lex contractus*. The Tribunal found that no "strong and legitimate interest of the United States" was present in the case to justify the application of the RICO statute, *id*.

46 The proponents of this approach tie it to the idea that arbitration clauses are autonomous from the rest of the contract, *see e.g.*, "It has also been held that in international matters an arbitration clause is allowed per se in virtue of the general principle of its autonomy, an independent rule which gives efficacy to the arbitration clause independent of the law applicable to the contract and to the parties to the contract, with the sole limitation of international public policy, in particular as to the arbitrability of the dispute." Case No. 8938 of 1996, 24 Y.B. Comm. Arb. 177 (1999).

47 US Federal Racketeer Influenced and Corrupt Organization Act (RICO), 18 U.S.C. § § 1961–1968 (1970).

48 *Id*. at § 1962.

49 *Id*. at § 1964.

50 Case No. 8385 of 1995, Clunet 1056 (ICC Int'l Ct. Arb.).

51 JOANNA JEMIELNIAK, LEGAL INTERPRETATION IN INTERNATIONAL COMMERCIAL ARBITRATION 208 (2014). The sole arbitrator decided that application of the RICO statute would be against predictability in international commerce and therefore, "it would be inappropriate to apply rules which solely respond to *state interests*" *Id*. [emphasis added].

52 Translated from French, available at http://www.trans-lex.org/850100.

53 *Id*.; *see also* ANA M. LÓPEZ RODRÍGUEZ, LEX MERCATORIA AND HARMONIZATION OF CONTRACT LAW IN THE EU 127 (2003).

54 Case No. 6320 of 1992, *supra* note 45.

issues.[55] Based on this, the claimant invoked the RICO Act and asked for treble damages.[56] The applicable law was not the US law. However, the reasoning of the tribunal shows us that it adapted what we are considering as the first approach to transnational public policy. They noted that the contractual choice of law is governed by the claiming party's domestic law and not US law. However, it rejected the RICO treble damage provision as a provision specific to the United States that does not constitute a principle of international public policy:

> The conclusion might be different if the national mandatory law would have to be considered as reflecting a principle of international public policy. However, such a qualification cannot be made for the treble damages rule of the RICO statute, whose application is at stake here. In fact, as mentioned above, this rule is specific to the United States and is not found either in other major national legal systems or in international conventions.[57] [58]

2. National courts' international public policy

The second approach gives less discretion to tribunals. Under this theory, the tribunal should investigate whether a rule under the national law amounts to a transnational public policy. In other words, the tribunals can disregard certain mandatory rules only if the courts (and other authorities and sources) in that specific jurisdiction have not found it to be a transnational public policy norm. For example in France, the Cour de cassation placed the emphasis on the *French conception* of international public policy when dealing with international arbitration.[59] French public policy in the

---

55 *Id.* at 64.
56 *Id.*
57 *Id.* at 101.
58 A similar challenge arises in cases where claimants seek punitive damages. For instance, in an ICC case, the Arbitral Tribunal rejected the punitive damage claim because it would violate the public policy of Switzerland, the place where arbitration took place (the seat of arbitration). Interestingly enough, the applicable law was New York Law: "Damages that go beyond compensatory damages to constitute a punishment of the wrongdoer (punitive or exemplary damages) are considered contrary to Swiss public policy, which must be respected by an arbitral tribunal sitting in Switzerland even if the arbitral tribunal must decide a dispute according to a law that may allow punitive or exemplary damages as such . . . ", Case No. 5946 of 1990, 16 Y.B. Comm. Arb. 113 (1991). The Tribunal here did not reject the punitive damage claim based on transnational public policy but on the Swiss public policy ground.
59 France, Cour de cassation, Chambre civile 1, 23 Janvier 1979, 77-12825, quoted in JEMIELNIAK, *supra* note 51 at 196; *see also* the case X (SpA) v. Y (Srl) in Swiss Federal Supreme Court: "[A] Swiss judge, who does not live in a no man's land but in a country attached to a given civilization where certain values are privileged as opposed to others, is led to identify these principles with his own sensitivity and on the basis of the essential values

context of international disputes limits itself to the values that public opinion finds universal.[60] In the language of one scholar, "international public policy ... is confined to violations of really fundamental conceptions of legal order in *the country concerned*."[61] The *Hilmarton* case is an enlightening example of this approach. A French company hired the English company Hilmarton to provide legal and tax help in respect of the former's investment in Algiers. The agreement between the French company and Hilmarton also stipulated that the latter would "coordinate administrative matters" with Algiers officials. In the ensuing arbitration, seated in Geneva, the tribunal found that the agreement violated Algerian mandatory rules (a ban against corruption). The Swiss court, however, rejected the argument by the arbitral tribunal as "arbitrary" and found that such agreement would not violate the public policy of Swiss law.[62] [63] In another case, in which Spanish law was applicable, the arbitral tribunal concluded that "the Spanish Law for Civil Procedure (LEC) is not part of Spanish international public policy."[64] According to the defendant, Spanish Civil Procedure provides certain limitations as to the submission of disputes to alternative fora, including arbitration.[65] The tribunal did not find that the provision would be applicable in "matters of international arbitration"; nor would it form "part of Spanish public policy affecting this arbitration."[66] In another ICC case, the tribunal applied the Swiss law approach to the case because "the attitude of Swiss law towards secret commission agreements is

---

shared by this civilization; his is the Swiss component of the public policy reservation.", X (SpA) v. Y (Srl), ASA Bulletin, vol. 24 no. 3 (2006) 550060 (Swiss Federal Supreme Court) quoted in *id*, at 206.
60 France, Cour de cassation, Chambre civile 2, Mai 25, 1948, Lautour, quoted in *id*.
61 Pieter Sanders, *Commentary in* Sixty Years of ICC Arbitration, A Look at the Future 364 (1984). He believes that "for the sake of international commercial arbitration the distinction between domestic and international public policy is of great importance" and that it is related to the prevailing thought that international public policy is "more restricted" that national public policy, *id*.
62 Bundesgericht [BGer] [Federal Supreme Court] April 17, 1990, Hilmarton v. OTV, Rev. Arb. 315, 320–21 (1993), English translation available at 19 Y.B. Com. Arb. 214, 216 (1994).
63 The Supreme Court of India, in a famous case, *Renusagar*, adopts this approach as well: "[I]n the view of the absence of a workable definition of 'international public policy' it would be difficult to construe public policy as used in Art. V of the New York Convention to mean international public policy. Hence, as used in the Indian Foreign Award Act, the expression means the doctrine of public policy as applied by the courts of India, and must be construed narrowly," Renusagar Power Co. Ltd. v. General Electric Co., Supreme Court of India, October 7, 10 Arb. Int'l 2, 141 (1993).
64 Case No. 5485 of 1987, 14 Y.B. Comm. Arb. 164 (ICC Int'l Ct. Arb.).
65 *Id*. at 157–58. ("Note General Editor Translation of Spanish legal texts provided by Mr. A. Tejada. Art. 57 of the Spanish Code of Civil Procedure (LEC) provides 'Express submission shall be understood as that made by the parties renouncing clearly and definitively their own jurisdiction and precisely designating the judge to whom they may submit'").
66 *Id*. at 163.

in accordance with international public policy."[67] In this case, a party violated its fiduciary duty by promising to influence the principal's decision in exchange for remuneration.[68] Even though Swiss law was the governing law, the tribunal had to show that it was part of the international public policy of Switzerland.[69] [70]

3. Lex Mercatoria

The third approach belongs to those who believe in *lex mercatoria*, or independent transnational commercial laws.[71] This approach stems from the idea that (a) each international arbitration dispute has a transnational element to it, even if parties do not explicitly refer to any international laws or rules; and (b) arbitration is an autonomous legal order that does not owe its juridical stature to any national laws.[72] Proponents of this approach find these two issues to be tied together. They argue that, due to the international character of arbitration in the cross-border context, we need certain transnational rules to preserve such character.[73] As noted by some scholars,

---

67 Case No. 6248 of 1990, 19 Y.B. Comm. Arb. 132 (ICC Int'l Ct. Arb.).
68 "There is no doubt under Swiss law that a contract by which a party bound by distinct fiduciary duties towards a principal promises against a remuneration to secretly influence such principal's decisions for the benefit of the promisee or another party different from the principal, is contrary to *bonos mores*." *Id.* at 131–32.
69 *Id.*
70 Another example is Case No. 8420 in which Italian law was the applicable law to the merits of the dispute. Yet, the Tribunal argued that for the issue of arbitrability, it needed to look at *lex arbitri* or the law governing the arbitration clause. As a result, the Tribunal rejected the relevance of the Italian Code of Civil Procedure, which prescribed that the dispute should be handled by the Italian courts. The Tribunal argued that the "wording of Arts 409 and 413 of CCP [Italian Code of Civil Procedure] showed no indication of fundamental legal principles that would take precedence over Art. 177 PILA [Swiss Private International Law Act]." Case No. 8420 of 1996, Y.B. Comm. Arb. 328–29 (ICC Int'l Ct. Arb.).
71 For a discussion on *lex mercatoria, see generally*, KLAUS PETER BERGER, THE CREEPING CODIFICATION OF THE LEX MERCATORIA (1999); Alex Stone Sweet, *The New Lex Mercatoria and Transnational Governance*, 13 J. OF EUROPEAN PUB. POLICY 627 (2006). For a criticism on the application of *lex mercatoria* in international commercial arbitration *see* W. MICHAEL REISMAN, SYSTEMS OF CONTROL IN INTERNATIONAL ADJUDICATION AND ARBITRATION 134–39 (1992). ("*Lex mercatoria* is a claim by certain members of the business community and arbitrators to break free of that process and to determine, for themselves and often on a case-by-case and sometimes ex post facto basis, what law and policy they will apply, without regard to the interests of the territorial communities which may thereby be affected.")
72 JEMIELNIAK, *supra* note 51 at 203; *See also* K. Lipstein, *Conflict of Laws before International Tribunals: A Study in the Relation between International Law and Conflict of Laws*, 29 TRANSACTIONS OF THE GROTIUS SOCIETY: PROBLEMS OF PEACE AND WAR, PAPERS READ BEFORE THE SOCIETY IN THE YEAR 1943, 51, 62 (1943) (". . . international tribunals possess no *lex fori* in matters of private law. The *lex fori* of international tribunals consists of international law as developed by custom and treaties").
73 Emmanuel Gaillard, *Thirty Years of Lex Mercatoria: Towards the Selective Application of Transnational Rules*, 10 ICSID REV. 208, 223 (1995).

124 *Transnational public policy in arbitration*

traditionally such rules are only complementary to the applicable law. From 1960 onwards, some scholars opined that such transnational rules are autonomous and independent from national laws.[74] Consequently, tribunals should take into account public policy stemming from such autonomous transnational legal order.[75][76] Under this approach, the mere designation of an international dispute resolution mechanism in a contract automatically subjects it to transnational rules.[77]

An example for this approach is an ICC arbitration case between a Brazilian and an American party in which Brazilian law was the applicable law.[78] The Brazilian party objected to the arbitration proceedings, arguing that the Brazilian Constitution prohibited such arbitration proceedings[79] as being against Brazilian public policy.[80] The tribunal, however, rendered a decision based on transnational public policy considerations, stating that such provisions would be unacceptable when applied to international commercial contracts.[81][82] In a similar case, an ICC arbitral tribunal refused to

---

74 Gilles Cuniberti, *Three Theories of* Lex Mercatoria, 52 COLUM. J. TRANSNAT'L L. 369, 373–74 (2013). Some scholars believe that *lex mercatoria* does not have practical significance anymore, Christopher R. Drahozal, *Contracting Out of National Law: An Empirical Look at the New Law Merchant*, 80 NOTRE DAME L. REV. 523, 523 (2005).

75 "As they are not restricted by any one legal system, arbitrators are free to retain a truly transnational conception of international public policy," Gaillard, *supra* note 73, at 222.

76 Interestingly enough, these scholars argue "most arbitrators have common ethics and common notions of how business should be conducted. That leads them in the same direction," Lalive, *supra* note 1 at ¶ 104, quoting Professor Lando.

77 "[One] process for the internationalization of a contract consists in inserting a clause providing that possible differences which may arise in respect of the interpretation and the performance of the contract shall be submitted to arbitration," TOPCO/CALASIATIC, January 19, 1977, Award, ¶ 44 fn. 53, quoted in Kjos, *supra* note 13 at 75; *see also* Jaenicke, *The Prospects for International Arbitration: Disputes Between States and Private Enterprises* in INTERNATIONAL ARBITRATION: PAST AND PROSPECTS 155, 158 (A.H.A. Soons ed., 1990) (arguing that reference to international dispute resolution automatically subject the contract and dispute to international law).

78 Case No. 4695 of 1984, 11 Y.B. Comm. Arb. 149 (ICC Int'l Ct. Arb.) (Parties from Brazil, Panama, and USA v. Party from Brazil, Interim Award).

79 "The law cannot exclude from consideration by Judicial Authorities any infringement of individual right." According to the defendant's expert, "this constitutional guarantee of access to judicial resolution of disputes is a fundamental public policy of Brazil." *Id.* at 155.

80 *Id.* at 155–56.

81 *Id.* Surprisingly, the Tribunal went further to determine a good policy for Brazil as well: "A country like Brazil, more and more involved in the fabric of international trade, both an importer and as an exporter, not just raw materials, but of manufactured products as well, cannot place itself in a position of 'splendid isolation'"; "A further confirmation of the fact that the recognition and enforcement of arbitration clauses in international commercial contracts is not against Brazil public policy but, on the contrary, in full conformity with it," *id.* at 156.

82 Cases involving corruption have commonly invoked international public policy, *see e.g.*, Case No. 5622 of 1988, 19 Y.B. Comm. Arb. 114 (ICC Int'l Arb.) ("In fact, the Law of Algeria lays down a general principle which must be respected by all legal systems wishing to fight corruption. This is why the violation of this Law, which concerns

stay the arbitration pending a proceeding related to a constitutional challenge before the Ecuadorian courts.[83] Despite the fact that the governing law was Ecuadorian law, the tribunal found it against "international public policy" to give international arbitration such a secondary status to national courts.[84] A similar stance was taken regarding the Iranian constitutional constraint on arbitration. In ICC Case No. 3896, the Tribunal invoked "a general principle, which today is universally recognized" to reject the argument that the arbitration proceeding was invalid because it did not meet Iranian constitutional requirements.[85] In another case, the French Court of Appeals found that, based on the "principles of international arbitration" and the European Convention on Human Rights, it was correct for the court system to help constitute an arbitral body.[86] In this case, one party refused to appoint its arbitrator while the agreement was silent on this issue.

---

international public policy, is contrary to the notion of morality based on Art. 20(1) CO, which is part of Swiss public policy); Case No. 1110 of 1963, Y.B. Comm. Arb. 47 (ICC Int'l Arb.) (The Sole Arbitrator declined his jurisdiction in this case, because "a case like this, involving such gross violations of good morals and international public policy, can have no countenance in any court either in the Argentine or in France or, for that matter, in any other civilised country, nor in any arbitral tribunal"); *See also* Case No. 8891 of 1998, J.D.I. Clunet 4/2000, 1076 (ICC Int'l Arb.); Case No. 3913 of 1981 in COLLECTION OF ICC ARBITRAL AWARDS 1974–1985, 497, 562 (Sigvard Jarvin & Yves Derains eds., 1994) (ICC Int'l Arb.).

83 Case No. 10947/ESR/MS of 2002, 22 ASA Bulletin 308, 332 (ICC Int'l Ct. Arb.).

84 "We acknowledge that the Ecuadorian Courts are well placed to know and correctly apply Ecuadorian law. We consider that, all things being equal, this weighs in favour of a stay being granted. However, to grant a stay now until the final resolution of the Nullity Proceeding simply for this reason (notwithstanding that we have decided that we have jurisdiction, were first seized and that the other requirements of article 9 of the LDIP are not made out), would be to reduce international arbitration to second rank status. We do not consider that this is required (directly or by analogy) by the decision in the *Fomento* case. On the contrary, we consider that acting in a way which gives international arbitration such a status would run counter to international public policy," *id.* at 330.

85 "It is superfluous to add that there is a general principle, which today is universally recognized in relations between states as well as international relations between private entities (whether the principle be considered a rule of international public policy, an international trade usage, or a principle recognized by public international law, international arbitration law or *lex mercatoria*), whereby the Iranian state would in an event—even if it had intended to do so which is not the case—be prohibited from reneging on an arbitration agreement entered into by itself or, previously, by a public entity such as AEIO," Case No. 3896 of 1982, 111 Clunet 58 (1984) (Framatome v. Iranian Agency of Atomic Energy). A similar argument can be found in Case No. 1939 of 1971, 1973 Rev. Arb. 122, 145 (1973). (Italian Company v. African state-owned entity: "International Public Policy would be strongly opposed to the idea that a public entity, when dealing with foreign parties, could openly, knowingly, and willingly, enter into an arbitration agreement, on which its co-contractor would rely, only to claim subsequently, whether during the arbitral proceedings or on enforcement of the award, that its own undertaking was void.")

86 The French Court decision is cited in the judgment of First Civil Court of Switzerland in the judgment of January 10, 2013, available at http://www.globalarbitrationreview.com/cdn/files/gar/articles/10_janvier_2013_4A_146_2012l.pdf.

126 *Transnational public policy in arbitration*

Based on international public policy and the denial of the justice doctrine, the Paris Court of Appeals appointed that party's arbitrator.[87][88]

Another fascinating case pertains to piercing the corporate veil. X, a company incorporated in Maine, had a contract with Y, a Belgian company, to provide know-how and services to Y for the construction of a plant in Bulgaria.[89] Company Y became insolvent and the question for the arbitrator was whether the corporate veil of the parent company, Z Company, could be lifted.[90] The sole arbitrator decided that the applicable law for the contract (New York) would not govern this issue because it involved a third party, i.e. Y.[91] The arbitrator also rejected the notion that the law of the place of arbitration was pertinent, because the place of arbitration "is often chosen with neutrality concerns in mind and does not have any particular connection to the parties."[92] The tribunal, then, proceeded to apply the law that "best fits the need of the international business community" which it found to be *lex mercatoria*:[93]

> Applying international principles offers many advantages. They can be applied in uniform fashion and are independent from the particularities of each national law. They take into account the needs of international relations and allow a fruitful exchange between systems that are sometimes overly linked to conceptual distinctions and those that are seeking a pragmatic and fair solution to specific cases. It thus

---

87 *Id.*

88 Some tribunals refuse to apply *lex mercatoria* or UNIDRIOT Principles: in ICC Case No. 4650, the Tribunal refused to apply *lex mercatoria* even absent parties' agreement as to the applicable law, Case No. 4650 of 1985, 12 Y.B. Comm. Arb. 110–11 (ICC Int'l Ct. Arb.). In another ICC case, the Tribunal invoked Article VII of the Geneva Convention to declare that arbitrators should apply a certain law and not *lex mercatoria* or UNIDROIT principles, Case No. 9419 of 1998 (ICC Int'l Ct. Arb), available at http://www.unilex.info/case.cfm?pid=2&do=case&id=664&step=FullText. In ICC Case No. 5835, the Tribunal rejected the respondent's argument that, employing the implied negative choice method, the national laws of neither party should be applicable. Instead the Tribunal applied Kuwaiti law, which it believed had the closest connection to the dispute, while taking into account "principles generally applicable in international commerce," Case No. 5835 of 1996 (ICC Int'l Ct. Arb.) available at http://www.unilex.info/case.cfm?pid=2&do=case&id=654&step=FullText.

89 Case No. 8385 of 1995 cited in JEAN-JACQUES ARNALDEZ ET AL., COLLECTION OF ICC ARBITRAL AWARDS. 1996–2000 474, 562–63 (2003).

90 *Id.*

91 *Id.* at 563.

92 *Id.*

93 The arbitrator briefly looked over laws of New York and Belgian and quickly concluded that these two legal systems, if applicable, would reach the same result: "Even though the tribunal considers that it is preferable to apply the principles of international commerce dictated by the needs of the international market, it comes to the conclusion that the result is the same regardless of the application of New York Law, Belgian Law or of international principles," *id.* at 564.

constitutes a unique and ideal opportunity to apply what is increasingly referred to as *lex mercatoria*.[94]

To briefly conclude, the notion of transnational public policy emerged out of a need for predictability and speed in cross-border litigations.[95] As we discussed, the motive underlying all the intellectual endeavors and tribunal decisions seems to be directed towards *limiting* the scope and intrusion of national public policy.[96] [97] As some tribunals have expressly declared, "the only restriction to be observed by the arbitrator is that of international public policy."[98] If fully adhered to, this approach leads to the undermining of national public policy and legal orders. In other words, transnational public policy acts as a tool for tribunals to disregard what they deem to be parochial in an otherwise applicable rule of a national law. This trend is worrisome, especially considering the fact that increasingly the reviewing function of national courts has diminished.

Yet, only in two circumstances might it be legally correct for arbitral tribunals to resort to transnational public policy:

1   The relevant national law allows for arbitral tribunals to take into consideration mandatory rules as well as trump public policy only if they are truly transnational.
2   Parties allow the tribunals to decide the case based on *amiables compositeurs* or *ex aequo et bono*, meaning based on fairness and justice.[99]

However, even in these two cases, transnational public policy still remains very amorphous and indeterminate. On the one hand, the test to discover

---

94   *Id.* The Tribunal referred to Dow Chemical v. Isover Saint Gobain (ICC Case No. 4131 of 1982) and Westland Helicopters Limited v. AOI, etc., (ICC Case No. 38791/AS) as precedents, which lifted the corporate veil invoking international principles, *id.* at 565.
95   "To compromise the principle by permitting the arbitrators to have regard to transnational principles of public policy introduces an element of discretion which could do much to undermine the certainty which is so essential to international commerce," Michael Pryles, *Reflections on Transnational Public Policy*, 24 J. INT'L ARB. 1, 6 (2007).
96   Professor Catherine Kessedjian enumerates the reasons that render it necessary for arbitrators to apply transnational public policy. First, the scope and subject matter of disputes referred to arbitration is ever increasing. Second, courts are reluctant to review awards based on public policy. Therefore, "it would be a disservice to the parties, to the arbitration process and to society at large to say that arbitrators can only look at issues which have been posed by the parties." Catherine Kessedjian, *supra* note 5 at 861–63.
97   The same stance is taken in investment arbitration: "Arbitral tribunals should therefore pay little, if any, heed to arguments from the host country that rely on their own national law to override a rule or principle of transnational public policy," Hunter Martin & Gui Conde Silva, *Transnational Public Policy and its Application in Investment Arbitrations*, 4 J. WORLD INVESTMENT 367, 372 (2003).
98   Case No. 8420 of 1996, *supra* note 70 at 333.
99   JEMIELNIAK, *supra* note 51 at 204; W. Michael Reisman, *Law, International Public Policy (So-called) and Arbitral Choice in International Commercial Arbitration* in INTERNATIONAL ARBITRATION 2006: BACK TO BASICS? 849, 851 (Albert Jan van den Berg ed., 2008).

transnational public policy remains a vague test (searching for common values across various legal systems). On the other hand, it is not clear which *legal order* tribunals try to protect by applying the notion of transnational public policy in these two instances.

C. Transnational public policy in enforcement

Public policy plays a major role in the enforcement of arbitral awards. The discussion on the substance of this notion is not different from choice of law. However, enforcement merits a separate discussion for several reasons:

1 Several international instruments regarding arbitration, including the New York Convention, explicitly refer to public policy as a ground for refusal for enforcement.[100]
2 Public policy, and for that matter transnational public policy, enter the scene of arbitration at the very end of the process (unlike finding the applicable law and overriding mandatory rules, which occur during the arbitral proceedings).
3 The discretion to discern public policy falls squarely within the authority of national courts (versus applying the mandatory rules which are conducted by arbitral tribunals).

Many arbitral awards merely meet national courts at the end of the arbitral process, which is the enforcement stage. Courts lend their authority to render arbitral awards enforceable provided that the awards do not offend their public policy. Since the encounter between arbitral awards and courts in the context of international arbitration is quite brief, national courts have shown a tendency to apply a *limited* version of public policy. This restricted approach is what is often called transnational public policy, in which the courts apply certain aspects of their domestic norms that they deem appropriate for the international setting. The French courts are at the forefront of this approach. In *Grands Moulins de Strasbourg*, the French Court of cassation declared that "international public policy . . . is a less strict notion of public policy than the notion applied by . . . French domestic law."[101]

However, this trend is noticeable in other jurisdictions as well. For instance, in the United States, the courts have resorted to the notion of "international comity" on various occasions to demonstrate that the limited

---

100 Convention on the Recognition and Enforcement of Foreign Arbitral Awards, art. v(2)(b), June 10, 1958, 330 U.N.T.S. 3.
101 Sté Grands Moulins de Strasbourg v. Cie Continentale France, Court of cassation (France) March 15, 1988, Y.B. Com. Arb. 129 (1991); *See also*, Sté de Telecommunications Internationales du Camerun v. France Télécom, Court of Appeal, Paris, January 16, 2003, Rev. Arb. 369 (2004).

aspects of domestic policies are applicable in the international context.[102] In other cases, for example in the *Ameropa AG* case, courts have emphasized that the "national policy is not synonymous with public policy."[103] In another case, the Southern District of Texas took a much narrower approach in the context of enforcement for kickbacks in contracts. The District Court did not find providing kickbacks offensive to the "most basic notions of morality and justice" (this phrase is used to gauge the parameters of public policy in enforcement of arbitral awards in many US cases).[104]

In these cases, the courts made it clear that the public policy doctrine cannot be the avenue for courts to review the substance of awards. Inevitably, courts have to take a more nuanced approach to supervening public policy elements in order to maintain a limited reviewability for courts. Also, due to the increasing importance of international arbitration, courts in various jurisdictions aim to convey that their jurisdiction is "arbitration-friendly."[105] This is also partly due to the fact that arbitral tribunals should consider the public policy of the place of enforcement, if it can be determined or predicted during the arbitral proceedings.[106]

To conclude, public policies emanate from a legal order. Parliaments or other relevant authorities enact laws in order to protect the public life shaped in a certain geographic location. No cross-border and systemic public sphere exists (yet) at the transnational level. Even if we believe that some form of transnational legal order exists, there is no authoritative body determining or discovering the policies of such legal order. The accumulation of the shared public policy of states simply leads to an imposition of certain policies of a handful of states. More importantly, domestic public policy at times aims to control market behavior by imposing restrictions and policies from manufacturing to consumption. This is in contrast with the proponents of transnational public policy who would seem to dictate certain parameters of globalization (e.g., *lex mercatoria*) via such a vague notion.

---

102 *See generally* Joel R. Paul, *The Transformation of International Comity*, 71 LAW & CONTEMP. PROBS. 19 (2008).

103 Ameropa AG (Switzerland) v. Havi Ocean Co. LLC (UAE), 2011 WL 570130, 1, 3 (S.D. New York, 2011) (rejecting that the sanction regime against Iran would constitute a public policy ground based on which the award can be set aside). The Court followed another similar case in which a similar argument was raised related to the Cuban sanctions regime, Belship Navigation v. Sealift, 1995 WL 447656, 1, 7 (S.D. New York, 1995).

104 Tamimi Global Company Limited v. Kellogg Brown & Root LLC et al., US District Court, Southern District of Texas, House Division, 2011 WL 1831719, 1, 3 (S.D. Texas, 2011).

105 *See generally* Chi Manjiao, *Is the Chinese Arbitration Act Truly Arbitration–Friendly: Determining the Validity of Arbitration Agreement under Chinese Law*, 4 ASIAN INT'L ARB. J. 104 (2008); Vasudha Sharma & Pankhuri Agarwal, *Rendering India into an Arbitration Friendly Jurisdiction-Analysis of the Proposed Amendments to the Arbitration and Conciliation Act, 1996*, 3 N.U.J.S. L. REV. 529 (2010).

106 Derains, Barraclough, and Waincymer are among the scholars who believe that arbitral tribunals should consider the public policy of the place of enforcement, JEMIELNIAK, *supra* note 51 at 202.

130 Transnational public policy in arbitration

As we also saw, transnational public policy acts as a limiting factor on national public policy in both choice of law and enforcement. Yet, at least at the arbitral level, the method for applying limited or truly transnational public policy remains highly vague and subjective. Some scholars believe that when parties choose a legal system they do not intend to apply it in its *entirety*.[107] Others believe that the parties not only opt for the substantive rules of a legal system but for its policies as well.[108] Yet, we should recall, in the discussion of public policy, the *intent* of parties is the least relevant issue. In fact, mandatory rules—public policy as other supervening rules—aim to limit the intent of parties and not the opposite. Parties' intent cannot restrict the application of the mandatory nature of certain rules even in the international setting. If national legal orders decide to limit the application of their public policy, or parties opt for an amorphous legal order (such as *lex mercatoria*) discussion of transnational public policy becomes relevant. Yet, even in these scenarios, the supervening elements of international law, the seat of arbitration, and the place of enforcement limit the choice of parties.

---

107 POUDRET & BESSON, *supra* note 37 at 609.
108 Reisman, *supra* note 99 at 850 (" . . . the applier, whether judge or arbitrator, must view the prescriptions which he or she is called upon to apply not as black-letter rules but as authoritative communications conveying information about (i) the policy or policies to be achieved as well as (ii) an indication of the range of circumstances in which those policies are to be applied").

8 The development of transnational public policy in international law

So far, we have reviewed the notion of transnational public policy from various angles. We started by looking at the history of this notion and then analyzed it based on the two main theories of international arbitration. In the last chapter, we carefully examined the practical implications of transnational public policy in today's transnational litigation. In this chapter we aim to analyze the substance of such notion and its conceptual framework. In other words, the question still remains as to what constitutes the *substance* of transnational public policy. This chapter first analyzes the more established norms, such as *jus cogens*, human rights, and norms against corruption. The last part predicts new fronts of public policy in today's international law.

A. Established norms

1. Jus cogens

Jus cogens is the most widely-known yet most controversial and discussed concept in international law.[1] Due to the variety of interpretations, it has proven to be an almost impossible task to pin down its boundaries and applications. Certain norms are believed to fall under "easy cases" of *jus cogens*. For instance, the Third Restatement of the Foreign Relations Law of the United States enumerates eight prohibitions that ostensibly fall within the category of preemptory norms.[2] In public international law, a

---

1 *See e.g.*, Alfred Verdross, *Jus Dispositivum and Jus Cogens in International Law* 60 AM. J. INT'L L. 55 (1966); Hilary Charlesworth & Christine Chinkin, *The Gender of Jus Cogens*, 15 HUM. RTS. Q. 63 (1993); Nicholas Onuf & Richard Birney, *Peremptory Norms of International Law: Their Source, Function and Future* 4 DENV. J. INT'L L. & POL'Y 187 (1974); GENNADIĬ MIKHAĬLOVICH DANILENKO, LAW MAKING IN THE INTERNATIONAL COMMUNITY 211–52 (1993); the Vienna Convention refers to peremptory norms of general international law (jus cogens), Vienna Convention on the Law of Treaties, art. 53, May 23, 1969, 18232 U.N.T.S. 332 (1980).
2 Section 702: "A state violates international law if, as a matter of state policy, it practices, encourages, or condones (a) genocide (b) slavery or slave trade (c) the murder or causing the disappearance of individual (d) torture or other cruel, inhuman, or degrading treatment or punishment (e) prolonged arbitrary detention (f) systemic racial discrimination."

consensus could be inferred on the prohibition of use of force as *jus cogens*.³ Yet, the penumbra of the notion of *jus cogens* has proved to be overbearing, which in turn has created strong skeptics amongst scholars.⁴ The purpose of this piece, however, is not to review the expansive literature on *jus cogens*. It aims to comprehend the role of grundnorms such as *jus cogens* in today's international litigation.

The idea behind *jus cogens* seems to be on a par with transnational public policy. Both concepts signify overarching norms that have the normative authority to suspend routine effects of treaties, contracts, and obligations.⁵ In other words, both notions are designed structurally to create a "state of exception" in the Carl Smittian sense.⁶ They also both act as a metanorm to create a hierarchy without which a legal system would not exit. The vagueness associated with *jus cogens* and transnational public policy contributes to their structural function. As Anthony D'Amato has noted, a "lack of content is far from disabling for a protean supernorm."⁷ For him "the sheer ephemerality of *jus cogens* is an asset, enabling any writer to christen any ordinary norm of his or her choice as a new *jus cogens* norm, thereby in one stroke investing it with magical power."⁸

Putting aside his pejorative tone on the scholarship on *jus cogens*, I would like to dwell on the word "enabling" in his discussion. Vague concepts such as *jus cogens*, public policy, justice, etc. are enabling speech acts that foster a temporary normative hierarchy in order to simulate the sovereign role of the "state of exception" in international law. *Jus cogens*, similar to transnational public policy, is a myth; yet it is a myth or fiction without which international law, or, to be more precise, public international law, would survive. The notion of "public" is inevitably intertwined with the hierarchy of norms and the state of exception. Furthermore, unlike the plethora of academic discussions attributing *jus cogens* to natural law, following the "enabling" logic we realize that positive international law is dependent on the vague grundnorms such as *jus cogens*. In a legal system such as international

---

3 Nico Schrijver, *Challenges to the Prohibition to Use [Of] Force: Does the Straightjacket of Article 2(4) UN Charter Begin to Gall Too Much?* in THE SECURITY COUNCIL AND THE USE OF FORCE 31, 41 (Niels Blokker & Nico Schrijver eds., 2005); W. Michael Reisman, *Law, International Public Policy (So-called) and Arbitral Choice in International Commercial Arbitration* in INTERNATIONAL ARBITRATION 2006: BACK TO BASICS? 849, 855 (Albert Jan van den Berg ed., 2008) ("the only *jus cogens* upon which the drafters of the Vienna Convention could agree was the prohibition of the use of force in Article 2(4) of the UN Charter.").
4 George Schwarzenberger, *International Jus Cogens?* 43 TEX. L. REV. 455, 455–56 (1964). ("The evidence of international law on the level of unorganized international society fails to bear out any claim for the existence of *jus cogens*.")
5 *Id.*
6 GIORGIO AGAMBENM, STATE OF EXCEPTION 1–2 (2005).
7 Anthony D'Amato, *It's a Bird, It's a Plane, It's a Jus Cogens*, 6 CONN. J. INT'L L. 1, 1 (1990).
8 *Id.*

law where "legitimacy"[9] is pivotal, the positivism/natural law dichotomy seems to disappear, leaving an intertwined body of norms. The disappointing performance of the International Court of Justice vis-à-vis *jus cogens* could be explained by this approach.[10] In addition to the political dynamics involved in each case, the norm *jus cogens* is employed by the Court and parties to create a hierarchy and system of law. Yet, the Court has almost never ruled on it.[11]

2. Human rights

Unlike *jus cogens*, human rights norms are more graspable with a strong presence in various regimes of international law. The Permanent Court of International Justice and the International Court of Justice have grappled with human rights issues in several cases,[12][13] adopting various methods in

---

9 THOMAS FRANCK, THE POWER OF LEGITIMACY AMONG NATIONS 15–18 (1990).
10 *See e.g.*, Application of the Convention on the Prevention and Punishment of the Crime of Genocide Case (Bosnia & Herzegovina v. Yugoslavia) 1996 I.C.J. 595 (July 11); Jurisdictional Immunities of the State (Germany v. Italy, Greece Intervening) 2012 I.C.J. 99 (Feb. 3).
11 However, a fine line exists between *jus cogens* and transnational public policy. Theoretically, *jus cogens* are derived from customary international law. Transnational public policy, on the other hand, is constituted by the "public policy" of states, which have transnational effects and converge in international law practice. In short, *jus cogens* are custom-based while transnational public policy is legislation-based. Furthermore, transnational public policy seems to have a procedural component as it is related to the last stage of each dispute. In a few instances, the International Court of Justice seems to conflate these two notions in its analysis of *jus cogens*. For instance, in *Germany v. Italy* the Court did not find that *jus cogens* norms could trump state immunity because the latter is a procedural matter: "Moreover, as the Court has stated…, the law of immunity is essentially procedural in nature." Jurisdictional Immunities of the State (Germany v. Italy, Greece Intervening), *supra* note 10 at ¶ 58.
12 *See e.g.*, cases: Case Concerning the Barcelona Traction, Light and Power Company (Belgium v. Spain), 1970 I.C.J. Rep. 3 (Feb. 5); Corfu Channel Case, 1949 I.C.J. Rep. 4 (April 9); South West Africa, Second Phase, (Ethiopia v. S. Africa; Liberia v. S. Africa), 1966 I.C.J. Rep. 6 (July 18), United States Diplomatic and Consular Staff in Tehran Staff (US v. Iran), 1979 I.C.J. Rep. 10 (December 15); Military and Parliamentary Activities in and against Nicaragua (Nicaragua v. US, 1986 I.C.J. 14 (June 27); East Timor (Portugal v. Australia), 1995 I.C.J. 90 (June 30); Legality of Use of Forces (Yugoslavia v. US), 1999 I.C.J. 916 (June 2); Arrest Warrant (Dem. Rep. Congo v. Belgium), 2002 I.C.J. Rep. 3 (April 11). *See generally* SHIV BEDI, THE DEVELOPMENT OF HUMAN RIGHTS LAW BY THE JUDGES OF THE INTERNATIONAL COURT OF JUSTICE (2007).
13 For a discussion on human rights in the International Court of Justice, *see* GENTIN ZYBERI, THE HUMANITARIAN FACE OF THE INTERNATIONAL COURT OF JUSTICE, ITS CONTRIBUTION TO INTERPRETING AND DEVELOPING INTERNATIONAL HUMAN RIGHTS AND HUMANITARIAN RULES AND PRINCIPLES (2008); Rosalyn Higgins, *Human Rights in the International Court of Justice*, 20 LEIDEN J. INT'L L. 745 (2007); Nigel Rodley, *Human Rights and Humanitarian Intervention: The Case-Law of the World Court*, 38 INT'L & COM. L.Q. 321 (1989); Stephen Schwebel, *Human Rights in the World Court* in INTERNATIONAL LAW IN TRANSITION: ESSAYS IN MEMORY OF JUDGE NAGENDRA SINGH 267 (Raghunandan Swarup Pathak ed., 1992); Stephen Schwebel, *The Treatment of Human Rights and of Aliens in the International Court of*

each of these cases.[14] Yet, they have applied what I like to call the *gradational method* to the norms of human rights. By this term, I mean that they weigh various norms and interests at play when dealing with human rights matters. The two Courts have repeatedly mentioned that many of these norms are temporal and subject to the development of international law.[15]

In the context of international dispute resolution, tribunals have shown reluctance to enter into issues related to human rights.[16] In two situations, the issues of human rights are discussed in investment law. I should disclaim that I am not discussing human rights matters, such as the right to property and expropriation, that fall squarely and explicitly within the purview of investment arbitration. Given our discussion on transnational public policy, the aim is to focus on other regimes that might constitute *public policy* or *ordre public* in international dispute resolution.

In the first category, distressed countries, mainly Argentina, have pled human rights issues in the cases brought against them by investors. Argentina argued that the emergency measures it took in the wake of its economic depression (2001–2002) were critical to protect the fundamental human rights and *jus cogens* of its people.[17] In other words, Argentina's argument rested on the proposition that the human rights obligations of states trump their investment obligations. With the exception of the *Continental Casualty* tribunal,[18] several tribunals disagreed with Argentina's human rights

---

Justice in FIFTY YEARS OF THE INTERNATIONAL COURT OF JUSTICE: ESSAYS IN HONOUR OF SIR ROBERT JENNINGS (Vaughan Lowe & Malgosia Fitzmaurice eds., 1996); SHIV BEDI, THE DEVELOPMENT OF HUMAN RIGHTS LAW BY THE JUDGES OF THE INTERNATIONAL COURT OF JUSTICE (2007).

14 For a discussion on the self-executing feature of rights enshrined in the UN Charter *see* Egon Schwelb, *The International Court of Justice and Human Rights Clauses of the Charter*, 66 AM. J. INT'L L. 337, 338–51 (1972).

15 *See e.g.*, Island of Palmas Case (Netherlands v. US), 2 R. Int'l Arb. Awards 829, 845 (1928) ("[a] judicial fact must be appreciated in the light of the law contemporary with it, and not of the law in force at the time such a dispute in regard to it arises or falls to be settled"); Legal Consequences for States of the Continued Presence of South Africa in Namibia (South West Africa) Notwithstanding Security Council Resolution 276 (1970), Advisory Opinion, 1971 I.C.J. Reports 16, ¶ 53 (June 21) ("viewing the institutions of 1919, the Court must take into consideration the changes which have occurred in the supervening half-century, and its interpretation cannot remain unaffected by the subsequent development of law, through the Charter of the United Nations and by way of customary law").

16 ERIC DE BRABANDERE, INVESTMENT TREATY ARBITRATION AS PUBLIC INTERNATIONAL LAW 146 (2014).

17 *See e.g.*, CMS Gas Transmission v. Argentina, Simens v. Argentina, Sempra v. Argentina.

18 Continental Casualty v. Argentina ¶ 261: ("In summary, in order to evaluate the relevance of that concept applied within [the] Fair and Equitable Treatment standard and whether a breach has occurred, relevant factors include: …ii) general legislative statements engender reduced expectations, especially with competent major international investors in a context where the political risk is high. Their enactment is by nature subject to subsequent modification, and possibly to withdrawal and cancellation, within the limits of respect of fundamental human rights and *ius cogens*.")

argument, finding that "no question affecting fundamental human rights"[19] existed or it was not an "argument that, *prima facie*, bears any substantiation to the merits"[20] of the case. They seemed to *categorically* reject the relevance of human rights issues in cases in which the sovereign takes regulatory measures, which constitute the majority of investment cases. Some other tribunals find it relevant and potentially significant.[21] In *Sempra v. Argentina*, the tribunal dug deeper into this issue by tying it to "constitutional order" and Argentina's responsibility to maintain such an order.[22] Yet, the tribunal found that Argentina could have accommodated such constitutional rights of its own people by "means of temporary measures and renegotiations."[23]

Another scenario that concerns human rights has emerged in the context of investment law, relating to situations where investor personal rights have been violated and/or investment has been procured through the violation of human rights. The *Phoenix v. Czech Republic* tribunal famously declared:

> nobody would suggest that ICSID protection should be granted to investments made in violation of the most fundamental rules of protection of human rights, like investments made in pursuance of torture or genocide or in support of slavery or trafficking of human organs.[24]

The human rights abuse of investors came up in a recent ICJ case. In the case of *Ahmadou Sadio Diallo (Republic of Guinea v. Democratic Republic of Congo)*, Guinea brought a case employing diplomatic protection on behalf of its citizen, Ahmadou Sadio Diall, a businessman based in Congo (then known as Zaire), who was imprisoned and expelled from Congo following his demand for payment of debts due to him. The court found the claim admissible, yet declared that such violations of human rights fell under investment regime protection and that the role of diplomatic protection was "somewhat faded."[25] The court's reasoning indicates that cases such as

---

19 CMS v. Argentina, ¶ 121.
20 Simens v. Argentina ¶ 79.
21 EDF v. Argentina, ¶ 912 ("The Tribunal does not call into question the potential significance or relevance of human rights in connection with international investment law.").
22 Sempra v. Argentina ¶ 331.
23 Sempra v. Argentina ¶ 332.
24 Phoenix v. Czech Republic ¶ 78.
25 Case Concerning Ahmadou Sadio Diallo (Republic of Guinea v. Democratic Republic of Congo), 2007 I.C.J. 1 (May 24), ¶ 88 (hereinafter the "Ahmadou Sadio Diallo case"). ("The Court is bound to note that, in contemporary international law, the protection of the rights of companies and the rights of their shareholders, and the settlement of the associated disputes, are essentially governed by bilateral or multilateral agreements for the protection of foreign investments, such as the treaties for the promotion and protection of foreign investments, and the Washington Convention of 18 March 1965 on the Settlement of Investment Disputes between States and Nationals of Other States, which created an International Centre for Settlement of Investment Disputes (ICSID), and also by contracts between States and foreign investors. In that context, the role of diplomatic

Barcelona Traction and *Diallo*, which include the human rights violations of investors, should be adjudicated at investment tribunals if relevant bilateral or multilateral investment treaties exit. In other words, the human rights order applies to investment cases, especially in the context of the abuse of investors' rights.

As discussed, two scenarios are discernible in the applicability of international human rights in international dispute resolution—mainly investment arbitration. Under the first situation, the distressed host countries resort to international human rights to explain their adopted regulatory behavior. Under the second scenario, the investors invoke human rights law in situations where their rights have been allegedly breached by host states. It is hard to draw a general inference on the applicability of human rights law in international dispute resolution. Yet, it seems that human rights issues that are related to pre-investment or procurement of investment tend to borrow rules from other international legal regimes. This holds true for the next discussion as well, which is on corruption and fraud.

3. Corruption and fraudulent conduct

Issues related to corruption and fraud occur frequently in the context of international dispute resolution.[26] Yet, fraudulent conduct and corruption present distinct problems while yielding different consequences in international law.[27] In the area of international arbitration, transnational public policy is repeatedly employed by tribunals to refer to instances where corruption and fraud were involved. A very prominent example is the investment arbitration case *World Duty v. Kenya*. The dispute arose out of a 1989 agreement for the construction, maintenance, and operation of a duty-free shopping center at Nairobi and Mombasa Airports. The claimant argued that its investment was unlawfully expropriated and that Kenya breached the agreement. The respondent challenged the validity of the agreement with the preliminary objection that the contract was secured through bribery to the then president of Kenya. The tribunal first had to determine whether the payment was a bribe or whether it should be considered a "personal

---

protection somewhat faded, as in practice recourse is only made to it in rare cases where treaty régimes do not exist or have proved inoperative.")

26 For the causes, consequences, and reform of corruption, *see generally* SUSAN ROSE-ACKERMAN, CORRUPTION AND GOVERNMENT (1999). Issues of corruption in cases of intermediary services have appeared before US courts as well, *see e.g.*, Northrop Corporation v. Triad International Marketing, 593 F. Supp. 928 (1984); Mohammed Habib and Middle East Services v. Raytheon Company and Raytheon Services Company, 616 F.2d (2014); Lockheed Aircraft Corporation v. Ora E. Gaines, 645 F.2d 761 (1981).

27 MICHAEL REISMAN & CHRISTINA SKINNER, FRAUDULENT EVIDENCE BEFORE PUBLIC INTERNATIONAL TRIBUNALS 5 (2014). Due to the complexity of issues introduced by arguing "fraud" in international law, Reisman and Skinner call it the "international law's quintessential 'f' word," *id.* at 7.

donation for public purposes,"[28] as the claimant argued. The tribunal held that the payment was bribery.[29] It then proceeded to examine the impact of the bribery on the agreement. It concluded that bribery is sanctioned in almost all legal systems with severe punishments while national courts find the practice against their public policies.[30] There are a number of international conventions and agreements strongly condemning the act of bribery, as well.[31] The tribunal explained the international public policy as "no more than domestic public policy applied to foreign awards and its content and application remains subjective to each State."[32] It set forth arguments—backed by court practices and legal doctrines—to distinguish it from transnational public policy. It eventually concluded that bribery is indeed against transnational public policy.[33] [34]

Another investment case which grappled with the issue of corruption and fraud is *Inceysa v. El Salvador*. Inceysa was awarded first place in a bid organized by the Ministry of the Environment and Natural Resources of El Salvador. The bid was related to a service contract for the installation, management, and operation of mechanical inspection stations for emission control. Following several problems between the parties, in 2003 Inceysa filed a claim in ICSID for damages based on breach of contract. El Salvador responded, *inter alia*, that the contract was obtained through fraud,

---

28 World Duty Free Company Ltd v. Republic of Kenya, ICSID No. ARB/00/7, Award (Oct. 4, 2006), ¶ 133–36.
29 *Id.*
30 *E.g.*: "Thus, in the *European Gas Turbines v. Westman* case, the French Court of Appeal of Paris ruled, on 30 September 1993, that "a contract having influence-peddling or bribery as its motives or object is, therefore, contrary to French international public policy as well as to the ethics of international business as conceived by the largest part of the members of the international community (Abdulhay Sayed — Corruption in International Trade and Commercial Arbitration — Kluwer Law International — 2004 — page 307 [sic]." Id at 147.
31 "In order to render more effective this general condemnation, a number of international conventions were concluded during the last decade. The first was adopted within the framework of the Organisation of American States on 29 March 1996. A convention on combating the bribery of foreign public officials in international business transactions was then concluded within the Organisation for Economic Cooperation and Development on 21 November 1997. It has thus far been ratified by 36 States. Afterwards, two conventions on corruption—one relating to criminal law and one dealing with civil law—were adopted by the Council of Europe on 27 January 1999 and 4 November 1999. The first has been supplemented by a Protocol of 15 May 2003. Those three instruments are in force. The first has been signed by 45 countries and ratified by 31 countries; the second has been signed by 39 countries and ratified by 25 countries." *Id.* at ¶ 143.
32 *Id* at ¶ 138.
33 "In light of domestic laws and international conventions relating to corruption, and in light of the decisions taken in this matter by courts and arbitral tribunals, this Tribunal is convinced that bribery is contrary to the international public policy of most, if not all, States or, to use another formula, to transnational public policy." *Id.* at ¶ 157.
34 Interestingly enough, as noted by scholars, this approach would result in the host country to be unjustly enriched, ANDREAS KULIK, GLOBAL PUBLIC INTEREST IN INTERNATIONAL INVESTMENT LAW 321 (2012).

forgery, and corruption. Specifically, it was alleged that Inceysa misrepresented its company in the bid process by providing false information about its financial condition, experience, and its partner in the tender process. The tribunal agreed with the respondent about the fraud and forgery by Inceysa during the bidding process. It found that the non-exclusion of Inceysa from the protection of the bilateral investment treaty would lead to a violation of international public policy. The tribunal, unlike other fora, attempted to define international public policy:

> International public policy consists of a series of fundamental principles that constitute the very essence of the State, and its essential function is to preserve the values of the international legal system against actions contrary to it.[35]

In another famous case, *Plama v. Bulgaria*, the tribunal invoked the notion of international public policy even in a situation in which the alleged conduct was against Bulgarian law. Following the *World Duty* and *Inceysa* cases, this tribunal declared that investments obtained through fraudulent misrepresentation and the falsely stated qualification of investors[36] are against international public policy:

> Claimant, in the present case, is requesting the Tribunal to grant its investment in Bulgaria the protections provided by the ECT. However, the Tribunal has decided that the investment was obtained by deceitful conduct that is in violation of Bulgarian law. The Tribunal is of the view that granting the ECT's protection to Claimant's investment would be contrary to the principle *nemo auditur propriam turpitudinem allegans*[37] invoked above. It would also be contrary to the basic notion of international public policy—that a contract obtained by wrongful means (fraudulent misrepresentation) should not be enforced by a tribunal.[38]

There are other cases which followed this approach and found the claims inadmissible due to their violation of international public policy.[39] Yet,

---

35 Inceysa Vallisoletana S. L. v. Republic of El Salvador, ICSID No. ARB/03/26, Award, ¶ 245 (August 2, 2006).
36 "What is clear is that Mr. Vautrin was determined not to disclose his role in the privatization and, by doing so, he deliberately misrepresented to the Bulgarian authorities the true identity of the investors in Nova Plama." Plama Consortium Limited v. Republic of Bulgaria, ICSID No. ARB/03/24, Award, (August 27, 2008), ¶ 129.
37 No one can be heard to invoke his own turpitude.
38 Plama v. Bulgaria, *supra* note 36 at ¶ 143.
39 *See e.g.*, Metal-Tech Ltd. v. The Republic of Uzbekistan, ICSID No. ARB/10/3, Award, ¶ 194–95, 308, 336 (October 4, 2013); Waguih Elie George Siag & Clorinda Vecchi v. Egypt, ICSID No. ARB/05/15, Dissenting Opinion of Professor Francisco Orrego Vicuña, 5 (June 1, 2009). For a brief discussion on whether states should be prevented from raising

scholars have criticized the practice of arbitral tribunals referring to transnational public policy in cases involving fraud and corruption.[40] In fact, with a multitude of sources including domestic law as well as international law expressly prohibiting corruption and fraud, tribunals' resorting to the unsettled theory of transnational public policy seems irrelevant. Yet, two possible theories could potentially explain this trend. Tribunals are trying to set a persuasive "precedent," since corruption and fraud are some of the most common pervasive issues in today's international arbitration.[41] Since domestic law is nuanced and not all states are signatories of international instruments prohibiting corruption, by introducing the concept of transnational public policy, tribunals hope to foster a *jurisprudence constante* in this area. Another hypothesis is that increasingly international arbitral tribunals are viewing themselves as the guardians of "global public interest" especially considering that the World Court seems to be in decline.[42] Tribunals seem to desire to create systemic implications and long-term impact with their decisions.[43] In the language of the *Glamis* tribunal "a case-specific mandate is not a license to ignore systemic implications."[44] This approach has been criticized on the ground that tribunals can exceed their case-specific mandates only under very limited circumstances.[45]

---

corruption claims if they have not first prosecuted them domestically, *see* Brody Greenwald, *The Viability of Corruption Defenses in Investment Arbitration When the State Does Not Prosecute*, EJIL: TALK! April 15, 2015, available at: http://www.ejiltalk.org/the-viability-of-corruption-defenses-in-investment-arbitration-when-the-state-does-not-prosecute/.

40 Donald Francis Donovan, *Investment Treaty Arbitration,* in MANDATORY RULES IN INTERNATIONAL ARBITRATION 286, 286–90 (George A. Bermann & Loukas A. Mistelis eds., 2011).

41 *See generally* ALOYSIUS P. LLAMZON, CORRUPTION IN INVESTMENT ARBITRATION (2014).

42 KULICK, *supra* note 34 at 77–84. *See also* GUS VAN HARTEN, INVESTMENT TREATY ARBITRATION AND PUBLIC LAW (2008).

43 Several scholars have addressed the issue of precedents and their role in international arbitration, *see e.g.*, Stephen W. Schill, *International Arbitration as System-Builders*, 106 AM. SOC'Y OF INT'L L. 295 (2012); Irene M. Ten Gate, *The Costs of Consistency: Precedent in Investment Treaty Arbitration*, 51 COLUM. J. TRANSNATION'L L. 418 (2013); Brian King & Rahim Moloo, *International Arbitrations as Lawmakers*, 46 N.Y.U. J. INT'L L. & POL. 875 (2013).

44 Glamis Gold v. US, NAFTA Ch. 11 Arb. Trib. 2003), Award, ¶ 6. (Jun 8, 2009), available at http://www.state.gov/documents/organization/125798.pdf.

45 "But I will argue that investment tribunals should eschew mixing that 'case-specific' approach with a 'systems-implication' approach or with a modicum of it or even with a 'greater contextual awareness' approach (all *Glamis* terms), other than for (i) thoughtful consideration of previous awards that are on-point; (ii) consideration of the objects and purposes of the BIT or investment chapter in question, but only within the scope prescribed by the canon of treaty interpretation; and (iii) disciplined supplementative interpretation but only when confronted by a *lacuna* in the applicable law. Subject to these narrow exceptions, international investment tribunals should confine themselves to a case-specific methodology." Michael Reisman, *"Case Specific Mandates" v. "Systemic Implication": How Should Investment Tribunals Decide?* 29 ARB. INT'L 131, 131–132 (2013).

B. Transnational public policy in the twenty-first century

The world is changing, as is international law. Sooner or later, new fronts will be discussed under the category of transnational public policy. I suspect that these new fronts will depart from the traditional approach that focused mainly on human rights abuses and corruption. With increasing globalization, economic challenges and concerns will occupy more room in the global public interest.[46] Thus far, expropriation, fair and equitable treatment, as well as states' regulatory barriers have been the centerpieces of the global regulatory scheme in the context of international dispute resolution. The paradigm seems to be shifting as the neoliberal hegemony has had to confront several regional and a major global recession. On the one hand, the *realpolitik* security measures of the US, especially following 9/11, shattered the illusion that the era for power politics has passed. On the other hand, futile collective measures to restructure the economies of distressed countries has shown the world that the present investment and trade regimes do more harm than good when a country experiences an economic recession.[47]

1. Economic sanctions

Despite the triumph of neoliberalism and the end of structural bipolarity in international relations, we have witnessed a growing number of economic prohibitions in the form of national economic sanctions and UN Security Council Resolutions.[48] Indeed, the progress of increasingly intensified security measures can be traced through the Resolutions and sanctions imposed following the collapse of the Soviet Union.[49] The literature is largely silent

---

46 Free movement of capital, as the central norm for globalization has faced several important limitations, Farshad Ghodoosi, *The Limits of the Free Movement of Capital, The Status of Customary International Law of Money*, 7 N.W. INTERDISC L. REV. 287, 324–25 (2014).

47 Furthermore, the world is witnessing more than ever the externalities of maintaining a global economy and global consumerism. Environmental issues are the forefront of these concerns.

48 "In the minds of the drafters of the new world legal order 'complete or partial interruption of economic relations' would restore—or at least contribute to the restoration of—international peace and order. This tool of coercion and compliance in international law has largely remained dormant and under-utilized until the post Cold-War era. Only in 1966 and 1977 did the Security Council impose sanctions against Southern Rhodesia and South Africa respectively. It was the end of bi-polarity in international order that shifted the paradigm towards the liberal use of economic sanctions." Farshad Ghodoosi, *The Sanction Theory: A Frail Paradigm for International Law?* HARV. INT'L L. J. ONLINE (January 27, 2015).

49 Some scholars find it problematic to use the term "sanctions" for national and regional restrictive economic measures, W. MICHAEL REISMAN, THE QUEST FOR WORLD ORDER AND HUMAN DIGNITY IN THE TWENTY-FIRST CENTURY 405 (2012) (explaining that the term economic warfare is more accurate when a state or states applies certain restrictive economic measures instead of an international body).

on the clash between investment and trade law and economic sanctions. I have addressed this issue in a separate piece.[50] In summary, the Security Council Resolutions and economic sanctions do not enjoy the status of *jus cogens*.[51] Yet, their interference in cross-border investment is inevitable, be it with the targeted state or a third party state. I have concluded that, except in situations where the Security Council Resolutions expressly sanction individuals or entities, sanctions are reviewable, to varying degrees, by international tribunals.[52]

Relevant to our discussion, in cases where Security Council Resolutions address a problem, the framing of them as a transnational public policy by arbitral tribunals seems redundant and unnecessary. Security Council Resolutions are binding on international tribunals. However, in one scenario the framework of transnational public policy might seem pertinent: imagine that, in a concerted effort, several nations decide to "boycott" or "outcast" a recalcitrant state that is violating the basic human rights of its own people.[53] The question is whether an arbitral tribunal can find an investment contract between the targeted state and a third state unenforceable due to transnational economic sanctions and public policy. In other words, in this situation can the tribunal refuse to enforce the contract because it violates the sanctions regime (transnational public policy) endorsed by a large group of states?

In the trade context, there have been cases involving economic sanctions and/or Security Council Resolutions. In *Beverly Overseas SA v. Aleman et al./Privredna Banka Zagreb*, the claimant sought to enforce a promissory note associated with a contract dealing with the arms trade to Croatia. The Swiss Federal Tribunal ruled that the contract was invalid particularly because of UN Security Council Resolution 713 of September 25, 1991 prohibiting the supply of arms to ex-Yugoslavia territories.[54] In another instance, however, the Swiss Supreme Court rejected the Israeli government's argument that sanctions against

---

50 Farshad Ghodoosi, *Combatting Economic Sanctions in Times of Political Hostility, A Case Study of Iran*, 37 FORDHAM INT'L L.J. 1731, 1774–83 (2014).
51 *Id.* at 1775.
52 *Id.* at 1780–83.
53 Outcasting theory in international law is gaining force; for instance Oona Hathaway and Scott Shapiro argue that international law is law because it enforces its obligations through outcasting: "...very little of international law meets Modern State Conception of international law—very little (if any) of it is enforced through brute physical force deployed by an institution enforcing its own rules. But what is interesting is not so much what international law is not, but what it is. And that is law that operates almost entirely through outcasting and external enforcement." Oona Hathaway & Scott Shapiro, *Outcasting: Enforcement in Domestic and International law*, 121 YALE. L. J. 252, 302 (2011). For a criticism on this approach, *see* Ghodoosi, *supra* note 50.
54 Decision 4C.172/2000 of 28.03.2001, ASA Bull (2001) quoted in CHRISTOPH BRUNNER, FORCE MAJEURE AND HARDSHIP UNDER GENERAL CONTRACT PRINCIPLES: EXCEPTION FOR NON-PERFORMANCE IN INTERNATIONAL ARBITRATION 277 (2009).

Iran were against Swiss public policy.[55] In this case, the defendant, an Israeli-owned Swiss Company, argued that enforcement of an arbitral award in favor of Iran ($97 million) would violate fundamental principles of international law (transnational public policy).[56] The Court, however, did not find that international sanctions again Iran would violate *Swiss* public policy because the defendant's argument rested on general considerations of international politics not relevant to the *Swiss* legal order.[57]

On a related topic, the issue of state recognition, an interesting case appeared before an ICC arbitral tribunal. The defendant, the Republic of X, argued that because the international community did not recognize the territory's status as a state, it would be a violation of transnational public policy for the tribunal to establish jurisdiction.[58] By adjudicating the dispute, the tribunal would recognize the territory as a state and, thus, violate transnational public policy.[59] The tribunal disagreed: "the question of recognition or non-recognition, on the one hand, and that of the application of non-application of international public policy, on the other hand, by international arbitrators should be distinguished."[60] By reducing the scope of transnational public policy to *jus cogens*, the tribunal argued that the recognition of states is not a *jus cogens* norm.[61]

2. Sovereign debt

Sovereign debt restructuring is another pervasive problem for the global economy. In a global market, states increasingly need to develop their capital markets, which they mainly do through issuing bonds. Yet, governments sometimes default, for several reasons including domestic mismanagement as well as the brutality of international capitalism.[62] The saga between

---

55 Company X v. Company Z, Swiss Federal Court, Judgment, January 21, 2014 available at http://www.globalarbitrationreview.com/cdn/files/gar/articles/4A_250_2013.pdf. For a discussion of the decision, *see* Leo Szolnoki, *Swiss court rejects award challenge over Iran sanctions*, GLOBAL ARB. REV. March 6, 2014, at http://globalarbitrationreview.com/news/article/32478/swiss-court-rejects-award-challenge-iran-sanctions/.
56 *Id.*
57 *Id.*
58 Case No. 6474 of 1992, 25 Y.B. Comm. Arb. 279–80 (ICC Int'l Ct. Arb.) (Supplier v. Republic of X, Partial Award on Jurisdiction and Admissibility).
59 *Id.* at 282–83.
60 *Id.*
61 "In order to accept the defendant's objection and contention, on that account, the Arbitral Tribunal would have to be persuaded that it is *bound*, either under the Resolutions of the United Nations or under 'a separate principle of international law', i.e., in particular under the concept of '*jus cogens*,' to decline to exercise jurisdiction over the present dispute." *Id.* at 285.
62 For a history of sovereign bonds, *see* NIALL FERGUSON, THE CASH NEXUS, MONEY AND POWER IN THE MODERN WORLD 1700–2000 (2001).

Argentina and its debt-holders[63] illustrates the importance of creating more organized sovereign debt restructuring.

The debate on restricting sovereign debts has had several phases since World War II.[64] The latest phase started with the Mexican peso crisis that aimed to "bail out" many private creditors.[65] Efforts have been put into institutionalizing the restructuring process of sovereign debts, albeit in vein.[66] Although a latecomer to the game, international arbitration has affected sovereign debt more than any other international regime.[67] In a highly controversial case, *Abaclat v. Argentina*, an investment tribunal held that it had jurisdiction to hear the claims of 60,000 Italian bondholders against Argentina's default.[68] The decision marked a turning point in investment arbitration.[69]

However, this development encountered a backlash, first from a group of scholars who believe that international arbitration is not equipped to handle matters related to portfolio investment and bond defaults.[70] They find it outside of the purview of international arbitration's authority and mandate, which deals with foreign direct investment. Recent cases also show this trend of backtracking on the expansion of arbitral discretion

---

[63] See e.g., Guillermo Vultin, *The Latest Chapter in Argentina's Debt Saga*, BROOKINGS (June 19, 2014) at http://www.brookings.edu/blogs/up-front/posts/2014/06/19-argentina-debt-consequences-vuletin; Jude Webber, *Argentina Holdout Saga, Who has a Dog in the Fight?* FINANCIAL TIMES (April 25, 2013) at http://blogs.ft.com/beyond-brics/2013/04/25/argentina-holdout-saga-who-has-a-dog-in-the-fight/; John Carreyrou, *Hedge Funds Clash Over Argentina Debt*, WALL STREET JOURNAL (February 11, 2014) at http://online.wsj.com/articles/SB10001424052702303874504579372923716382850.

[64] LEX RIEFFEL, RESTRUCTURING SOVEREIGN DEBT: THE CASE FOR AD HOC MACHINERY 3–5 (2003).

[65] Id.

[66] IMF suggested that a body is tasked with international bankruptcy. Yet, both creditors and debtors have not welcomed this proposal. FEDERICO STURZENEGGER & JEROMIN ZETTELMEYER, DEBT DEFAULTS AND LESSONS FROM A DECADE OF CRISES 81 (2006).

[67] The literature on this topic is rampant, see e.g., William Burke-White, *The Argentine Financial Crisis: State Liability Under BITs and the Legitimacy of the ICSID System* in THE BACKLASH AGAINST INVESTMENT ARBITRATION: PERCEPTIONS AND REALITY 407 (Michael Waibel et al. eds., 2010); Karen Halverson Cross, *Arbitration as a Means of Resolving Sovereign Disputes*, 17 AM. REV. INT'L ARB. (2006); Joanna Simões, *Sovereign Bond Disputes Before ICSID Tribunals: Lessons From the Argentine Crisis* 17 LAW & BUS. REV. AM. (2011); Robert M. Ziff, *The Sovereign Debtor's Prison: Analysis of the Argentine Crisis Arbitrations and Implications for Investment Treaty Law*, 10 RICH. GLOBAL L. & BUS. (2011); Jessica Beess und Chrostin, *Recent Developments: Sovereign Debt Restructuring and Mass Claims Arbitrations before the ICSID: The Abaclat Case*, 53 HARV. INT'L L.J. 505 (2012).

[68] Abaclat and others v. Argentina Republic, ICSID Case No. ARB/07/5, Decision on Jurisdiction and Admissibility ¶ 660 (Aug. 4, 2011).

[69] See e.g., S.I. Strong, *Mass Procedures as Form of "Regulatory Arbitration"—Abaclat v. Argentine Republic and the International Investment Regime*, 38 J. CORP. L. 259 (203).

[70] "Article 25's definition [ICSID Convention] is not infinitively elastic. Sovereign bonds do not display the typical features of an investment," Michael Waibel, *Opening Pandora's Box: Sovereign Bonds in International Arbitration*, 101 AM. J. INT'L L. 711, 722 (2007).

over sovereign bonds. However, in addition to legal arguments, it seems that political and economic policy is also being taken into consideration. For instance in the case of *Istrokapital SE v. Hellenic Republic*, the tribunal declined jurisdiction on claims arising out of interests in bonds. The tribunal argued:

> In sum, sovereign debt is an instrument of government monetary and economic policy and its impact at the local and international levels makes it an important tool for the handling of social and economic policies of a State. It cannot, thus, be equated to private indebtedness or corporate debt.[71]

Hence, sovereign debt restructuring seems to be another new front for transnational public policy. Tribunals might soon be inclined to respect concerted efforts of states to execute sovereign debt restructuring by denying holdouts based on transnational public policy considerations.

To conclude, in all the instances above, transnational public policy aims to solve the problem of "coordination" in international law. This is at sharp contrast with the traditional view on transnational public policy, which is mainly centered on *ethical* grounds.[72] The traditional approach seems to endeavor to protect what can be aptly called "global public morality." However, I predict the notion of transnational public policy will shift towards "global public interest" with the aim to control and, at best, minimize the problem of coordination in today's international law. I believe "economizing" the vague notion of transnational public policy will have several benefits for international dispute resolution. First, it will clarify the notion to a level that makes it more palpable for parties and scholars. Second. tribunal decisions will contribute to fostering a body of persuasive jurisprudence that can gradually address some coordination problems in today's international law. Finally, the methods employed to analyze the circumstances will include "balancing" and the "proportionality test," which in return will make the decisions understandable and subject to easier scrutiny by scholars.

---

71 Poštová banka, a.s. and ISTROKAPITAL SE v. Hellenic Republic, ICSID Case No. ARB/13/8, Award ¶ 324 (April 9, 2015).

72 Some scholars suggest establishing public policy grounds based on the International Covenant on Economic, Social and Cultural Rights, DIANE A. DESIERTO, PUBLIC POLICY IN INTERNATIONAL ECONOMIC LAW: THE ICESCR IN TRADE, FINANCE, AND INVESTMENT 387 (2015). ("Social protection commitments under the ICESCR should operate as normative foundations to States' numerous economic decisions especially in the international sphere—in designing treaties and contract, voting in international institutions, and State practices at home and abroad.")

Conclusion

In the last several decades, a major part of international law scholarship shifted its focus to transnational law. Since Philip Jessup coined the term transnational law in his famous Storrs Lectures at Yale,[1] the enquiry of international law—by many scholars and practitioners—switched to norms that transcend traditional national/international and private/public dichotomies.[2] The idea behind this movement was that transnational norms become effective through a complex process involving various international and national actors. The relentless triumph of neoliberalism and globalization encouraged eminent scholars such as Harold Koh to assert that "a complex new order has supplanted the realist world order dominated by sovereign states."[3]

It is hard to disagree that a new order has dominated the world we live in, specifically in the post-Cold War era. Transnational norms and practices travel across borders much easier and faster than before. The seemingly unstoppable expansion of arbitral institutions and rules serves as a good example. Yet, transnationalism appeared to gear towards less national legal order involvement without creating robust transnational governance. Anne-Marie Slaughter refers to the paradox of globalization and international law:

> this is a globalization paradox. We need more government on a global and a regional scale, but we don't want the centralization of decision-making power and coercive authority so far from the people actually to be governed.[4]

---

1 *See generally* PHILIP JESSUP, TRANSNATIONAL LAW (1956).
2 For a brief history of the evolution of transnational legal process, *see* Harold H. Koh, *Transnational Legal Process*, 75 NEB. L. REV. 181, 186–91 (1996).
3 Harol H. Koh, *Opening Remarks: Transnational Legal Process Illuminated* in TRANSNATIONAL LEGAL PROCESSES: GLOBALIZATION AND POWER DISPARITIES 327, 327 (Michael Likosky ed., 2002).
4 Anne-Marie Slaughter, *A New World Order* in THE GLOBALIZATION READER 283, 286 (Frank Lechner & John Boli eds., 2015).

The discussion on transnational public policy in international dispute resolution is a case in point. The importance of public policy concerns—such as policies reflected in anti-competition law, tax law, corruption, and environmental concerns—is undeniable. Yet, the practice and some supporting scholarship show the extent to which transnationalism aims to marginalize public policy considerations emanating from national laws. The need for speed and predictability has eclipsed a serious discussion on the scope and impact of the marginalization of the public policy exception. This is coupled with the reluctance of national courts to play an active role, potentially for the fear that their respective jurisdiction would not be considered an "arbitration-friendly" forum. This has resulted in a weak and elusive public policy doctrine which is losing its status as the only internal and jurisprudential control mechanism in arbitration. This might be a worrisome development in today's globalized world.

Index

Abaclat v. Argentina 143
acceptance of public policy argument 114-17
Adams v. Howerton 48
adjudication, decline of faith in 53
age of statutes 27-31
Ahmadou Sadio Diallo case 135-6
Aitchison, W. 57
Akerlof, G. 37
Alabama Claims arbitration 82-3
Alexander VI, Pope 79
alternative dispute resolution (ADR) 1-2, 3; paradigms 49-62; phases of in the US 49; *see also* arbitration
American approach to international arbitration (statism) 93, 94, 99-107
American Civil War 82-3
American legal realism 15-16, 29-31
Ameropa AG v. Havi Ocean Co. LLC 129
ancient Greek civilization 78-9
anti-suit injunctions 104-5, 107
arbitral tribunal-chosen law public policy 114-17
arbitration 3, 49-77; doctrine of public policy in 62-73; international *see* international arbitration theories, international commercial arbitration; reasons to arbitrate 49-62; US Supreme Court 73-7
Argentina 134-5, 142-3
arguments of policy 45-8
arguments of principle 47
arms trade 141
asymmetry of information 37-9
Austria 69
authority signal 101
Ayres, I. 36

Bacock v. Jackson 89
Baltimore & Ohio Southwestern Ry v. Voight 34
Barak, A. 45, 46
Beals v. Saldanha 68
Belgium 105
Bell, J. 46-7
Bennett v. Bennett 10
Beresford v. Royal Insurance Company Limited 19
Berman, H.J. 50
Beverly Overseas SA v. Aleman et al./ Privredna Banka Zagreb 141
Boundary Commission 81-2
Brams, S. 58
Brandeis, L. 28-9
Brazil 124
bribery 136-7; *see also* corruption
British Debts Commission 81-2
Bulgaria 138
bureaucracy 51
Bush, R.A.B. 60-1

Calabresi, G. 23, 28
Canada 68
Cardozo, B. 25, 27
Carr, E.H. 91
charismatic legitimacy 51
Cheng, T.-H. 103
Chevron USA, Inc. v. Natural Resources Defense Council, Inc. 31
China 65-6
choice of law 110-17, 130; approaches to transnational public policy 117-28; empirical data on success rate 113-17
Chromalloy Aeroservices v. Division of Chromalloy Gas Turbine Co. 106
classical approach 22-7
classical liberalism 22

148 Index

Colombia 106-7
common international values 119-21
common law *see* English common law
communication 101
compromise, possibility of 58
conflict of laws 11, 86-90
Congress system in Europe 80
consensus model 46
consent: consent-based paradigm of ADR 52-5; contract formation 8-9
Continental Casualty v. Argentina 134
contract law 8-10, 13-14, 98-9; classifications of public policy 19-20; law and economics approach 33-42
control intention 101
Convention on the Recognition and Enforcement of Foreign Arbitral Awards (New York Convention) 54, 63, 77, 84-5, 89, 106, 128
conventional interest arbitration 57-8
Cooke v. Turner 7
coordination 144
Corporacion Mexicana de Manenimento Integral v. Remex-Exploracion y Production 106, 107
corporate veil, lifting the 126
corruption 120-1, 136-9
cost-benefit analysis 3, 44-5
critical legal scholarship 32-3

D'Amato, A. 132
debt, sovereign 142-4
decision-making 101-2
default rules 35
Derains, Y. 98-9
disparate-impact discrimination 35
distressed countries 134-5, 140
Doctor's Associates, Inc. v. Casarotto 77
Donovan, D.F. 75, 100
Dunham v. Gould 41-2
Dworkin, R. 26, 46-7
Dyer, J. 5

Eastern Association Coal Corporation v. UMWA 62-3
economic sanctions 140-2
economic and social life 64-6, 73
economics of public policy doctrine *see* law and economics approach
Ecuador 125
Egerton v. Brownlow 7, 13, 48
Egypt 106
El Salvador 137-8

encounter commone ley 5
enforcement 1, 3, 38, 89, 90; proceedings in national courts 105-7; transnational public policy in 109, 128-30
English common law 5-20; definition of public policy 11-14; paradigm shift 5-8; taxonomy 14-20; unruliness of public policy 8-11
Epstein, R. 38
established norms 131-9
ex ante approach to public policy 25
ex dolo malo non oritur actio 6
ex post phase 25

Falk, R. 100
First Peloponnesian War 78
Folger, J.P. 60-1
foreign judgments and awards 12, 13; set-aside awards 105-7
formalism 22-5
France 70, 105-6, 121-2, 125-6, 128; Code of Civil Procedure 70
Frankfurter, F. 28
fraudulent conduct 136-9
Fried, C. 41
Friedman, D.A. 20
Fuller, L. 25, 26
fundamental principles of law 69-70, 73
Furmston, M.P. 19-20

Gaillard, E. 94-7, 99
game theory of arbitration 56-9
Gellhorn, W. 14-15, 16
General Act of the Pacific Settlement for International Disputes 84
general morals 17-18
general security 17
Geneva Convention on the Execution of Foreign Arbitral Awards 89
Germany 70
Ghodoosi, F. 140
Gilmore, G. 28, 29
global public interest 139, 140, 144
globalization 140; paradox of international law and 145
Goode, R. 94
governing law public policy 114-17
government policies 11, 12-13
Grace v. Rubber Workers 62
gradational method 134
Great Depression 27
Gregory VII, Pope 50

Hague Conferences on Private International Law 83, 86
Hague Convention for Pacific Settlement of International Disputes 83-4, 85
Hall Street Associates, LLC v. Mattel, Inc. 76-7
Hardwicke, Lord 5-6, 46
Hathaway, O. 141
Hilmarton v. OTV 105-6, 122
Hobbes, T. 22
Holmes, O. W. 15-16, 30, 45
Holzer v. Deutsche Reichsbahngesellchaf 44
Hong Kong 68-9
human rights 133-6
Hurd, H. 26, 27

illegality of a contract 9-10
immigration 31, 43
implied negative choice 111-12
in pari delicto 39
Inceysa v. El Salvador 137-8
individual life, value of 18
information asymmetry 37-9
institutionalization of ADR 54-5
intent: legislative 18-19, 46-8; of parties 130
interest-based paradigm of ADR 55-9
international arbitration theories 91-107; judicialization and state power 91-3; practical significance 104-7; statism 93, 94, 99-107; transnationalism 92-3, 94-9, 104-7
International Center for Settlement of Investment Disputes (ICSID) 85
International Chamber of Commerce (ICC) International Court of Arbitration (ICCA) awards 113-17
international comity 128-9
international commercial arbitration 108-30; approaches to transnational public policy 117-28; public policy in 110-17; transnational public policy in enforcement 109, 128-30
international commissions of inquiry 85
International Court of Justice 85, 133-4
international dispute resolution 78-90, 146; early modern era 80-5; emergence of the notion of public policy 85-90; pre-modern developments 78-80
international investment arbitration 100, 103
International Law Commission (ILC) 84

International News Service v. Associated Press 29
international public policy 70-3; national courts' 119, 121-3
interpretation 22-4
interstitial legislator model 47
investment cases 134-6
Iran 125, 141-2
Israel 141-2
Istrokapital SE v. Hellenic Republic 144
Italy 71

Jay Treaty: arbitrations 80-2, 83; comissions 81-2
Jessup, P. 145
judges' role in policy-making 15-16
judicial activism 43-4
judicialization 91-3
jus cogens 103, 131-3, 142
justice, basic notions of 66-9, 73
justiciable disputes 85-6

Karpinski v. Collins 39
Kenya 136-7
Keohane, R. 92
Kessedjian, C. 127
kings 50, 79
Koh, H. 102, 145
Krasner, S. 92
Kurth, M.H. 66-7

Lalive, P. 71-2, 97-8, 108
Lasswell, H. 16, 101
Lauterpacht, H. 85-6
law and economics approach 33, 34-48; in law 34-7; incompleteness 43-5; policy arguments in courts 45-8; public policy 37-42
League of Nations 84
legal order 96, 109, 129; *see also* choice of law
legal and political disputes 85-90
legal realism 15-16, 29-31
legislation-based doctrine of public policy 14-15
legislative intent 18-19, 46-8
legitimate domination 51
lex arbitri 112, 113
lex causae 112-13
lex fori 87, 98
lex loci arbitri 113
lex mercatoria 119, 123-8
liberalism, classical 22

150 *Index*

Liebman v. Rosenthal 43-4, 45
Locke, J. 22

Malley v. Briggs 12
mandatory rules 11, 13, 35-6, 98-9; international commercial arbitration 117-28, 130
Mann, F.A. 94
Marbury v. Madison 12
Marcus Brown Holding Co. v. Feldman 24
Maritime Claims Commission 81-2
Mayer, P. 99
McDougal, M. 16, 101
mediation 60-1
Mexico 107
Microsoft 40
Mitchel v. Reynolds 5
Mitsubishi Motors Corp. v. Soler Chrysler-Plymouth, Inc. 3, 12-13, 72, 73-6
Monolocalism 94
Montesquieu 45
Moore, M. 26
morality: basic notions of 66-9, 73; law and 26, 30; public 3, 43-5
Moravcsik, A. 92
multiculturalism 31-2

national courts 89, 90, 128, 146; approaches to public policy exceptions 63-73; enforcement proceedings in 105-7; international public policy 119, 121-3
national law 112, 113
national policy 68
negative externalities 3, 35, 39-40, 43-4
New Deal 28
New Haven School of Law (NHSL) 100-2
New York Convention 54, 63, 77, 84-5, 89, 106, 128
New Zealand 68
non-acceptance of public policy argument 114-17
non-governing law public policy 114-17
non-justiciable disputes 85-6
Nordenfeldt v. Maxim 7-8
normative approach to law 26
norms 101-2; established 131-9; ordinary and overriding mandatory norms 104

objective approach: choice of law 111; enforcement 63
objective public policy matters 104
ordinary norms 104
outcasting 141
overriding mandatory norms 104
Owen v. City of Independence 12

paradigm shift 5-8
paradox of globalization and international law 145
Parsons & Whittemore Overseas Co. Inc. v. RAKTA 67
participation 59
parties in the contract, protection of 35, 37-9, 42
paternalism 35, 37-9
Patriot Act 19
Paulsson, J. 103-4
Pemex case 106, 107
People v. Hawkins 24-5
Permanent Court of Arbitration 83
Permanent Court of International Justice 133-4
Phoenix v. Czech Republic 135
piercing the corporate veil 126
Plama v. Bulgaria 138
policy arguments in courts 45-8
policy content 101
political and legal disputes 85-90
pollution 39
popes 50, 79
Portugal 79
positivism 96
Posner, E. 41, 42
post-ADR movement 60-1
post-decision phase 1
postmodernism 33
Pound, R. 16-18
precedent setting 139
pre-referral phase 1
primary fora set-aside decisions 105-7
principles: arguments of principle 47; fundamental principles of law 69-70, 73
private international law 86-90
procedural natural law 26
proceeding phase 1
protection: of parties in a contract 35, 37-9, 42; of third parties 35, 39-40, 42
public interest 3; in general progress 18; global 139, 140, 144
public morality 3, 43-5
public policy doctrine 2-4, 145; in arbitration 62-73; courts' approach 63-73; definition 11-14; emergence in international dispute resolution

85-90; history of in English common law *see* English common law; history of as regulatory planning in the US *see* regulatory planning; in international commercial arbitration 110-17; leading role of 43-8; taxonomy 14-20; unruliness of 8-11; *see also* international public policy, transnational public policy
public security 3, 44-5
punitive damages 121

racketeering 120-1
RAKTA 67
rational legitimacy 51
rationalism 25-7
rationality 58-9
rationalization of law 51
realism 91; American legal realism 15-16, 29-31
Redfern, A. 108
redistributive justice 35, 41-2
regime theory 91-2
regulatory planning 21-33; age of statutes 27-31; classical approach 22-7; new approach 31-3
regulatory state 28-9, 31-2
Reisman, M. 99-103, 130, 139
res publica 6
resistance-based paradigm of ADR 59-62
Resnik, J. 74
reviewability of awards 76-7
revisionism 31, 32
Rice, W. 35
Richardson v. Mellish 6, 15
rights model 46-7
Roman Empire 79
royal law 50
Russia 64-5

same-sex marriages 48
sanctions, economic 140-2
Sanders, P. 122
Scalia, Justice 63
Schwartz, A. 37-8
Sempra v. Argentina 135
set-aside decisions 105-7
Shapiro, S. 141
Shavell, S. 57
Slaughter, A.-M. 145
Smit, H. 109
social and economic life 64-6, 73
social institutions, security of 17

social interests 16-18
social regulation 27
social resources, conservation of 18
sovereign debt restructuring 142-4
Spain 71, 79, 122
Sparta 78
'Special Connection' theory 118-19
state of exception 132
state interest 7-8
state power 91-3
state recognition 142
statism 93, 94, 99-107
Statute of the International Court of Justice 97
statutes 23-4; age of 27-31
structural tension 50-2, 54, 59-60
subjective approach: choice of law 111-12; enforcement 63
subjective public policy matters 104
substantive law, choice of 110-13
supervening rules *see* mandatory rules
Switzerland 70-1, 105-6, 118, 122-3, 141-2

taxonomy 14-20
TemoRio S.A. E.S.P. v. Electranta S.P. 106-7
textual interpretation 24
third parties, protection of 35, 39-40, 42
traditional legitimacy 51
transnational law 145
transnational public policy 4, 108-9, 146; approaches to 117-28; development in international law 131-44; in enforcement 109, 128-30; international arbitration theory 92-3, 94-9, 104-7; in the twenty-first century 140-4
treble damage provision 120-1
tying arrangements 40

UNCITRAL Model Law on International Commercial Arbitration 68, 110
unconscionability doctrine 10-11, 37-8
Underhill v. Van Cortlandt 67
unfair competition 18, 40
United Kingdom (UK): *Alabama* Claims arbitration 82-3; Jay Treaty arbitrations 80-2, 83
United Nations Charter 84
United Nations Security Council Resolutions 140-1
United Paperworks International Union v. Misco 62

United States (US): *Alabama* Claims arbitration 82-3; Arbitration Act 62, 66, 77; Constitution 19, 23; courts' approach to public policy exception 66-8; enforcement of awards in national courts 106-7; Federal Racketeer Influenced and Corrupt Organization Act (RICO) 120-1; history of public policy as regulatory planning *see* regulatory planning; Immigration and Nationality Act (INA) 48; international comity 128-9; Jay Treaty arbitrations 80-2, 83; Patriot Act 19; phases of ADR 49; phases in approach to arbitration 66-7; Sherman Act 18, 74, 75; Third Restatement of the Foreign Relations Law 131
United States v. Microsoft Corporation 40
United States v. Procter & Gamble 12

United States Supreme Court 3, 12-13, 62; public policy in arbitration 73-7
unruliness of public policy 8-11
usury 9, 41-2

values 102; common international values 119-21
Vienna Settlement of 1814–1815 80

Washington Convention 85
Washington Treaty 83
Weber, M. 51
welfare state 27-9
Westphalian approach 94-5, 96
Westphalian international system 79-80
World Duty v. Kenya 136-7

Yugraneft Corporation v. Rexx Management Corporation 68